P9-CKL-558

ENTERING THE HEART OF GOD

Praying the Lord's Prayer in Our Day

by
Charles E. Irvin

xulon
PRESS

Copyright © 2005 by Rev. Charles E. Irvin

Entering the Heart of God
by Rev. Charles E. Irvin

Printed in the United States of America

ISBN 1-59781-426-1

All rights reserved solely by the author. The author guarantees all contents are original and do not infringe upon the legal rights of any other person or work. No part of this book may be reproduced in any form without the permission of the author. The views expressed in this book are not necessarily those of the publisher.

Excerpts from THE JERUSALEM BIBLE, copyright © 1966 by Darton, Longman & Todd, Ltd. and Doubleday, a division of Random House, Inc. Repinted by permission.

"Primary Wonder," "Sojourns in the Parallel World," by Denise Levertov, from SANDS OF THE WELL, copyright © 1994, 1995, 1996 by Denise Levertov. Reprinted by permission of New Directions Publishing Corp.

"In Whom we Live and Move and Have Our Being," by Denise Levertov, from SANDS OF THE WELL, copyright © 1996 by Denise Levertov. Reprinted by permission of New Directions Publishing Corp.

www.xulonpress.com

ACKNOWLEDGMENTS

Publishing this book would not have been possible without the help of a number of people whose encouragements, criticisms, and comments motivated me to press on with my hope to share these reflections on Jesus' prayer you will find in this book. The encouragements of Patrick O'Brien, Fr. Larry Delaney and Heidi Saxton, along with the criticisms of Msgr. Robert Lunsford, and the editing skills of Marybeth Hicks and Ann Stapleton Jacob made this book possible. I am deeply grateful for all of their contributions.

Table of Contents

PREFACE

This book is a series of meditations on the major words and phrases of the Lord's Prayer. As you read it you will feel its texture to be more like sackcloth than silk. The sections are thematically, not logically, connected. The result? The transitions between them are edgy.

The Lord's Prayer comes from the heart of a Person who was truly a man and truly the Son of God. The lance of suffering pierced his heart, but pierced though it was, it was not broken. It was opened.

These reflections emanate from a priest with a heart likewise molded through suffering. Priests are fully men, men whose lives fill up with the experiences of ordinary people. Priests are not shielded from those things all people experience in life, including those dreadful things that touch everyone and make us wonder about God's love and presence in our lives.

Because of my many years in the priesthood, I know there is little difference between my life and yours. Our common joys, sorrows, sufferings, and triumphs are astonishingly similar. I know this to be true from the countless stories I have heard from men and women I have cared for throughout the years of my priesthood. I know this is true from what has come my way in my own life.

I point this out because many folks assume that priests are somehow "different." Some people think priests don't know or understand what it means to live life "in the world" and therefore cannot speak to what is in the hearts and souls of ordinary people who struggle with the real issues life often sends our way. Lest there be any doubt, let me reveal to you that priests seek out and enter into the heart of God just as all believers do.

Allow me to give you a glimpse into my life and background so that you will know I am with you as your friend, reflecting here together on the words of the Lord's Prayer and journeying into its deeper meanings.

For all of you who have suffered because of alcoholism and addiction, know that I am your brother. Alcoholism was in my family, in my childhood home and, yes, in my own personal life. Depression is something I have experienced, as have many other people. If you ever have felt overlooked, lonely, and inferior, I am your brother. I have experienced those feelings also.

Growing up as an only child in a dysfunctional home, my early life was less than ideal, a whole lot less. I remember my parent's "marriage" as a marriage only in a minimal sense of the word. Because of my father's abuse of alcohol, or substitutes for it, I watched my mother carry on in isolation as she worked to raise me to feel loved and secure. My father loved me also (and I knew it), but... well, he had his problems.

At the age of twenty-three, I suffered two terrible losses. In January of 1956, I lost the girl I hoped to marry. Our relationship ended abruptly and inexplicably, leaving me with questions and with deep doubts about myself and about life. Dark thoughts of self-destruction tried to capture my soul. By God's grace they were defeated.

A few months later, doctors diagnosed my father with lung cancer. Early in August of that same year, he passed over into eternal life. Even though my relationship with my father was troubled, I loved him deeply. His death was a devastating blow to me. There was so much in our relationship that needed healing, and now he was gone. I was in deep despair and wanted to know why an all-loving God allowed such pain and suffering to come to a faithful young man such as myself.

My mother, who had herself experienced great suffering in her life, was filled with wisdom and compassion. Her faith was strong, very strong. Seeing me in emotional pain she brought forth from her prayer book a verse she knew as "The Prayer of an Unknown Confederate Soldier." Perhaps others know it by another name.

I asked God for strength, that I might achieve,
I was made weak, that I might learn humbly to obey....
I asked for health, that I might do greater things,
I was given infirmity, that I might do better things....
I asked for riches, that I might be happy,
I was given poverty, that I might be wise....
I asked for power, that I might have the praise of men,
I was given weakness, that I might feel the need of God....
I asked for all things, that I might enjoy life,
I was given life, that I might enjoy all things....
I got nothing that I asked for -- but everything I had hoped for,

Almost despite myself, my unspoken prayers were answered.
I am among all men most richly blessed.

Mother didn't talk with me about what this prayer meant. She didn't need to. In suffering as in love, hearts speak to hearts, and this prayer spoke directly to my heart, challenging me to think about God's goodness and love for me and for others, a love and presence that hides deep within our losses and pain. I began to experience my Catholic faith as never before, finding within the Mass the Suffering One whose heart poured out compassion for all of God's estranged children.

Time and God's good graces eventually healed my wounds. I continued to pursue my education and became a lawyer. Thoughts about life, love, and God kept surfacing from deep within me and later on I experienced God calling me to leave my career in law and seek out Christ's priesthood.

Throughout my life, I continue to struggle with pain, rejection, and loneliness, as everyone does from time to time. Along the way, however, I have learned that God's presence, comfort, and love are always available to us in prayer and in the Eucharist.

Earlier in my life, my prayers were all about what God could give me. My attitude reflected a greater question about religion, attending Mass, and being Catholic. "What's in it for me?" This is a valid question even though it is a spiritually immature one. A better question might be, "Why is there something in it for me?" Prayer has a purpose, and that is what this book is all about.

The Purpose of Prayer

Somewhere along my own journey I began to ask: Is prayer all about disposing God to do things for me, or is it about putting myself at the disposal of God? The second half of that question makes the direction of our fundamental consideration obvious. Prayer is really all about locating ourselves in relation to God, not the other way around.

This book looks into the essential meaning and purpose of the verses we know as the Lord's Prayer, or the "Our Father." Even though the Lord's Prayer at first appears to be about what we want from God, I hope that, upon deeper reflection, we will see that it is really all about how we can place ourselves at God's disposal. When I pray the Lord's Prayer as Jesus prayed it, I seek to respond to our Father's offer and invitation. Prayer is not "all about me" but rather "all about God."

The most frequently asked questions about prayer are, "Why are my prayers unanswered? Often it appears that I don't get what I pray for," and "Why is God silent, distant and seemingly uncaring?" and "What is prayer, anyway?" We must deal with these questions before we can move on to deeper reflections about prayer.

Prayer Changes Us, Not God

If prayer is to change anything at all, it is to change us, to change our minds, our attitudes, and the way we live. Genuine prayer puts us at God's disposal. It allows us to see what God dreamed we could be when He created us. Ask yourself what's more real, the self you see, or the self God sees? The self God sees is what we can be, not what we have been, or done, or accomplished. Prayer, in other words, takes hold of the Presence and gives us power over ourselves, not power over God. Prayer gives us the chance to see ourselves in God's eyes and therefore to live with self-respect, in peace, and with the power not only to change ourselves but also the power to heal, to love, and to free others so they can see themselves in the same Light of God. Prayer liberates us. That is good news!

Intercessory prayer for others should, I believe, be seen in that light. God wants us to pray for our family, friends, those who are hurting, and even our enemies. Why? In order to change His mind about them? No! It's in order that we might find our selves along with them in God's love for us all. If we call down God's love upon others, we are recognizing God as our Father, which properly locates us in our relationships with Him and with others. Hopefully such prayers will change our ways of dealing with others and deepen our communion with them.

Our prayers are answered in God's way, not ours. The Spirit's main work is to change us, to make us care more, and to get us to focus on what others are going through instead of seeing the world only from our own perspective.

Prayer is that place where we stand before the Icon, the Icon that is God's Word made flesh, and there discover the Presence in order that we can, in turn, become icons revealing God's presence to others. Because of Christ, and in Christ, we are in the image and likeness of God. Through the Sacraments of the Church, we are incorporated into Him... we live in Him, and He lives in us. His Body and Blood mingle with and become part of ours.

During Mass, at the "Presentation of the Gifts," the priest takes the wine-filled chalice and, mingling a few drops of water into the wine, prays, "Through this mingling of water and wine, may we come to share in the divinity of Christ who humbled himself to share in our humanity." That humanity, represented by the water, is yours and mine. Then the wine, with the drops of water mingled in it, is consecrated and by God's power changed into the Blood of Christ. Prayer allows a "mingling with God" to occur so that all we have watered down in life can be changed into His true and real presence among us.

Not only does prayer change us, but prayer doesn't change anything other than us. It calls us to lose control, to surrender, and to let God's presence well up more powerfully and more brightly from deep within us, where He was in the first place, and is now abiding.

Christian spirituality doesn't so much provide us with answers as it challenges us with a journey, a great adventure. Discipleship isn't so much a status, like "being

xiii

a student," as it is a way of life. Following Jesus is an active, not passive, adventure along His way, with His truth, and in His life. It's a way of living, a way of seeing, and a way of relating, relating to one's self, relating to others, and relating to God.

Along that way God healed my broken heart and later called me to serve Him as a priest of Jesus Christ. Living out life in His Priesthood has caused me (necessarily caused me) to share in the losses and sufferings of so many people, as well as allowed me to witness their resurrections into new life and their victories over sin and death. Because I have seen it and experienced it, I know that Christ lives on in His Mystical Body, the Church, in people who are searching for the One who brings peace, hope, and life to us all. This book shares insights I have learned in the past thirty-eight years along Christ's way, in His truth, and living in His life.

Prior to undertaking the task of writing this book, my prayers were usually directed to Jesus Christ, God the Son. Writing this book has led me to pray much more frequently now to God our Father, a Father whom I now love in a closeness I never before experienced. Entering more thoughtfully and prayerfully into the way Jesus prayed, into what He taught and lived, has brought me into the heart of His Father and mine, into His Father and yours, into our Father.

Won't you walk with me for a while now as we venture into the richness of the prayer that Jesus taught us? In it, we will be together entering into the heart of God, the God who is our Father.

xiv

ENTERING THE HEART OF GOD

Praying the Lord's Prayer in Our Day

Part 1

Prayers of Adoration

OUR...

Self is the only prison that can ever bind the soul.
Henry Van Dyke, **The Prison and the Angel**

Whose God is God, mine or ours? Do "we" have our God and "they" have theirs? The word "Our" may well be the most significant word in our Christian Community of Faith.

Take yourself back to the earliest moments in your life and the earliest ideas that you learned. Surely you recall those moments when you learned what was meant by "my" and "mine." Those were life-defining moments, were they not? They shaped and formed what we, as adults, understand as the concept of sharing. Their influence extends down through the days of our lives to this very moment; their influence is hidden within what we mean when we pray "Our" Father.

I recall a life-defining moment back when I was in the second grade. I can't remember what I had taken from another child but my second grade teacher, standing in front of the class, pointed her finger at me and told everyone that I had taken whatever it was and that I lied to her when she asked me if I had taken it. Over sixty years later I can still feel the shame. But I also, because of that moment, came to understand what "my" and "mine" really mean. Perhaps that lesson also contributed to my lifelong inclination to be a giver rather than a taker.

1

Not many weeks after that schoolroom lesson in life, the Japanese bombed Pearl Harbor. Thereafter the word "our" took on a breadth and depth of meaning that is still with me. All Americans of that time understood "our," I am sure, in a new and life-changing way.

"Our" is a terribly powerful word. When we hear someone say, "You are one of ours," our hearts can be taken to the heights of happiness. But when we are told the opposite, "You are not one of ours," we can be plunged into the depths of depression and unhappiness. It's wonderful to be chosen; it's devastating to be told we are not. The experience of being rejected, excluded, or not wanted has an effect that echoes in our hearts and minds for the rest of our lives. It can be the soil out of which grows hateful and antisocial behavior toward others, perhaps even leading to neuroses and worse. These days the word "our" is losing its grip on us. What is "mine" as distinguished from what is "yours" seems to be of greater concern for people than what we acknowledge to be "ours."

Into a world shot through with conflicts between "I," "mine," "you," and "yours," God sent Christ Jesus to us, not just to end conflict and division but to help us see what is "ours" and to give us His Father as ours. That Christian vision immediately offends many people. They will likely stay offended until they understand who Jesus was and is. But understanding who Jesus was and is would take us into a journey that is way beyond the scope of this book.

2

The very first word of the Lord's Prayer immediately presents you and me with a problem. I need to experience and know "my" God in a personal way. I need to experience and know Jesus Christ personally and uniquely as my Lord and Savior. At the same time I must let others have their own personal and inner relationship with God. I should not and cannot demand that others experience God as I do in order that they might be saved. Christianity is, after all, not an imperialistic religion. It calls and *invites* others to be aware of God personally in Christ Jesus. It invites us into a huge, diverse, worldwide family made up of individuals, a family in which God our Father loves each one of us with all of His love.

> Now once he was in a certain place praying, and when he had finished one of his disciples said, "Lord, teach us to pray, just as John taught his disciples." He said to them, "Say this when you pray:
> "Father, may your name be held holy, your kingdom come; give us each day our daily bread, and forgive us our sins, for we ourselves forgive each one who is in debt to us. And do not put us to the test."
> **Luke 11:1-4** [See also **Matthew 6:9-13**]

"Our" seems to be the most important word in this entire prayer. This opening word is, for some, the most upsetting of the Lord's Prayer. We want to belong. At the same time we want to keep all our options open, be in charge of our destiny, and set our terms, all of which seem contrary to surrendering into and belonging with others. The autonomous self is threatened by the word "our." It is quite challenging to be independent while at the same time being available to others, others who need us in so many ways and at such different levels.

3

"Our" and "My"

Early in my life my heart was frozen many times by the word "our." Being "chubby" and athletically challenged, I was told out on the school playground, "We don't need you," which translated really meant, "We don't want you numbered among us. We have our team and you're not good enough to be on it."

"Our" was thus used in a limiting way, as a possessive and narrowing word, an exclusive word -- not an inclusive word broad enough to include me. Immediately Jesus confronts us with one of life's most basic issues: Are we going to be inclusive or exclusive? Is our faith community going to exclude or include? Do I limit my heart only to those who are in my circle?

My childhood experience of family illustrates, perhaps, this desire for belonging. Mom and dad were unbounded in their love for me. I am largely who I am because of the limitless love they gave me. I am ever so grateful to God for the parents He gave me. Because of them my heart is large and can both hold and give a lot of love. But I was an only child and this generated a unique form of longing to belong to others. I really missed having brothers. I especially missed having sisters. I was jealous of my friends who had them. Dare I wonder if Jesus (being an only child Himself) shares with me that same hunger, that same longing?

The word "our" is a two-edged sword. It can be used inclusively, or it can be used to exclude. I have heard some Christians speak of "our God" with the implication

4

that He is not "your God." We have our God, they are saying, and you have yours. God is "ours," they think, believing they have a monopoly on His love. "We decide," they say to themselves, "who is saved and who is damned because God is on our side, not on yours." As with so many other issues in life, this is at root a control issue. We think we decide what God is thinking, saying, and doing. He is ours. We possess His love. We decide who is "in" and who is "out." Our God, you see, is my God. All of this, of course, perverts the meaning of the word "our" as Jesus used it in His prayer.

Love, too, is often corrupted and used as a means of manipulation. Love is granted or withheld under the terms of the strategies and tactics we deploy upon those whom we allegedly love. Marriage and commitment, love and control are at times intertwined like the pasta on a plate under a seemingly tasty spaghetti sauce. Abortion, euthanasia, stem cell harvesting, and any number of other medical issues confront us with issues of control, often cloaked in words of love. "It's the loving and compassionate thing to do," we are told. But really it's the controlling thing to do.

"Our" indicates that God wants to be the loving Father of you and me, His children. It tells us that no one of us (or group of us) has a monopoly over His love and attention. He is not exclusively the Father of Christians, all others thereby being "outsiders." Only in the risen Christ do Christians share in Christ's unique and prior claim on God our Father. Our Father loves all of His children with all of His love. Our claim on our Father's love is warranted only in Jesus' claim. He shares with us His belonging to His Father. Jesus makes His claim become our claim on our Father's life, along with our claim on His love.

Our religion and our faith are not solitary, confined to our selves alone. My faith, and yours as well, is shaped and formed by the faith of others. My faith comes to me through a community. Likewise in that community my faith contributes to the faith of others and becomes a part of theirs. Individualistically oriented Americans have a problem with Catholicism because the Church calls us to a faith that is both communal and individual. The community shapes and forms the individual; the individual contributes to the form and shape of our communal Church. We do not make our family of faith. God made it and He gives it to us in His Christ, which is why the Church is not simply a human institution.

> For as he (viz., Lucifer) was endowed with divine splendour, and shone forth among the other higher powers by the bounty of his Maker, he believed that he had acquired the splendour of that wisdom and the beauty of those powers, with which he was graced by the gift of the Creator, by the might of his own nature, and not by the beneficence of His generosity. And on this account he was puffed up as if he stood in no need of divine assistance in order to continue in this state of purity, and esteemed himself to be like God, as if, like God, he had no need of any one, and trusting in the power of his own will, fancied that through it he could richly supply himself with everything which was necessary for the consummation of virtue or for the perpetuation of perfect bliss.
> **JOHN CASSIAN**, The Twelve Books on the Institutes of the Coenobia and the Remedies for the Eight Principal Faults

"My" is a word that separates me from the others around me and the world around me. It isolates and differentiates, making me "different." There is nothing wrong with that when being different is located in a contextual whole. In the extreme, however, being "different" can put me outside of a communion of life and love with others. My uniqueness is generated by and nurtured in my family's life.

"My" is an ambiguous word because in it I am individuated. I am a unique person. God made me unique. If I do not love God as who I am then He will never be loved as only I can love Him. This being so, I am called to know, to love, and to relate to "my" Father in heaven. God wants my individuality, to be loved by the individual that I am. God wants me to be the "me" that He gave me and that I develop in my response to Him in His family.

Jesus speaks of "my Father." One finds one's individuation in personally belonging to others! My character and personality are formed in my belonging to my family. We need to see that the Trinity of Persons is composed of individuated Persons precisely and paradoxically in the fact that they totally belong to each other. In your mind you can distinguish between the Persons of the Trinity, but you can't separate them and still call yourself a follower of Christ. Being made in the image and likeness of God, then, we are likewise individuated in our belonging to others. It is in our belonging to others that we develop our own unique and individuated character and personality. It's a hard lesson for us to learn. In our lust to be totally in control it's hard to be vulnerable to, and shaped by, others.

7

God made me to love Him uniquely and individually as I am. How can I not speak about my Father? I belong to Him -- in His heart and in mine we belong to each other. In the "our" Jesus uses we all belong to each other -- the Father, Jesus, you, and me. This was the path that Jesus of Nazareth followed in His journey through life. Everything He did or said was located in His constant reference to His Father. Everything Jesus accomplished was grounded on that fundamental relationship. There are times when it is appropriate, and in fact needful, to address God personally: "O my God I am heartily sorry for all my sins..."; "O Lord, hear my voice and let my cry come unto Thee...." Private, personal, and individualized prayer is just as important as corporate, communal prayer, and at times it may be more so.

Still, "my" can be the word of the devil; it is Satan's favorite word. Note the temptations he presented to Christ in the desert: "All these are *mine*," he said. "And I will give them to you."

What happens when a child learns the word "mine"? A spirit of possessiveness enters his heart. How soon little children think they can take for themselves what belongs to others. What a blow to the tyrannical little ego it is when the child learns he cannot! The undeveloped, self-centered ego makes the assumption, "I can possess what I want -- anything I desire is mine." Paradoxically, and at the same time importantly, the child needs to learn that the words "my" and "mine" are belonging words, they tell others that I belong by contributing and sharing what is

8

mine with those who surround me. We spend our lives striking that balance.

"Our" means that I sacrifice myself for the sake of others; I give myself over to something greater than me... for our common good... for the nation and family to which I belong and in which I find my life.

We all have within us (if we dare take the time to enter into reflective silence) an awareness of being more than simply the sum of our sensory and bodily stimulations. I am who I am as a person because of those powers and faculties that inhere in my soul. My soul is the core of what is "me." I can think, and I can reflect on what I am thinking; animals cannot do that.

While "soul" is the core of me, it is somehow found and revealed in my belonging to others. I find what is "mine" in learning what is "ours." I possess what is mine when I possess what is found in the reality of what we mean when we use the word "our." This is why Christianity is not a "me and Jesus" religion, but rather a "we and Jesus"

> Before all things, the Teacher of peace and the Master of unity would not have prayer to be made singly and individually, as for one who prays to pray for himself alone. For we say not "My Father, which art in heaven," nor "Give me this day my daily bread;" nor does each one ask that only his own debt should be forgiven him; nor does he request for himself alone that he may not be led into temptation, and delivered from evil. Our prayer is public and common; and when we pray, we pray not for one, but for the whole people, because we the whole people are one. The God of peace and the Teacher of concord, who taught unity, willed that one should thus pray for all, even as He Himself bore us all in one.
> **St. Cyprian**, d.258, Treatise IV On the Lord's Prayer, 8.

9

encounter with the living God. Once again the Way of Jesus is found in approaching and receiving our Father.

We speak often of "our" sins as well as "my" sins. But we must remember that "my" sins, my own personal and private sins, have an effect on others. All sin is social; there's no such thing as an "isolated" or private sin. Sins are not private at all! All sins, even so-called solitary sins, have an impact on those around me. They affect my attitude toward others along with the way that I live in relating to others.

Solitary and private sins influence how I regard others. They lower the esteem in which I hold others, reduce the dignity that others have in my mind and in my attitudes. Internal sins and so-called "private" sins of racism have an external effect. Internal and individual sins of lust, envy, and pride affect the way I treat others. They show up in my external actions and reactions toward others. Lust makes others merely objects of pleasure for my own personal gratification. This is why "victimless" sins do not exist; everyone is touched and diminished by "private" sins. They have an impact on the whole communion, the whole community, and the social order in which I act.

"Our" and the Autonomous Self

What is mine and what is God's is the fundamental question presented us in the Book of Genesis, the book that ushers us into the drama in which we face and hopefully overcome all of life's challenges to us --

10

challenges to our ego, our pride, and our autonomy. Are we equal to God, or are we not? Are we our own autonomous gods, or are we not? The drama is set against the background of our response to the meaning of the word "our."

"Our" occurs three times in the Lord's Prayer. "Us" occurs five times. "My" never occurs. Thus the "our" is not a possessive word but rather an indicative one. It reveals God's nature and who He is. He is the One who is always for you and for me. Jesus' prayer is a communal prayer; His entire life was communal.

In our contemporary culture the mass media exalts the virtues of being self-assertive and self-sufficient. We must remember, however, that there are other virtues, too. Being self-sufficient needs to be placed in the context of these other virtues. Self-realization is popular these days, but by itself is a bogus way of living. It is impossible for me to make myself real all by myself. There is much that is proper and good about self-affirmation, and many folks need it, particularly those who have been victimized by others. But while self-affirmation is good in many instances, in other cases it can lead individuals to live unbalanced lives, lives in which self-affirmation is skewed into an aggressive self-assertion that destroys wholesome relationships with others.

In asserting my own individualistic and self-centered rights I can trample upon and destroy those rights that belong to others. In asserting my self-centered entitlements I may take away from my community's common good. I may diminish its values and weaken its bonds. Isn't this one of the chief problems in our contemporary world?

The world has led us to believe that everything we need is within our own power to grasp and achieve. Happiness, we are told, lies within us. In America, you can be anything you want to be, if only you work for it, we are told. Bookstore shelves buckle under the weight of self-help works. Subtly they replace God-help books. The truth is that God has sent His Son to save us, not to show us how we can save ourselves. It is God who saves us, a truth that is in complete opposition to the prevailing dogmas of our highly individualistic and secularized culture.

Yet how can you save yourself if you are sinking in a pond of quicksand where the more you thrash around the more it sucks you down in its suffocating grip? The only way out is to grasp the hand of someone who stands on rock and, hands gripped together, you pull together in order to be lifted out and saved. Our deliverance, our salvation, comes from a power outside of ourselves. We simply cannot save ourselves; the more we try the more we are pulled down. The combination of humility, trust, faith, and surrender to our Higher Power is the only path to our salvation. Paradoxically, independence comes to us from our dependence on God. We win by surrendering -- surrendering our wills and our lives into the care of God.

But where do we find God? "Up" in the cosmos? "Out there in space," as if He were some distant Force in the universe?

Jesus reveals to us that we are as far away from God as we are removed from those who surround us. This is why being too individualistic can cast us into the hell of isolation and loneliness. In our age of hyper-individualism, is it any wonder that so many of us are lonely? Radical individualism takes us away from God and damns us to living lives only for our selves. Individuals living in isolation are cut off from communion. They are literally ex-communicated. The result of this rampant individualism is that we are rejecting the very life of God, the God who is a community of interdependent Persons.

Thus we see that the way we treat those around us is the way we treat God. It's not the other way around! The way we treat God doesn't necessarily mean that we'll treat those around us very well. We have only to look at people who are "hyper-religious" and see how they treat others around them. When asked why he was not a Christian, Mahatma Gandhi replied, "I love your Christ. It's you Christians that I can't stand!"

The greatest indicator of original sin is the condition of our society. Original Sin is in our origins and is something that we share. It, too, is ours. It's in our DNA coding; it's in our genes. We are conceived in a collectivity and history of human self-centeredness, greed, and aggressive self-assertion over and against others. Abuse of others is a deep wound in our souls, a wound that weakens us and takes us more deeply into self-centeredness. It results in the breakdown of communication and then the breakdown of community.

13

What follows is consequent loss of communion along with a concomitant loss of understanding, empathy, and compassion.

Original sin is at work amongst us. We see it every day in the news about what we humans are doing to each other and to the world that has been given us. We are all desperately in need of redemption because our society and culture is so fractured. Talk of finding "redeeming qualities" is commonplace in our mass media. That's all very nice. But as the media projects its images and its icons into our living rooms, whose values are shaping our attitudes and ways of thinking? For sure, they are not God's values.

Where do I find and receive the power to govern my destiny? Does it come from my autonomous self, or does it come from belonging with others in life's great causes? That is the question of our day and a great many consequences flow from how we as Americans and Christians answer it. It is childish to think I can self-generate that power all by myself.

"Our" and the Family of Jesus

I wonder how many people really mean "our" when they pray this prayer. My fear is that far too many of us really don't believe we can know God as

> Because we all have the same Father we are bonded together as one.
> **St. Cyril of Alexandria**

"Father," as Jesus teaches us to relate to God, because we only know the sort of "Father" we ourselves conceptualize. Indeed the very word "father" is in trouble these days because so many sons and daughters have had painful relationships with their own earthly fathers and stepfathers.

We all belong to our Father together, even though some of us don't want to. Others simply don't bother to care.   Still others devote their whole lives to it. Underneath all our thoughts and feelings, however, we belong to each other because we come from the same Creator and Father of us all.

I wonder if, because of Jesus, you see the Father that is ours? Or do you see only the Father that you individually see? Indeed some modern philosophers question whether anything "out there" can be seen and known at all, and then shared in the same way I see and know external reality. Is it possible for two or more people to see and know something in the same way? Many people deny that is possible, insisting that no one can see and know something in the same way as others do. If that is the case, then, why bother even praying to "our Father"?

Most Christians, and certainly Catholic philosophers and theologians, still insist that Truth can be known, understood, and shared by all of us in a common-union. We still hold to the notion that together we can see, know, and experience God as our Father. If we don't hold to that, then the Lord's Prayer is meaningless.

"Our" is used when speaking of the family of faith called the Church. Catholics speak of "our Church" more often than they speak of "my Church." And even though Christians are divided by denominational boundaries we all pray to our Father, for there is one faith, one Lord, one baptism, and one God and Father of us all. "Our

> It is truly right to give you thanks, it is fitting that we sing of your glory, Father of infinite goodness.
> Through the gospel proclaimed by your Son you have brought together in a single Church people of every nation, culture, and tongue.
> Into it you breathe the power of your Spirit, that in every age your children may be gathered as one.
> Your Church bears steadfast witness to your love. It nourishes our hope for the coming of your kingdom and is a sure sign of the lasting covenant which you promised us in Jesus Christ our Lord. Therefore heaven and earth sing forth your praise while we, with all the Church, proclaim your glory without end:
> Holy, holy Lord, God of power and might...
> **Preface for Eucharistic Prayer: "The Church on the Way to Unity"**

Father" denotes belonging; it signifies family, our family of faith.

When you make a commitment to belong to a parish you are committing yourself to tolerate or at least "put up with" others in that community who are different from you, who belong to another political party, who are of a different race or ethnic background. You may not agree with the person who sits next to you, but you still share the "Greeting of Peace" with them just before you share your Holy Communion with all the others who make up the Body of Christ. Does everyone in your parish have to be just like you in your thinking, agree with your view of

16

our government's social policies, your local school board's policies, etc.?

To love God and to love our neighbor can never be separated from each other. To love God and not want to live in communion with others -- not even want to be with them in church -- is to live in spiritual isolation. To live in isolation is to live a privatized, delusional life. To live apart from the Church is to live in a false and self-delusional spirituality.

The scandal of the Church is that it is so filled with all that is human. To reject the Church is to reject what is so very human, to cast it off instead of loving it enough to redeem it, which is the way and the life of Christ Jesus.

The history of the Church is a saga filled with failure and sin, glory and holiness. Historical humanity is found, redeemed, and celebrated in a historical Church. Human history and the history of the Church are filled with light and darkness, sanctity and depravity, people who are sincere as well as people who are hypocritical. Do we love them, or leave them?

The Father we address in the Lord's Prayer is the One God and Father of us all. He belongs to us all; as a family of faith we belong to Him because we find our origins in His creative love. Each of us is involved in His loving activity. And when we pray to Him as our Father we acknowledge that we belong to Him in His sons and daughters.

Our Father is the Father of all living people, of all living creatures. "Our" of Jesus' prayer dissolves boundaries, opens gates, and recognizes that God's love has no

17

dimensions. It is immeasurable; it is limitless. We are presumptuous when we try to contain it within our man-made limits.

"Our" speaks of the groups to which we belong -- family, school, team, and nation, to name just a few. In the Declaration of Independence we declared that we are "endowed by our Creator with certain unalienable rights." "Our" speaks of a Common Good that we all share together, a Commonweal, with values, wealth, and treasure, that we preserve, protect, and defend in a shared social order. "Our" speaks of neighborhood and what we share because we are neighbors.

God saves us by the fact that we belong -- we belong to His people. We are members of His family. It is there, in that place, that He acts on me -- and it is in that reality that He sanctifies me, justifies me, and saves me.

Salvation is not an individualistic thing. Salvation comes to us from God. He offers; we respond. We are saved. I am saved because I belong; I belong to Christ in His Mystical Body; I belong to His family; I belong to His Church. I belong to the God whom we address as our Father. He is not just my Father, He is our Father.

"Our" and the Vision of Jesus

It is important to recognize the place and situation in which Jesus taught His disciples this prayer. St. Matthew, in his Gospel, has Jesus teaching this prayer to the crowds gathered on the Mount of Beatitudes high above all that

18

separates, high up in a sweeping panorama that gathers everything into one, broad, and all-encompassing vista.

We also need to be aware that Jesus spent considerable time at the Temple in Jerusalem, in the Court of the Gentiles, teaching men and women coming from anywhere and everywhere. The Jewish people of Christ's time knew it as the House of Prayer for All Peoples.

Is, then, our religion, our spirituality, and our approach to God exclusive or inclusive? Is God our Father only as Catholics understand him? Or

> Look with favor on the offering of your Church in which we show forth the paschal sacrifice of Christ entrusted to us.
> Through the power of your Spirit of love include us now and forever among the members of your Son, whose body and blood we share.
> Renew by the light of the gospel the Church of N. [diocese/place].
> Strengthen the bonds of unity between the faithful and their pastors, that together with N. our pope, N. our bishop, and the whole college of bishops, your people may stand forth in a world torn by strife and discord as a sign of oneness and peace.
> **Eucharistic Prayer** for "The Church on the Way to Unity."

Jews? Or Muslims? Or Jehovah's Witnesses, Mormons, or Unitarians? We have to look into our souls and ask ourselves if we are possessive of God... the God we are tempted to make exclusively ours.

"Our" is such a significant word in the prayer Jesus taught us, the central descriptive word for what we mean by "home" and "family." I don't think it is a coincidence that Jesus positioned "our" as the first word in His prayer. We need to note, too, the words of His disciple's request: "Lord, teach us how to pray...." The plural again.

19

Jesus gave us a unique way of living, along with transcendent truths and a limitless life. Joining our lives into Christ's really means that He joins His life into ours. If that is so, then we are brothers and sisters at a level we cannot completely comprehend. In His holy sacrifice we are His blood brothers and sisters, sharing a Spirit of Life that cannot possibly be the result of our own making. That being so, then all that we call Justice and Brotherhood has a grounding beyond any human reach (thank God!). Our history of dealing with transcendent ideals has been pretty shameful, to say the least. We have badly smeared all that is transcendent with our own stains. What a wonder it is, then, that God allowed Himself to become one with our humanity!

In following Jesus, you and I don't hear only about His Father, nor do we simply obey His laws and commands. It is much more than that. In the Jesus of Nazareth who was raised in His resurrection to be the Spirit-filled Christ of glory, we receive a

> In the Offertory, as the priest pours a little water into the wine he says: "By the mystery of this water and wine may we come to share in the divinity of Christ, who humbled himself to share our humanity."
> **Liturgy of the Eucharist**

share in His very life! In Baptism, Confirmation, and all of the other Sacraments, the life of God the Son is fused into our lives, both individually and collectively. He takes on our humanity in order that we may become a part of His divinity. We are baptized and confirmed into His Spirit-filled, resurrected humanity.

Thus when we worship God in the Mass, replete with its rich symbolisms, we should see our individuality in the hosts of bread processed to the altar in the offertory procession of the Mass. These individual hosts, given as gifts, present us to God on His altar, the altar of sacrifice upon which His Son continually gathers us into Himself to take us home to our Father in Heaven. Crushed, ground, and baked together, these grains of wheat encapsulate and then represent you and me in the offertory. Each host is thereupon consecrated in the central and most sacred prayer of the Mass, the Eucharistic Prayer. Each one of us then becomes a living cell in the Mystical Body of Christ, mingled into His Spirit-filled humanity. My faith becomes part of another person's being because my individuality becomes a part of the whole Christ, and then is received by another who shares in Christ's, and now our, Holy Communion. Just as each Person in the Holy Trinity retains His individuality while living in the unity of God's being, so also, in Holy Communion, we each retain our individuality while now living in oneness in God.

All of this being so, when I receive Holy Communion am I prepared to swallow all those who compose it? If I wish to receive the whole Christ I must be prepared to swallow all the others who comprise Him in His Mystical Body.

If you and I are to see the face of God then we have to see His face in the faces of those around us. For He has told us that's where He can be found, that's where His Presence resides. "I was thirsty, I was naked, I was in jail, I was sick, I was lonely, etc. and you cared for me." He is found in us, not in me alone.

21

Finally, we are His children. We are not childish passive dependents; we are sons and daughters who recognize we are in need, that we need His Fatherly presence, power, and love. We are His family and He gives each one of us all of His love. Justice, peace, compassion, forgiveness, and restoration to new life are not just poetic ideals; they are divine imperatives, requirements for living in the family that addresses God as Our Father.

* * * * * * *

PRAYER

O Father, I want to be alone and I want to belong; I want to share and I do not want to share; I am afraid of loneliness and yet I fear commitment. "Ours" is such a challenge to me and to what I hold as "mine."

You belong totally to your Son and your Holy Spirit; you are plural and yet individual. O God, help me to live in your image and likeness, help me to live as you live. Remove my fears and in my individuality give me the will to be dependent upon others so that I may live your life in mine and be generous as you are generous.

* * * * * * *

QUESTIONS

What things do we as humans share with others?
Who does God not love?
What is the reasoning behind your answer?
What is exclusively mine?
What of me can God not have?

① Every thing
② Selfishness
③ We do not own anything or anyone - We are all children of God, therefore we must be willing to let go of anything or anyone, if it separates us from "God, Our Father".
④ Nothing
⑤ Nothing

FATHER...

He fathers-forth whose beauty is past change:
Praise him.
  Gerard Manley Hopkins, "Pied Beauty"

Images of Fatherhood

Once, while on an airline flight, I watched a big six-foot, two-inch young man in his twenties, built like a football player, as he walked up and down the aisle of the plane

> Childless indeed is pagan philosophy – always in pains of childbirth, it never engenders living offspring.
> **St. Gregory of Nyssa**

while holding his one-year-old child to his breast, covering the child with kisses and cuddling him, all the while cooing soft reassuring sounds. That child was wrapped in love, secure in the arms of his daddy, utterly protected and at peace.

In the ancient world, no one ever addressed the Almighty, Everlasting, and Omnipotent Creator of the universe and all living creatures within it, as "papa." Such audacity would have been beyond the limits of any rational, thinking person. Yet that is precisely what Jesus did! While there are a few Old Testament references that speak of God as a father by virtue of His creative and protective power (see Psalm 68:8, Psalm 103:1; Isaiah 63:16; Isaiah 64:8), Jesus was the first to speak of God as "Abba," a title of intimate kinship. This was something quite unprecedented in any of the world's great religions.

24

Jesus made God personal for us; He revealed to us the heart of God as "Father."

Do we feel that way about God? Dare we think of God as Father? Jewish people are suspicious, and rightly so, of any depictions or visualizations of God. Why? Because we humans have an enormous propensity to fashion idols for ourselves. If you don't think so, take a close look at what media outlets offer us today. Idols abound. It is in that context that we moderns blithely and foolishly attempt to fashion God into our own image and likeness.

How merciful the Lord is to us, how kind and richly compassionate. He wished us to repeat this prayer in God's sight, to call the Lord our Father and, as Christ is God's Son, be called in turn sons of God! None of us would ever have dared to utter this name unless he himself had allowed us to pray in this way. And therefore, dear friends, we should bear in mind and realize that when we call God our Father we ought also to act like sons. If we are pleased to call him Father, let him in turn be pleased to call us sons.
St. Cyprian of Carthage (d.253), No. 11-12:CSEL 3. 274-275

Jesus gave us two predominant images to consider with respect to the fatherhood of God. The first shows us how to be a child of God, and the second reveals to us the kind of Father God is. "He who sees me sees the Father," Jesus tells us (John 12:45). He frequently used the phrase "my father in heaven" along with many references to "the one who sent me." This repetition indicates how important this concept of God as Father was to Jesus and how important that image of God should be for us, also.

Imagination is the process of imaging; this process is crucial in how we relate ourselves to God. Imagination is so important that Jesus taught predominantly in parables and stories, rather than theological tracts. Our fundamental relationship with God is grounded on the images we have of Him.

It took me a long time to feel close to God as a father, as my heavenly Father. My earliest awareness was conditioned in such a way that I approached God as the "Supreme Judge" sitting on His heavenly bench, deigning to hear my pleadings. I felt unworthy to approach God, and in my prayers I approached Him for clemency and mercy, both for myself and for others, with great fear. My prayers and devotion focused on begging Him to withhold His wrath. I never missed Mass on Sunday, not out of love for God but to avoid going to hell. I approached Jesus my Judge in fear and trembling, looking to His Mother, Mary, for compassion, understanding, warmth, protection, and mercy. In one prayer I remember praying often as a child I asked Mary "to protect me from Jesus my Judge." Imagine that! Mary was supposed to protect me from Jesus! It was only later in life, when I began to see Jesus as my Friend, Brother, and the One who loved me, that I was able to picture and then approach God as my Abba...Papa.

To see God as Jesus wants us to see Him, we must let go of the baggage and negative associations we have with the word "father," but we must also relinquish the idealized image of the perfect father. Our human impressions are wholly inadequate. God our Father is strong, loving, and wise. He is head of the gigantic human family, the Father who provides us with our "Mother Earth," and the One who regards each of us as "the apple of His eye." When we face life's storms and the chaos that threatens our world, we can fly to Him to find refuge.

Because Jesus continually spoke of God as "Father," it is perhaps inevitable that we superimpose our own images of what it means to be a good father. Jesus never intended for us to replace revealed truth with our own subjective experience, however, but instead carefully set out to reveal what kind of a Father our God truly is. The most complete and perfect expression of this revelation was the Incarnation itself. Jesus declared, "He who sees me, sees the Father," and "The Father and I are one." To see God as our Father we need to see Christ Jesus as He relates to others and to us. Jesus, in His humanity, is the Icon of God.

What does it mean to be a father? The ideas that come to me are that such men are strong, loving, present to their children, and wise. Protectors and providers, they shape us and guide us as we grow. They give us refuge when necessary and then send us out into the world when we're ready. They give us care and support without making us passive dependents, leading us, and not manipulating us, challenging us while not making us cringe before them.

People honor me, a Catholic priest, by calling me "Father." Over the years I have come to realize that to be a good priest, one must be able to be a good father. But what does it mean to be a godly man and father?

A godly father is strong. Being strong does not mean that one beats children into submission. For me, being a good "father" has meant being near to God's children, being open and loving. What a blessing it has been for me

27

to see fathers express their affection for their children openly, not from an emotional distance.

A godly father is wise. A wise father is not merely a problem solver, however, for the employment of data and information does not comprise wisdom. Wisdom goes beyond data, information, analysis, and the implementation of what those elements indicate. To be sure, wise fathers teach, but they go beyond that and offer insight grounded in experience and love.

Mothers have equally important work to accomplish and missions to fulfill. Together, the two genders complement and fit each other much as pieces in a jigsaw puzzle. There is an "ought-ness" to their gender complementarity. This partially, and only partially, explains the urge within us to revere Mary, the Mother of God, as we do. Our souls impel us toward the complementary balance. The urge is toward family. The paternal along with the maternal gives us completeness, wholeness, and holiness.

Because God is our Father, we are all related to each other. Spiritually we are sister, brother, father, and mother to each other and for each other. This truth imposes obligations upon us, and makes it our duty to extend kindness, compassion, mercy, justice, truthfulness, and all manner of respect and caring to others, particularly to those whom we find "difficult." For them we should be Christ, the One whom God gave us as Brother, Lover, Savior, and Friend in order to bring us together back home to our Father in

> The best way to live is to trust the Lord; to keep peace in one's heart; to accept all things as being for the best; to be patient and good; never to do ill.
> **Pope John XXIII**

28

heaven. As members of His family we have ways of thinking, acting, and loving that heal us in our brokenness and in our fractured lives. This is the power of religion, healing us in our torn and dislocated ligaments of life.

Through His gift of love, God chose to make you His daughter or His son. You can call Him "Papa" -- Father -- because He first loved you. We did not love Him first, did not entice Him to declare a love for us that was not there from the beginning.

Only you can love our Father precisely as you. No other being, no other creature, or child of His love can love Him just as you can love Him. Did you ever think of that? If you don't love Him as you, God will never receive the love only you can give Him, the kind of love He envisioned in you before the world began. When you meditate on what that means you'll begin to get in touch with a stupendous truth. You are infinitely important to your heavenly Father and precious in His heart. If you were the only person on earth who needed to be redeemed, God our Father would have sent down His only Son to suffer and die just for you. You were bought back at a great price -- that's how important you are to your Father in heaven.

Problems with Fathers

Is it difficult for you to believe all this? If so, you are not alone.

Experiencing closeness with God presents an immediate difficulty for all too many of us. Many people have revealed to me that because of their relationships with their earthly fathers they have trouble feeling close to God as Father. With gentle probing they tell me that they experienced their own fathers as uncommunicative, distant, and even uncaring.

> O God, our help in ages past, our hope for years to come, Our shelter in the stormy blast, and our eternal home. Beneath the shadow of your throne your saints have dwelt secure. Sufficient is your arm alone, and our defense is sure.
> Hymn by **Isaac Watts**

Our many great spiritual mentors, from Jesus, Mary and Joseph down to the present day, tell us that God cares for us -- deeply cares for us. He listens to us; He loves us beyond anything we can imagine. Faith is the remedy and allows us to see what is spiritual and not of this world. Spiritual realities need to be seen spiritually, not as the worldly see things. Faith gives us vision -- good vision -- and good insight. Faith opens us up to God's love.

Our Ancient Enemy, Satan the Accuser, accuses God of being mean-spirited by denying us pleasure and the happiness of immediate gratification. Satan goes on to tell us that we are not entitled to God's love anyway because we're rotten and no-good failures. So he whispers, "Go ahead and do what you want to do. Indulge yourself, otherwise you'll miss what little pleasure is allotted to us in this life." Eat, drink, and be merry, he whispers, for soon you will die.

But God does not want us to give in to that lie. So eager was He to engage us in the truth, to show us His infinite power and tenderness, He pursued us all the way to Bethlehem. "The infinite and omnipotent God made himself little and limited," Pope John Paul II said (quoting the words of St. Jerome in the fourth century), "Look at him: He who holds the universe in His fist, is held in a narrow manger."

Jesus' Primary Image of God Our Father

Of all the images of God the Father given to us by Christ Jesus, none surpasses His parable of the prodigal son (see Luke 15). I think the most wonderful depiction we have of our Father among human artistic creations is Rembrandt's masterful painting of the return of the prodigal son, a return not only to his father but to his family of origin, to that world in which his character and personality were formed and shaped. In Rembrandt's marvelous vision, the boy with his head cradled in his father's hands looks as if he is returning to the womb. His return is complete -- back to his beginnings.

Like the father in the parable, God is always offering His love to us, always waiting for us to respond to His love. Our problem lies in accepting it. God never abandons us. When our feelings or decisions cause us to feel distance from God, the "distance" is not caused by God's withdrawal. We are the ones who have moved. Cannot God, then, use that sense of distance for our own spiritual good?

I must speak now of a great mystery, what mystics have called "The Dark Night of the Soul." Jesus entered into it on His cross. He cried out: "My God, my God, why have you abandoned me?" Many of us have experienced this.

31

We experience it when God thinks we are ready, when we reach that stage in our spiritual journey wherein all else falls away, when everyone else has abandoned us, and we have nothing other than God's will and God's love upon which to rely.

Does this mean that God is a capricious and "testing" Father? Not at all. He knows better than we do what we're made of, what's deep within us. Love, after all, calls us to do hard things. Love calls us to be faithful. To truly love, one cannot escape the cross.

All of us are mystics to some degree. We all reach points in our lives when, because of our human estrangement from others and from God, we plunge into the depths. "Out of the depths I cry out unto Thee," cries the Psalmist. It is a human cry that comes from the human heart, especially in times of transition from what is old to what is new. The elderly

> You are great, O Lord, and greatly to be praised: great is your power, and your wisdom is without measure. And man, so small a part of your creation, wants to praise you: this man, though clothed with mortality and bearing the evidence of sin and proof that you withstand the proud. Despite everything, man, though but a small a part of your creation, wants to praise you. You yourself encourage him to delight in your praise, for your have made us for yourself, and our heart is restless until it rests in you.
> **St. Augustine, CONFESSIONS**

experience it when their bodies and their powers begin to fall away as they approach the end of their lives and are forced to face the unknown and mysterious new. The young face it when the future looms too large to handle. This is due to no fault of our own but occurs because of our very nature as humans, living out our individual

32

odysseys as we pass through life and into the life our Father has prepared for each one of us. No dawn can come except through the night, and it is at its darkest and coldest just before dawn.

However far we may think of ourselves as distanced from God we can always return home to Him. He is our Father; we can never not be His sons and His daughters. In whatever condition we find ourselves, God's love is available to us unconditionally. No matter how we have squandered the treasures He has given us, He stands ready to share all He has with us. And, sinners that we are, when we actually do go back home to Him we are then truly "born again" as Christians in His Son. Perhaps that is the highlight of Rembrandt's insightful depiction.

Our Father has great expectations of each one of us. He waits and waits expectantly for us to turn to Him. In the parable Jesus says "But while he was still a long way off his father saw him" (Luke 15:20ff). How did the father see his wayward son? With hopeful waiting, expectant watching. It's as if after all that time he was still standing at the door, scanning the horizon, hoping, waiting for the day his son would return. He wanted to be the first to see him come over the hill.

Many fathers don't do this. Because of their own hurt, their hearts are not big enough to include the rejection of a child or even their child's need to seek independence. Fatherly indignation, along with manipulation and control, done in the name of "love," soon replace genuine love. Too many fathers resort to power, control, domination, and fear to keep their sons and daughters in line. And being "in line" means making their kids to do exactly what they want them to do, nothing more and nothing less. Mothers, too, can be guilty of the same.

Some parents go to war with an independent or strong-willed child to prove they are still in control. Other parents, when they face a child's rejection, respond in just the opposite but equally harmful way. They reject the child. The father in Jesus' parable does not react in either of these ways. He is big enough to contain the rejection of the son and to love him even still. He respects his son's freedom and dignity and doesn't go off to the distant city to find him and drag him back home. But neither does he cut off his son emotionally. He waits expectantly, longing for his return. And when the son finally hits bottom, and then comes to his senses, recognizes his need, and comes home to his father, the broken but still loving heart of the father is there waiting and watching, anticipating the return of his son. And while the son was still a long way off, his father sees him, and runs to him. I love that! It's a beautiful depiction of God.

Do you see this? Jesus is telling us that God our Father respects our dignity and freedom to choose whatever path we want and even to squander the good things He has given us. And He will allow us to live in whatever pigpen we have chosen to create for ourselves. He will not force us out of our moral, financial, relational, or spiritual pigpens. Nor will He ever abandon us.

This is the kind of Father Jesus is showing us. Our Father is big. He's generous. He waits expectantly for us to return home to Him. God our Father is much bigger than our puny imaginations depict Him. Nothing tells us more about God than Jesus' parable of the prodigal son.

Jesus Loving His Father

Is God a Father for us?

Some people have difficulty imagining a God who so intimately connects Himself to the human race. They may tolerate the idea of a Prime Mover, a First Cause. If pressed, they may even concede to a "Higher Power." Others feel that addressing God as "Father" is nothing but archaic patriarchy. Christ Jesus, God's eternal self-expression in our humanity, addressed God as "Father." For that reason alone we should do likewise.

To Jesus' contemporaries, the notion of God as "Abba" was preposterous blasphemy. In our day it is merely politically incorrect.

> God fulfilled the office of a true father. He Himself formed the body; He Himself infused the breath of the soul. Whatever we are, it is altogether His work.
> **Lactantius**

It's not enough for you and me to simplistically accept Jesus as our personal Lord and Savior. He asks more of us. Jesus came to reveal His Father to you and me. He asks us to surrender to His Father and trust Him as our Father. Jesus came to answer the question: "What kind of God is God, if there is a God?" Moreover

> The new man, born again and restored to God by grace, says "Father!" because he has now begun to be a son.
> **St. Cyprian of Carthage**

God the Son came down to us in order to take us back home with Him to our Father in heaven. God's Word came into us to bring His Father to us and to bring us into the bosom of our Father, Christ's Father -- and ours.

Many Christians don't pay much attention to being sons and daughters of the Father. By "accepting Jesus" as their Savior, they stop there and declare themselves to be saved. And yet Christ Himself said, "Not every one who says to me, 'Lord, Lord,' shall enter the kingdom of heaven, but he who does the will of my Father who is in heaven" (Matthew 7:21). The way we live and the way we act toward our brothers and sisters, all children of our Father, demonstrates whether we have become sons and daughters of the Father of our Lord, Jesus Christ. Accept Jesus as our Lord and Savior? Yes, absolutely! But that's only the beginning, and much more must follow on the way of Jesus back to our Father in heaven. Bringing us to His Father is the essential work of Jesus.

> Listen to the Savior: I regenerated you, unhappily born by the world to death. I set you free, I healed you, I redeemed you. I will give you life that is unending, eternal, supernatural. I will show you the face of God, the good Father.
> **St. Clement** of Alexandria

The Father Who Provides

There are so many types of prayer, including prayers of petition and confession, prayers of praise and thanksgiving. They needn't be eloquent or long. In fact Jesus

> In your prayers do not babble as the pagans do, for they think that by using many words they will make themselves heard. Do not be like them; your Father knows what you need before you ask him.
> **Matthew** 6:7-9

tells us to keep them short and to the point.

Even so, He invites us to talk with Him, *with* Him, not at Him. Our Father loves His children and wants to listen to them. He wants to hear us tell Him what's happening in our lives. He wants us to ask for His help and His love. What parent doesn't like that? What parent does not want to be wanted? And so it is with God our Father.

The same is true when we pray by asking God to do something for us. Consider the words and the attitude of St. Peter: "Lord, you know everything. You know that I love you" (John 21:15-17). With those simple words, Peter reveals his inner self to God. Christ didn't need Peter to say that, but Peter needed to hear himself say it.

And so it is with us. Again, the power of prayer is not so much the effect it has on God, but the effect it has on us. Prayer doesn't' change God's mind; it changes us. Prayer strengthens our faith in our Father in heaven who loves us in spite of ourselves. And so God wants us to pray, to seek out His love, to claim in faith His caring love for us. He wants to provide for us.

The Father Who Is Compassionate

God is compassionate. In the parable of the prodigal son St. Luke writes: "While he was still a long way off, his father saw him, and felt compassion for him..." Jesus is telling us here about His Father, your Father and mine.

Compassion is not about pity. This isn't about how the father simply felt sorry for the son. When one feels compassion, one is emotionally involved with another.

37

It's about being moved by the plight of another person. The father in Jesus' preeminent parable felt compassion for the son because he saw someone who was very different than the child who left and was now coming back home over that hill.

Compassion literally means, "to suffer with." That's the message given whenever you gaze upon a crucifix. Jesus, in His human body hanging there on His cross, is the supreme revelation of our Father's love for us, a love with height, breadth, and depth, the boundaries of which are truly limitless and beyond any human measurements. The cross makes no sense unless it is seen through the eyes of Love incarnate.

The boy who launched out on his own was a cocky, arrogant, selfish, I've-got-the-world-by-the-tail kind of kid with a big bank account and a big appetite. The one limping back over the hill was a different kid. He was broken, needy, ashamed, and humbled by experience. He was a softened, repentant young man who was a son, still a son! And the father lets him know the awesome truth: "I, too, know pain. I know how you feel. And I love you."

The father in this parable doesn't go to the son and say, "Look, stupid, you've made a mess of your life. Look at you!" No. Instead the father says, "We need to get you back again... we need to put you back together again the right away and get you fixed up." And so he was re-dressed.

It must be so difficult for a parent to let a child become broken, or mess up, or make big mistakes and to give them the freedom to learn through their experiences. And it must be even harder to let that child do so and still remain emotionally engaged with the child and feel compassion for his pain. It would be more natural to try and intervene, to save the child from his own bad judgment. Imagine what it would be like, failing that, to endure the child's rejection also.

You and I have known some fathers who have simply written off their "bad" children. God the Father is not like that. He respects our freedom, yet stays engaged with us emotionally. No matter what you have done, or where you are today, no matter how much you have made a mess of your life and your relationships, God's heart is breaking with you. He knows your pain and He loves you.

Jesus tells us more. "While he was still a long way off, his father saw him, and felt compassion for him, and ran to him." In ancient Near Eastern cultures a man never ran. In fact, a man never even showed his legs. Men wore robes and under those robes they wore long undergarments. You could never run in this kind of clothing without hiking it all up around your waist and exposing your entire leg. This would never be done. It would be a public disgrace. Men of dignity and respect, and certainly men of power, didn't do that. Others did the running.

But in the parable, the father runs to his son, bare legs exposed. Why? This father faces a choice. Either he lets his nearly naked, filthy, shame-filled son walk (or maybe even crawl) in front of all the onlookers, or he takes the public disgrace and shame upon himself instead by running to his son. This prodigal Father of ours is not uninvolved, distant, or remote as some would tell us. He came to us in His Son, hanging naked on His cross.

And so in Jesus' parable the father chooses, because of his great love for his returning son, to bear the weight of public humiliation so that his son doesn't have to bear it all himself. He hikes up his robes around his waist and takes off through the crowd, sacrificing his own respect and dignity in running to his son. What a scandal!

Again, what a picture of Jesus this is! So that we wouldn't ever have to bear the weight of public and eternal humiliation because of our moral failures and sin, Jesus was publicly killed on the cross to bear that weight of shame in our place. He was stripped naked and then humiliated. Like the father in this story, Jesus humbly sacrifices himself so that we could return home to our Father with dignity and know His welcoming love. That is the way, the truth, and the life to live; the one Jesus calls us to live.

But Jesus offers us even more to see. "While he was still a long way off, his father saw him, and felt compassion for him, and ran and embraced him and kissed him." Pay attention now to the words spoken by this father. Read the parable again and ask yourself when the father first speaks upon his son's return. Note, too, that in his actions alone he has spoken volumes about his love for his son.

When he gets to the son, what do you think his son is ready to hear? He might well have expected to hear "You no good, lousy, selfish fool. What have you done with all I gave you? Where is my money? What have you done?"

But his father says none of this. He doesn't shame his son. He hugs him, holds him close to his breast and kisses him again and again.

He is affectionate. God? Affectionate? Absolutely! Jesus taught the men and women who followed Him to not only call God "Father," but to call Him "Papa!" The Aramaic word is "Abba," which means "daddy." It's the affectionate term little children call their fathers. Jesus says, "call God by that name." Jesus wants us to know that God our Father, our heavenly Papa, will be affectionate with us when we come home to Him. He will not shame us. There will be no "I told you so's." He will welcome us with open arms, wrap them around us, and hold us close.

So when the two meet and embrace, the son launches into his well-planned, well-rehearsed speech. But he gets only the first two lines out. His father cuts him off and never lets him speak another word. Was that rude? Absolutely not. It was love. And it's the constant love of the father saying to him (and to us), "Yes, you have sinned... and, yes, you are not worthy. But you will never stop being my son and I will never stop being your father. You will never be my servant. You are my child. And no matter what you could ever do or say, you will always be my son."

Jesus wants us to know our Father in heaven like this too. He wants us to be assured of our identity as children of God. When we come to our senses and come home, we will not come home merely as servants, we will come home as children and will be His children always.

We need to notice something special here, something called "grace." Grace is an English word that comes from a Latin word "gratia," a word that means, "gift." Grace is always a gift. So notice the prodigal father's gift. He says, "Quickly, bring out the best robe and put it on him, and put a ring on his hand and sandals on his feet; and bring the fattened calf and kill it. Let us eat and be merry, for this son of mine who was dead has come back into our life again."

The robe in this Middle Eastern culture was not just a warm covering; it was a symbol of honor and dignity. The signet ring was a symbol of authority and gave access to all family property and money. The sandals represented sonship. Servants didn't wear sandals, but sons did. And the calf was a sign of special celebration. The "Lamb who was slain" comes to us in a celebration, the foretaste of the Messianic Banquet we celebrate in Holy Mass.

The father's forgiveness was total and full of grace. This was not something the son deserved, and certainly nothing he could ever have earned. He received it only because of the grace and the generous, giving love of the father.

The same is true for us. We could never earn the love of God and can never merit the forgiveness He has for us. It is only by gift, by grace, that we can come home to the Father and be cleansed and restored into relationship with Him. And yet (thank God!) that path is wide open for every one of us.

The father in the parable declares: "This son of mine was dead, and has come to life again; he was lost, and has been found."

He is not speaking in a literal sense but rather spiritually. This father understood the spiritual reality behind his son's behavior and feelings. He understood that the self-destructive path of selfishness and loose living his son had chosen wasn't merely unwise but was also a flight from God. He understood that the life the son was living would leave him spiritually dead and spiritually lost.

> Jesus said, "Take the stone away." Martha said to him, "Lord, by now he will smell; this is the fourth day." Jesus replied, "Have I not told you that if you believe you will see the glory of God?" So they took away the stone...
> When he had said this, he cried in a loud voice, "Lazarus, here! Come out." The dead man came out, his feet and hands bound with bans of stuff and a cloth round his face. Jesus said to them, "Unbind him, let him go free."
> **John 11:39-40, 42-43.**

So when the son comes home to his father, this spiritually wise dad knows there is something far greater happening on a deeper, spiritual level. This son is welcoming God back into his life. And the wonderful result is real life, the spiritual life for which God creates us.

To live apart from God the Father is to be spiritually disoriented, confused, and lost. We wander around in our world without purpose or meaning. To recognize our need, come to our senses, and return to the Father is life.

43

The son in Jesus' parable came home and found his father waiting for him, with love and with open arms of forgiving grace.

We can too.

God can't stand being apart from us. His infinite urge is to come to us, embrace us, and hold us close to His heart. It is that drive for union that impels the efforts, the works, of His Son and His Holy Spirit. In His nature He is "driven" to be Father. God created you to share love with Him, to share His inner life with Him. Our own life is meant to be a living union with God in Christ. It is, moreover, a life we share with the lives of others. We save our souls by sharing our souls in love, along with the gifts and treasures within them. For when we die, it's not what we have that will matter; it's what we have shared. How would God know you and recognize you if you arrived before His eyes without others?

As you travel on your path through life you may come upon a "Y" in the path and be confronted with making the decision to take one path and rely totally on God or choose the other path and rely on human powers, either your own or yours with others. It is a great gift when you choose to rely totally and completely on God. Such a moment is graced. Choosing to rely on God and God alone can cause others to mock you; it can cause you to judge yourself as weak or a failure.

But choosing to rely on God brings with it the experience of tremendous peace, relief, and freedom. Such moments often come amidst suffering and loss. They are echoes of Christ's last words on His cross:

"Father, into your hands I commend my spirit." To make that choice, to enter into that act, brings you a gift that can come only from God's heart, a new life for you.

I must confess that most of the time I have not really put myself in a position of complete reliance on God's loving providence and care for me. Oh, I've mouthed the words, but kept control to myself. I have actually relinquished control and given into God only when compelled to do so by life's events. Nevertheless, on those few occasions when I have freely and totally given myself over into God's control and care, I have experienced something that's truly wonderful -- God's closeness to me.

Having considered all that we have about God's tender, loving mercies, His compassion and His infinite forgiveness, we cannot overlook the fact that God is fair and just. The parable of the prodigal son concludes with the father going out to the elder son with all of the love and tender concern he gave to the younger son. We do not know, however, what became of that elder son.

This leads me to consider that perhaps God is infinitely just in that He accepts our decisions and allows our decisions to have consequences. The prodigal son received the fullness of his father's mercy and forgiveness. The self-righteous elder son, as far as we know, did not. The result? Terrifying justice! Into what a hell that elder son condemned himself! This was because in his hardened heart he could not find room for mercy and forgiveness.

Is God just? We've all heard the expression "This cries out to heaven for punishment." In our imperfect world some perpetrators of evil deeds have caused untold pain to others and have never been held to accountable and never suffered the consequences for their actions. There are punishments that must be meted out and the Father of us all must see to it that the scales of justice are balanced. Along with freedom of choice comes accountability. Only God knows what is truly necessary to restore the balance.

Is there a hell? I believe so. I believe so because in His justice God permits the consequences of our decisions, which I dread the most. Oh, the burden of freedom! Oh, the awesome consequences of freedom of choice! Perhaps this gives us a clue, a glimpse, into why Jesus freely chose His crucifixion and redeeming death on the cross, for His cross is ours as well.

God your Father knows you by name. He knows you through and through, knows you better than you know yourself. He has many things He wants to share with you. He wants to talk with you to teach you, to guide you, and to form you in the image of His Son. He has things He wants you to do. But how can you know them (and hence know Him) unless you give Him opportunities to encounter you, to reach your heart and soul? He called you into being in order to have His own relationship with you. It is in those encounters that you will find your destiny, your reason for being, the meaning and purpose of your life here on earth.

* * * * * * *

PRAYER

O Father, in your limitless power and might you brought all things into being and made us in your own image and likeness.

Truly you are a powerful Father. But you love us too with a mother's love, unconditionally, with boundless mercy and forgiveness. We have turned our backs to you, yet you ceaselessly pursue us as Lover. Help me to set aside my self-will and surrender to your all-powerful love. Help me to meet the destiny you prepared for me when you fashioned me in my mother's womb. Help me to be all that you dream I can be.

* * * * * * *

QUESTIONS

To what extent do I trust in and rely upon God to care for me?

What is God "supposed' to do for me, and how do I respond to God?

Why does the Psalmist, David, speak of Yahweh as "father" in Psalms 89:27 and 103:13?

What are the qualities of a good father?

47

① To tal Surrender — for Every thing —
② Nothing — He has already given us His Only Son — Thank U
③
④ Teacher, Supporter, trusting, always forgiving, never withholding His Love →

WHO ART...

It's all a dream, this talk of heaven bathed in light, and of a God who made it all, who is to be your possession in eternity! You really believe, do you, that the mist which hangs about you will clear away later on? All right, go on longing for death, But death will make nonsense of your hopes; it will only mean a night darker than ever, the night of mere nonexistence.

St. Therese of Lisieux,
"Night of Nothingness" in
Maurice & Therese - The Story of a Love

Picture yourself in a Philosophy 101 class and the professor is dealing with questions such as, What is, and what is not? What is real and what isn't real? What is truth? The famous question, "If a tree falls in the forest, is there a sound?" comes to mind here and it leads us to the statement of a student: "There is no God unless and until I experience him because I will not accept the testimony of others." Such is the stuff of the meditations we make here as we continue on our pilgrimage through the Lord's Prayer.

What's Out There?

Who has not looked up into a star-filled night sky and asked, "What's out there?"

Could it be there is a God? Some One who is not just "The Force" but One who cares? Is there One who is there behind what we can touch, taste, smell, feel, and measure? Is there a Refuge who, in the midst of our trials and powerlessness gives us courage, hope, and the will to carry on, to persevere through life's unfairness until we find justice, peace, and fulfillment? Could it be there is a God?

I don't think we convince people that there is a God by arguing with them and attempting to intellectually "prove" the existence of God. No. I think we bring people to an awareness of God, however dim, by asking questions, life's great questions, and then embarking with them on the great adventure of finding answers to those questions. Perhaps some people "argue themselves" into accepting God's existence but most, I believe, do not. Why? Because life itself remains (however intelligible) incomprehensible. There is a great deal we cannot explain, much less "prove."

Seeing Is Believing

This chapter was difficult to write because the existence of God cannot be proved by mathematics or by the scientific method. In mathematical problem solving the end result is one answer only. Scientific proof is established in much the same way; experimental procedures can be repeated with the same results obtained each time. When it comes to God's existence, however, we resort to arguments and "evidentiary hearings"; the

49

credibility of the evidence is accepted primarily through our own human experience. Our conclusions, therefore, are always open to question, since all human experiences are questionable in their nature. One is open to the idea that God exists because one has, in some way or another, experienced at least tangentially the Presence.

So is there a God? And if so, where is He?

The scientific method is not the only intellectual discipline that puts me in touch with those realities that exist outside of my own subjective self. Art and imagination can be quite effective, sometimes more so than science. History is another, along with anthropology, psychology, and literature -- all are routes to Reality. There are other intellectual searchlights we can turn on, and in their lights see the world around us. Enlightenment comes to us in many forms, via a number of intellectual quests.

> The First Vatican Council teaches, then, that the truth attained by philosophy and the truth of Revelation are neither identical nor mutually exclusive: "There exists a twofold order of knowledge, distinct not only as regards their source, but also as regards their object. With regard to the source, because we know in one by natural reason, in the other by divine faith."
> **Pope John Paul II**, Fides et Ratio

There is a whole body of evidence that points to realities beyond what facts, data, and information can only demonstrate. Realism puts us in touch with them. If we limit ourselves to accepting

> Be still, and know that I am God.
> **Psalm 46:10**

only those things that can be empirically "proved" then we cut ourselves off from those greater realities that lie beyond the horizons of what we can merely see and measure. Openness to other things, to new things, is the essence of intellectual curiosity. This openness is more realistic than the current dogmas of intellectuals who limit themselves to so-called objectivity. Objects are only a part of a total greater Reality.

There are those who tell us that as believers in God we have constructed an anthropological "God" in our own idealized image and likeness. He is much too human, they tell us, to be truly God.

This "anthropological problem" is God's problem, not ours. For if God is to be known and loved by humans He must come to us and present Himself to us humanly. The

> For all men were by nature foolish who were in ignorance of God, and who from the good things seen did not succeed in knowing him who is, and from studying the works did not discern the artisan;
> But either fire, or wind, or the swift air, or the circuit of the stars, or the mighty water, or the luminaries of heaven, the governors of the world, they considered gods.
> Now if out of joy in their beauty they thought them gods, let them know how far more excellent is the Lord than these; for the original source of beauty fashioned them.
> Or if they were struck by their might and energy, let them from these things realize how much more powerful is he who made them.
> For from the greatness and the beauty of created things their original author, by analogy, is seen.
> But yet, for these the blame is less; for they indeed have gone astray perhaps, though they seek God and wish to find him.
> For they search busily among his works, but are distracted by what they see, because the things seen are fair.
> But again, not even these are pardonable.
> For if they so far succeeded in knowledge that they could speculate about the world, how did they not more quickly find its LORD?
> **Wisdom 13:1-9**

only other available alternative is that He must come to us inhumanly... but of course that simply wouldn't work. So

51

God's incarnation was a "must" in His divine plan for our relationships with Him. Of course we know and encounter God anthropologically; of course we speak of God anthropologically. Being anthropoids, how else could humans interact with God? How else could God reach us and encounter us?

Blaise Pascal, the famous French mathematician and philosopher of the seventeenth century, once said: "The heart has its reasons which reason knows nothing of." When we speak of God we reason with our minds and realize with our hearts. God, after all, is not simply an idea, He is personal. What is personal is of the mind and of the heart.

Certainly we do we do not love others simply as objects, things that we possess. So why, then, should we relate to God only as an intellectual object?

You and I are persons. We are subjects, not objects. We are the subjects of each other's love, not objects to be loved. Objects are used and manipulated. To treat other persons only as objects is to misapprehend them. The same is true with respect to God. He cannot be only objectively apprehended in order to be "known."

We need the humility to recognize that in this our earthly life we can only "see" God obliquely (as Moses did) by turning aside from what occupies our immediate attention. We see, but we don't see all there is to see. Abraham, Moses, John the Baptist, and Mary all point to what is beyond that which is immediately present to us. From what beyond us in the next life they mediate to us the One whom we can only name as "The One Who Is."

All we can say about God, we can say only analogically. Having said whatever we have declared about God, we need to say more, to thirst and quest for more.

Christ Jesus reveals to us that God in His very being is relational, three Persons existing totally for each other in forming one Being. That being so, we can only begin to "know" God in our willingness to enter into a relationship with Him. You can only know Relational Being by being in relationship, not by remaining objectively and dispassionately outside of it and holding yourself aloof from everything that is not empirically and objectively known. The great danger of hyper-intellectualism is that it leads only to knowing "about" someone, which is not the same as knowing someone.

For the sake of argument, however, granting that God exists, how can we speak of God as being, or in being, when God is simply "ising"? He exists in the simple act of being. You and I are not pantheists; Christians don't posit God as simply "being everything." God is not everything, and everything is not God. But we do say that God is in everything, that He who is energy itself holds all materialized forms of energy in being, in His own existence as energy. It is in God's "ising" that things are. When you get down to the tiniest sub-atomic particle, what's left? Only energy!

Immediately a relativist will jump up and claim, "Believers are arrogant absolutists. There are no absolutes because everything is relative." This implies that anyone's opinion about Truth or Reality is just as good as anyone else's. Well, fair enough. That means that both our relativist friend and his statements are merely relative! Does the fact that something is relative require us to not take it seriously? If everything is relative, why should we take our relativist friend (or his thinking) seriously? Thus the relativist himself permits us to relativize his thinking.

In reality it is the relativist who is the arrogant one. Doesn't it demean human intelligence to claim we have been born blind and that truth is not our concern? Real arrogance consists in taking God's place in order to determine who we are, what we do, what we want to make of ourselves and of the world.

> Seek not to understand that you may believe, but to believe that you may understand.
> St. Augustine

Our relativist friends have done us the favor, however, of raising up to consciousness our consideration of the question of being. They speak for the present generation that now asks the question: "Does Truth exist, or is it a matter of private, personal (and therefore relative) opinion?" That issue has to be decided before we can even begin to talk about God, or recognize whether or not there is a God. Once past that we can finally get to the question, "What kind of a God is God, if there is a God, and what does He expect of us, if anything?"

Theologians tell us that God exists in His "ising," in the simple act of being. We cannot say He wasn't; we cannot say He won't be, or that He will be. All we can say is that He is. And if that is so, then He is present to everything that is, since all that is came to be from His "ising." When we use the word "God" we customarily use it as if it were

54

a noun, but really the word "God" is a verb. God in His being exists in the simple act of being.

Furthermore we must say that God exists as a personal being. A stone exists as a stone, a bird as a bird, an atom as an atom. But beings that exist in intelligence and in love are persons, personal beings. To be a person means that one's very nature is constituted by knowing and loving. Persons not only know, but they know that they know. Animals can't do that. Persons love, and know that they love, and they know others in their loving them. Animals can't do that, nor can any other extant thing. Only persons can reflect back on their actions and thereby understand themselves. That's what it means to have a soul.

God exists preeminently as a personal being, and Jesus reveals Him not only as the Father's expression of Himself in His Son but also reveals Himself in the effusion of Himself in love as the Spirit. God alone exists in that form of being; God alone exists in that form of "ising."

And He is transcendent, which is merciful. Being transcendent God is thankfully beyond the manipulation of our smearing human hands. Being nailed and then presenting His wounds to doubting Thomas, God's hands can fashion us beyond our reach. For me, this is a great relief because it means that I am a yoked cooperator, a co-worker, and am not responsible for everything. I am merely joined with God, and this is very liberating for me. I am not responsible for the universe; I'm only responsible for playing out my part in it.

Because of that fact no load is too heavy for me to bear. Weighty problems, concerns, questions, and losses with a specific density beyond my strengths can nevertheless be carried, for I carry them with God. "For with man it is impossible, but with God all things are possible." Nothing is so grave that, with God, it cannot be faced.

Finally, the wonder is that God thought me loveable enough and worthy enough to want me to pursue and eventually find Him. Imagine that! God, ever the lover, wants to be pursued and "caught." God wants you to want Him. In His eyes you must really be worth something.

With this said, we must return to the consideration that this book is about prayer, the great prayer that Christ Jesus tendered to us. It is a realistic prayer in that it opens us up to the greater reality, our realization, of the God and Father of our Lord Jesus Christ, the Father to whom He brings us. It has little to do with proofs and arguments because it transcends them and invites us into the world of experienced reality, that which Christ Jesus came to offer us.

In the Gospels Jesus speaks of His Father 164 times. Evidently Jesus had no doubt as to whether or not God the Father exists. We need to be clear-headed about this. Either Christ Jesus was a liar, a fraud, and a charlatan, or He was authentic and His claims about Himself and His Father were true. Either His disciples fraudulently fabricated a mythic Christ, along with the events of his life and his teachings, or they went to their deaths holding to their claims because they knew them to be true. Allegations that Jesus' disciples were frauds are absurd,

56

because not one of these figures, facing their own deaths, recanted or retracted their claims.

If God did not exist, it wouldn't make much sense for us to be sharing these thoughts, would it? The question for us, therefore, is not *whether* God exists, but *how* He exists for us.

Is our faith "blind"? Those who have no faith tell us that it is. Not seeing as we do, they claim we do not see. I argue that our faith is based upon probable evidence. I know faith to be a reasonable thing. It is grounded on a rational and reasoned response to the signs of God's Presence in the universe, and of His Presence around us. But what sort of "vision" is involved? The controlling issue is how we see. For what is Spirit requires spiritual eyes to be seen.

> Ever since the creation of the world, his invisible attributes of eternal power and divinity have been able to be understood and perceived in what he has made.
> **Romans 1:20**

Seventeen hundred years ago, after struggling with belief and the question of God's existence, Augustine of Hippo wrote in his *Confessions*:

> *Late, late have I loved You, O Beauty ever*
> *ancient and ever new!*
> *And behold You were within, and I was*
> *wandering outside, and there I sought You, and,*
> *deformed as I was, I ran after those beautiful*
> *things which You have created.*
> *You were with me and I was not with You.*
> *Those things kept me far from You, those things*
> *which could have no being but in You.*

57

You have called. You have cried out.
You have pierced my deafness and dispersed my
blindness.
You have sent forth your fragrance and I have
drawn my breath, and now I long for you, and
hunger after You.
Now my hope is nothing else but in your
boundless Mercy, O Lord, my God.
He who loves You, loves You for your own sake
and not for anything else.
Love, ever burning and never extinguished, true
Charity, My God, set me afire!

Faith and Human Experience

Perhaps no other argument supporting the notion of God's nonexistence is greater or more compelling than the problem of pain and suffering. It seems to me, however, that too often we get hung up on the fact of pain, its very existence, and then fail to move on to see one of the greatest things there is about being a human being, namely what we do with pain. It is our response to pain and suffering that makes us great and points to the possibility of a compassionate and loving God. One need go no further than to observe the responses to the tragic events of September 11, 2001.

Catholics see a response to pain and suffering every time they enter their church. It dominates their visual field as they look down the aisle toward the altar. It hits them –

the crucifix! – a Roman executioner's cross with a human body hanging nailed upon it. The cross is a cosmic key that, when inserted into Reality's black hole, unlocks our self-centered prison and opens us up to see how God Himself faced pain and suffering, then went through to the other side! God's self-expression, His Word made flesh, did that in order that we might respond to His love and join ourselves into His risen and Spirit-filled humanity and emerge victorious over sin, suffering and death. Thus yoked with him we penetrate nonbeing with everlasting life.

Prove to me that Love does not exist and I will accept the idea that God does not exist. Define Beauty for me. Define Wisdom for me. Only then can we declare that we have defined God (thereby eliminating our need for Him). Take control of the great Transcendentals and you will thereby eliminate the necessity and reality of God. Dissect your own self-awareness or mine and then give me a comprehensive definition of Goodness. Then, and only then, will I concede God's nonexistence (but not for one moment until then).

Pope John Paul II continually insisted that we are not pawns of political and economic systems. Nor are we each other's possessions. He pointed out that communism and unrestrained capitalism treat people as merely useful, either useful to the party or useful to the economic system. The danger of liberal capitalism's "cost of doing business" approach in valuing human labor is found in its treatment of human workers simply as units in the cost of production. It pays no heed to their intrinsic value. This degradation was likewise blatant in communism's view of human beings. Experience has taught us that both systems must treat God as irrelevant, not a part of life's equations.

Our present Western exaltation of individualism shoves God aside. Many people in modern Western culture believe that the individual governs everything and is subject to no one. Modern secular thinking has so enthroned the autonomous self that many people actually believe that they determine for themselves what is true, what is moral, what is just, even what is real! The autonomous self is so arrogantly imperial that it claims dominion over truth, even over reality itself.

> The insane man jumped into their midst and transfixed them with his glances. "Where is God gone?" he called out. "I mean to tell you! *We have killed him, you and I! We are all his murderers!* But how have we done it? How were we able to drink up the sea? Who gave us the sponge to wipe away the whole horizon? What did we do when we loosened this earth from its sun? Whither does it now move? Whither do we move?"
> **Friedrich Nietzsche**, The Gay Science

But isn't it true that you and I are subjects who receive realities that exist outside our individual selves? I do not determine them; they determine me. It is, of course, inescapable that some limited subjectivity is involved. Since we are not objects it is impossible for us to be totally "objective" in seeing, knowing, and understanding. Can one, for instance, be totally "objective" in discussing Love, or Beauty, or what is Good? Hardly! It must be recognized that the individual subject is only one-half the equation. Otherwise one becomes unbalanced.

Looking out into the greater world surrounding me and to what exists beyond planet Earth I've often heard my inner self asking, "Is that all there is?" There seems to be something within us that is always and forever wanting more -- more love, more knowledge, more answers to riddling questions, more of life, more than this world offers.

We have a built-in drive for the transcendent, no matter how beautiful and satisfying we find in the immanent which is present to us. Creation and the creatures within it are gorgeous. But Michelangelo's statue of David, for instance, does not stand alone. It presents its sculptor to us; it calls us to know the artisan. What sort of soul would sculpt such a stunning work of art? What sort of artist, from earth's clay, could form such a man? If we peer out into our surrounding world and perceive beauty, where does it come from? If we see order amidst chaos we ask, where does that order originate? If truth is conformity to reality, from whence comes reality? It is arrogant foolishness for me to claim that I create it by and for myself.

The ancient Greek philosophers taught us that what we find to be true calls out for Truth, just as experiencing love impels us toward Love, and what is wondrous calls us to seek out and find Beauty. We simply never get enough of what is present to us, what is merely immanent. That which is immediately in front of us lasts but for a short time. In our limitless drive for more we soon look for what is beyond.

When people claim they have no faith they are deluded. What sculptor, artist, architect, scientist, poet, or painter does not draw from others who have gone before them and their ideas and creations? All who draw on the works of others have faith in their reliability: they confidently draw upon them and build afresh upon them. We all live on faith in some way. We cannot pass through any day without having faith in those who have gone before us to give us what we have to work with today. Those who have gone before us give us their wherewithal upon which to build and further develop our lives today.

Faith and History

History presents us with the intellectual treasures that produced many of our world's cultures. There are certain fundamental questions that pervade them all: Who am I? Where have I come from and where am I going? Why is there evil? When I pass through death's door, what will I find? These are the questions that we find in the sacred writings of Israel, as well as in the Orient. Names such as Confucius and Lao-Tze come to mind, along with Buddha. The ancient Greeks give us the thoughts of Homer, Socrates, Plato and Aristotle. All of these great ones wrestle with questions that share a common source, the quest for life's meaning and my purpose in living in it. All of this stems from my consciousness that I am a human person. Where, then, did I come from and where am I going?

62

To determine where I am heading I must first know where I came from. History, then, is of enormous importance. Ignoring the lessons of history imperils all that I will yet attempt to do and deprive my mind of intellectual treasures and tools that are essential to successful living. How can I determine the value, the meaning, and the purpose of my life and its component elements unless I know my personal and communal history?

God's Revelation is imbedded in time and history. History is the arena wherein we see and reflect upon what God does for humanity. How otherwise can we discern God's coming to us in the things we know best and can verify most easily, the things of our everyday life? We cannot understand ourselves apart from this knowledge.

Our journey in quest for meaning takes us into our common human history. In that journey we come upon a universal and ultimate truth that stirs the human mind to stretch beyond that which is comfortable and into that which is challenging. Our capacities for reasoning continually extend the range of our knowledge in a journey that is endless, a journey that continues beyond the grave.

The Jews know that God exists because He has entered their history. History is where the evidence is seen and understood. Their survival as a people defies analysis. The normal principles of sociology and anthropology tell us they should not exist, that they could not have survived all that they have endured. The fact that they have defies all logic. The only plausible explanation is that they enjoy

God's care. Similarly, some see God's existence in the fact that the Church has for 2,000 years survived its clergy!

Science and Religious Belief

Albert Einstein was prophetic years ago when he declared that the day would come when imagination would be more important than knowledge. That day has come. Truth and Goodness come to us through the imagination of Beauty. It is Beauty that will redeem this present generation, perhaps more so than in any other era in human history. The souls of the people of our day thirst for Beauty, for in it we find the expression of God that truly informs the human spirit.

> Faith and reason are like two wings on which the human spirit rises to the contemplation of truth; and God has placed in the human heart a desire to know the truth—in a word, to know himself—so that, by knowing and loving God, men and women may also come to the fullness of truth about themselves."
> (cf. Ex 33:18; Ps 27:8-9; 63:2-3; John 14:8; 1 John 3:2).
> **Pope John Paul II** – *Fides et Ratio*

Beauty, image, imagination, and wonder were all a part of Albert Einstein's soul. Said he:

> *The most beautiful experience we can have is the mysterious. It is the fundamental emotion that stands at the cradle of true art and true science. Whoever does not know it and can no longer wonder, no longer marvel, is as good as dead, and his eyes are dimmed. It was the experience*

of mystery -- even if mixed with fear -- that engendered religion. A knowledge of the existence of something we cannot penetrate, our perceptions of the profoundest reason and the most radiant beauty, which only in their most primitive forms are accessible to our minds: it is this knowledge and this emotion that constitute true religiosity. In this sense, and only this sense, I am a deeply religious man... I am satisfied with the mystery of life's eternity and with a knowledge, a sense, of the marvelous structure of existence -- as well as the humble attempt to understand even a tiny portion of the Reason that manifests itself in nature.

Articles of faith cannot be used to validate or invalidate scientific theorems. Nor can scientific theorems and methods be used to validate or invalidate articles of faith. Both are subject to their own intellectual methods and criteria. Do we use the scientific method to establish and "prove" things of beauty? To establish justice? Determine what is good? Science may aid in those endeavors, but it cannot determine our conclusions. Using the scientific method, who has ever "seen" justice, or beauty, or the good? We have only seen the evidence of their presence.

To assert that our world resulted only from purposeless chaos is a belief, not a scientifically established fact. The belief that the world as it now exists resulted from a purposeful intelligence is a conclusion based on probable evidence. Neither view is based on scientifically established facts or proofs. It is not what is only possible that should govern our thinking or our actions; it is what is probable that should guide us.

The noise and clamor of this world's sensory and physical obsession need to be shut down in order for my soul's powers to come to the fore of my consciousness. My spiritual self has to be given credence and free reign in order for the higher contact with others to be made. The entombing stone of doubt needs to be rolled away, with all of its demands for proofs, in order for my soul to be liberated, its powers reawakened and set free so that I might rise to a newer and higher life.

Isn't it true that any scientist who is concerned about what brought our universe into existence speculates about an Intelligence that is the preeminent analogue of human intelligence? Can it be scientifically demonstrated that order can result from chaos?

Philosophy, Science, and Proofs

Imagine, now, that you and I are back in that classroom where Philosophy 101 is being taught. At some point the professor will pose the famous question, "If a tree falls in the forest, is there a sound?" We can be sure someone will ask, "What is sound? Sound is not sound unless a human being can hear it. It all depends upon what you mean by the term sound."

Hopefully another student will put another idea into play. "Suppose," he will say, "there's a recording machine nearby when the tree falls. Will it record the sound of the crashing tree even though there's no human being to hear it?"

There are those among us who claim, "There is no God unless and until I experience God. I define what's real and what's not real, what's true and what's not true." But there are others who assert that what is real is mediated to us by others. We have to accept the testimony of other entities, be they other people or the technological equipment we have fashioned to tell us what is "out there."

Hans Urs von Balthasar, one of the greatest philosophers of our day, has made the startling claim that, of all the great Transcendentals, it is Beauty that will redeem and save the people of our day, not Truth, or Wisdom, or any of the others. Transcendentals. Beauty will redeem our age, he suggests. Perhaps that is why John Paul II was so attracted to art, icons, and images. I think he agreed with Albert Einstein who prophesied years ago that imagination would one day be more important than knowledge.

The wonder is that there is any beauty and order in existence at all. Can it be reasonably argued that beauty "just happened by random chance," that from this molten mass of matter, hurtling through the cosmic void, beauty and nature's laws somehow just "emerged"?

It seems to me that science is one of the faith's greatest allies. It is not an enemy because science is based on faith, the faith that there is a way to Truth. Science seeks Truth and is based on the notion that there is an answer to life's greatest riddles. The drive for answers is in itself an aspect of faith, the belief that Truth is out there to be apprehended by our spiritual power of intelligence.

Science, reflective wonder, imagination, and questing all give powerful circumstantial evidence that there is an order that emanates from an all-powerful Intelligence that governs the universe and is the Source of all that exists. Mr. Spock, one of the main characters in the Star Trek series, exemplifies this in his problem-solving approach to the central issues presented in the Star Trek episodes. Kirk (the Scot word for church) relies on Spock, the theologian, in properly charting and setting the course of Starship Enterprise, the symbol of our planet as it hurtles through the universe.

To Love Is to Know, and to Know Is to Love

Imagine yourself deaf and blind, much like Helen Keller for instance. Picture yourself sitting all alone in a darkened room. Perhaps as a child you had suffered a major traumatic wound that left you blind, deaf, and disabled but still possessed of a keen mind and a profound intelligence. As a consequence you have heightened sensory awareness, and you have keen inner vision. She once wrote: "The best and most beautiful things in the world cannot be seen or touched... they must be felt with the heart." She reminds us that there is more to knowledge than facts, data, information, and proofs. The highest and best things we know, we know with the heart.

Now imagine someone else is in that same room with you, someone who very much wants you to be aware of his or her love for you. The normal means of communication are, of course, not available to you. The only path of communication available is spiritual; extra-sensory perception is the chief route to personal intercommunication between you and the one nearby who loves you.

It is much the same with God and us. It takes faith in the presence of the Other (God) in order for me to allow the two of us to enter into each other's presence. If I deny that the Other is there then I am in exactly the same position as the atheist. If I fill my soul with noise or otherwise divert my spiritual powers in sensual overloads then the only route to awareness and union with the Other is negated, and I am left in the prison of my isolated, autonomous self.

To make the question more personal: Is your life an absurdity? Is your life simply the result of blind forces set in motion by chance? In the long run, is your life meaningless and without purpose? Was I purpose-built, or not?

Even in the hearts of professed atheists there is something that rebels against the idea that all of the wonders brought into being by our intelligence and creative genius are purposeless, generated only by chaos, and doomed to return to nothingness. Perhaps the most well-known agnostic of our era, John-Paul Sartre, expressed a truth felt by us all, believers and non-believers alike, when he declared, "I do not feel that I'm a product of chance, a speck of dust in the universe, but rather someone who is expected, prepared, prefigured; in short a being by whom only a Creator could have put here."

Some thinkers assert that there are no absolutes, hence God is automatically excluded from being because if God is anything at all, He is Absolute. Truth? Justice? Beauty? God? They are not absolutes, according to some.

Others tell us that only scientific analysis employing empirical evidence can explain anything. Therefore God is not needed to explain anything. The modern scientist, many think, has replaced the medieval theologian in mediating reality to us.

> God transcends all creatures. We must therefore continually purify our language of everything in it that is limited, image-bound or imperfect, if we are not to confuse our image of God – "the inexpressible, the incomprehensible, the invisible, the ungraspable" – with our human representations. Our human words always fall short of the mystery of God.
> **Catechism of the Catholic Church**, 2nd ed., #42

Today's scientists and technicians are considered by many to be the high priests of "modern" reality. But when you talk with scientists themselves, they are much more modest. Many scientists are open to the idea of God as the Creative Intelligence from whence came the universe.

As a result of misunderstanding both the role and capabilities of science, epistemology (the study of how we know) today is in a fundamental crisis, one that is affecting us all. Truth? What is Truth? And how can you know what I know in the same way and with the same understanding? It is Truth itself that is on trial in our post-modern culture.

There is another major force undermining our human capacity to believe in and relate to God. The basic dogma

70

of modern secular humanism is that man and man alone is responsible for his destiny. This implies that salvation comes from man alone. Man is the sole agent in fashioning his destiny. Man's history is solely the result of the decisions of men and women. Technology will now replace God.

If this seems hard to believe, then take a look at the issues boiling around the conception and the termination of human life. Man and his technology can totally divorce birth, life, and death from any need of God. Indeed, the generation of human life can now be completely separated from sexual intimacy. Reproduction is something that can be done in the laboratory. Abortion and euthanasia are but symptoms and consequences of this more fundamental and practical atheism. All of these things can be controlled by technology. God is irrelevant.

God on Trial

Ours is a litigious society. Hard evidence is required for proofs. We are prone to require that other people "prove themselves" to us. This brings us to the familiar

> Faith is the confident assurance concerning what we hope for and conviction about things we do not see.
> **Hebrews 11:1-2**

challenge to "prove" that God exists. When challenged to "prove" the existence of God, my first response usually is "What type of evidence do you require?" There are many types of evidence that convince us, along with many levels of evidence. What level of evidence does the questioner demand?

71

In order to balance the argument, it seems that the same level of proof and quality of evidence demanded of believers should likewise be demanded of atheists and secularists who claim God does not exist. The truth is that they cannot "prove" that God does not exist any more than theists can scientifically prove God's existence.

There are rumors of angels and tracings of God's activities in our world. Nevertheless, no one has seen God except the One who came to us from God (John 6:46). Like jurors examining the evidence, we have testimonies about God and can examine the effects of His love and work. This brings us to the question we must all face: "Is the testimony and evidence credible?" It is not by accident that the bulk of the Gospels is presented in the format of a trial, using courtroom terms such as "evidence," "testimony," "proof," "judgment," and so forth.

Did you ever notice that Jesus' whole life was put on trial? And that concepts such as proofs, evidence, witnesses, judges, etc., surround everything Jesus said and did?

His death came about as a result of a trumped-up trial, complete with false witnesses, a corrupt judge issuing a crowd-pleasing sentence, and finally an execution. It is a sobering thought that the One we have judged will one day judge us.

* * * * * * *

PRAYER

O Father, you surround me with your presence. Like a spoiled child I sit in the midst of your many gifts. Captivated by fascination over their wonder, I fail to notice you. The mountains, seas, forests and flowers all speak of your grandeur and beauty, and yet I fail to see you and your love within them.

When life goes well with me, I am too busy to praise and thank you. When life is filled with misery, trails and sufferings I think you are absent, that you are not near, or that you don't even exist!

Help me to see You in those who surround me. Help me to have eyes to see you and ears to hear you. Help me to touch your face and look into your eyes in all those around me, for we are all made in your image and likeness.

How could beauty exist unless it came from you? How could I know truth unless it was found in you? How could anyone love unless our hearts were made in your love? Could anything come from nothing? Bring my soul to that quiet stillness in which you can hold me in your arms and I can find the love for which I was made.

QUESTIONS

What evidence leads me to conclude that God exists?
How can anything exist if there is no Original Cause?
Are there beings that exist apart from material, bodily
    form, or are "persons" found solely and exclusively in
    living, human bodies?
What does it mean to be a "person"?

(1) I exist, therefore God Exists.

(2) God Creates out of Nothing

(3) Yes.

(4) We have become living
Persons — because God
has a purpose for US here
on Earth — We are to make
a difference if we are
open to his Call.

74

IN HEAVEN...

Nigh and nigh draws the chase,
With unperturbed pace,
Deliberate speed, majestic instancy,
And past those noised Feet
A Voice comes yet more fleet –
'Lo! naught contents thee, who content'st not Me.'
Naked I wait Thy love's uplifted stroke!

Francis Thompson, "The Hound of Heaven"

Does Heaven Exist?

Lovers speak of it. We sing about it in love songs. Poets write poems about it. The Egyptians depicted it 4,500 years ago in their famous hieroglyphs. Countless artists have since. Truly, our hearts are made for it.

How can we write about and talk about heaven? Isn't it something to be experienced? Talking about it seems so dry, so inadequate. Can words ever describe unrequited love, or love fulfilled?

Our songs sing of it, hymns and love songs alike. They sing of belonging, seeing and knowing, caring, loving and being loved. Love songs fill us with hints about love's heavenly power. Lovers can feel like they're in heaven, their hearts overflowing with its ecstasies. Poets fill our blind eyes with impressions of it, their verses building bridges strong enough to transport us to heaven's

75

threshold. Picture the valentines you have received. Read love letters sent to you. Listen to Schubert's "Ave Maria."

Christ stands in both heaven and on earth. He has spanned the chasm between earth and heaven, mingling His divinity with our humanity. In Him we receive the things of heaven, God's gifts of infinite love to us here in our limited earthly lives. His Holy Spirit, given us in Christ, the One anointed in the Spirit, transports our earthly lives over into God's inner life. We are powerless to cause this transformation. God's power, God's love alone, causes this to happen; we do not.

Only music, art, and poetry seem to be strong enough to bear the enormity and gravity of such a stupendous grace. The language of data and information, being too fragile, buckles under such weight. Images and music have the strength to carry what words, facts and information cannot.

> I am enough of an artist to rely upon my imagination. Imagination is more important than knowledge. Knowledge is limited. Imagination encircles the world.
> **Albert Einstein**

If God is everywhere, then where is heaven? Could the answer be that heaven is everywhere? Could it be that it's possible to find myself in God's presence anywhere? And if so, then we need to figure out where hell is. But we'll talk of that a bit later. Heaven is not some distant location in the cosmos. Heaven, like love, is a state of being, a state in which we are living. It's a relationship we are in. Persons are made for heaven.

When you fall in love, you feel like you're in heaven. But suppose someone said to you, "Well, since you are in love, can you tell me where I can find it? Show me where I can find it." You can't, can you? The same is true for heaven, for if someone is in heaven, you can't locate where it is. Being in heaven is like being in love, it is outside of space, time, and our limiting measurements.

In being who we are, we are more relational than we are physical. We are made to belong in love to others more than we are made to simply converse with them, to merely occupy space next to them. We are made to live in caring for others, to live in acceptance and belonging. We are made to share ourselves with others.

If hell means that I am living with only my self to love and no one to whom I can give my self and my love, then heaven is hell's opposite. Heaven is living in such a way that I can fully disclose my self to a cherished other, or to others, and where they will receive my inner self, accept me, and cherish me in their love. So also heaven is living with someone (or others) whose very self or selves I want to be given to me in love. I'm in heaven when the others whom I love want to give themselves to me, who want to "belong" to me, share their life with me while I share my life with them. I'm in heaven when those whom I love want me to share my inner self with them.

Did you ever think that while we yearn and hunger to live like that, God hungers to live like that, only infinitely more so? He made heaven so He could live in love with us, so He could give Himself to us.

Living in heaven and living in love cannot be located somewhere on some cosmic map. God's love and God's heaven transcend space, measurement, location and time.

77

They are beyond our self-interested grasp, beyond the human limits and controls we try to impose upon others, upon life, and upon happiness.

Heaven is a state of being, a state in which we live and act as who we really are. For this reason we can enter it here on earth. Jesus told us, "You are not far from the kingdom of heaven" (Mark 12:34), and went on to teach us to pray for living and loving here on earth as life is lived and loved in heaven.

Jesus leads us into heaven, a heaven that begins here on earth, now. It's so very near to us; we have only to accept it. We cannot grab it or grasp it; we cannot earn, merit, buy, or achieve our way into it. Heaven comes to us as a result of the way we live.

When I die the only thing I can take with me is my soul, a soul clothed in Christ and adorned with His gifts. I take with me the character I have shaped and the heart that I have fashioned by what I have done in response to God's gift of life. As the saying goes, "God has given me the gift of life, and what I do with my life is my gift to God." The paradox is that in giving it to God He gives it to me. It's in the sharing that we experience heaven. This means that how I live here on earth has infinite and everlasting consequences. Actually doing the will of God here and now, actuating His presence and making it real for those in the world around me becomes immensely important for the kind of life I will live in eternal life.

I am your friend and my love for you goes deep.
There is nothing I can give you which you have not got,
    but there is much, very much that while I cannot give it,
        you can take.
No heaven can come to us unless our hearts find rest in today.
    Take heaven!
No peace lies in the future which is not hidden in this present little
instant.
    Take peace!
The gloom of the world is but a shadow.
    Behind it, yet within our reach is joy.
There is radiance and glory in the darkness could we but see -
    and to see we have only to look.
    I beseech you to look!
Life is so generous a giver, but we, judging its gifts by the covering,
    cast them away as ugly, or heavy or hard.
Remove the covering and you will find beneath it a living splendor,
    woven of love, by wisdom, with power.
Welcome it, grasp it, touch the angel's hand that brings it to you.
Everything we call a trial, a sorrow, or a duty, believe me,
    that angel's hand is there, the gift is there,
    and the wonder of an overshadowing presence.
Our joys, too, be not content with them as joys,
    They, too, conceal diviner gifts.
Life is so full of meaning and purpose, so full of beauty
    - beneath its covering - that you will find earth
    but cloaks your heaven.
Courage, then, to claim it, that is all.
    But courage you have, and the knowledge that
    we are all pilgrims together,
    wending through unknown country, home.
And so, at this time, I greet you.
Not quite as the world sends greetings,
    but with profound esteem
    and with the prayer that for you now and forever,
    the day breaks,
    and the shadows flee away.

A letter written by Fra Giovanni, 1513

While it is true that our Father is in heaven it is likewise
true that His Son is among us as the bridge-builder, the

79

Pontifex, to bring us back to His Father. In Christ, God's Presence is brought to us, or rather joined by the Holy Spirit into Christ we are brought back into the life of our Father. Christ's Father becomes our Father; we go back to the Father in Him.

The Father is not far from us. He is not distant, far-removed, and unattainable. He is near, much closer than we allow ourselves to believe.

Can we admit that we're powerless over sin and that our lives have become unmanageable? Do we really believe that a Higher Power greater than ourselves can restore us to spiritual and emotional health? Can we make a decision to turn our wills and our lives over into the care of our Father? Childlike submission is such a challenge to sophisticated adults who cannot understand or admit that one attains victory by surrendering. If recovering addicts can realize that, why can't recovering sinners, also?

The Beauty of Seeing

Theologians speak of the souls in heaven having "the Beatific Vision," which means seeing God and knowing God face to face, directly, immediately, without any one or anything between the soul and God. We have an inkling of what that means when we're in love, when we're gazing into the eyes of another and finding his or her love for us there. We're in heaven when we can see into our beloved's soul, when we can know, fully know, the one whom we love. Heaven means

> The heart has its reasons which reason does not understand.
> **Blaise Pascal**

80

full disclosure in order to have complete acceptance. Heaven is living in the experience of realizing how much you are loved for being just who you are.

Imagine the joy of seeing God gazing at us with the eyes of love! The beatific vision is not simply what we see, it also includes seeing what God sees, and to know with certitude that He loves us because we can see it in His eyes. We see and love others as He sees and loves them. We see and love ourselves as He sees and loves our inner selves.

One of my favorite biblical passages is that involving the Syrophoenician woman whose little daughter needed to be delivered from a tormenting spirit (see Matthew 15:21-28 and Mark 7:24-30). The Son of God saw in her a loveliness and a depth of faith that she didn't see in herself. She equated herself with the dogs; He saw a woman of tremendously attractive faith. His exchange with her should cause us to question how we see ourselves. All too often we sell ourselves short and consider ourselves to be next to worthless. God, on the other hand, sees in us what is worth dying for.

Another such character is St. Peter. It's hard to imagine how he felt about himself after all of his blustering misunderstandings of what Jesus was all about and his terrible betrayal of Jesus during His Passion and trial leading up to His Crucifixion. Yet by God's grace he recognized within himself a deep love of Jesus and came to realize Jesus' deep love for him.

Immediately after His Resurrection, Jesus encountered Peter and brought out of him a self-understanding that he

81

had probably never recognized before. Three times Jesus questions Peter: "Do you love me?" Three times Peter's response affirms that he does. Thereupon Jesus commissions Peter to act in His name, to bring His saving Presence to all (see John 21:15-19).

Heaven is seeing what God sees, seeing as God sees. It's loving what God loves and loving as God loves. Knowing the mind and heart of God, even though we cannot fully comprehend what He knows and loves, completely fills us to the limits of our own capacities. Our big task in our life here on earth is to develop and expand our capacities, which are limitless. Having a big heart, then, is all-important. Taking narrow, hard little hearts into the next life has infinite consequences for us. God works with what we give Him. Perhaps, after all, He doesn't damn us. Perhaps we damn ourselves. Why would He want to damn us when He loves us? It's we who do the damning.

Heaven's Vision

How can we ever describe all that it means to see and love all that God sees and loves? Yet such, I suppose, will be what the beatific vision is all about -- seeing ourselves, others, and all that exists as God sees them, and loving them as God loves them.

When have you experienced total happiness, even bliss? Isn't it when you've experienced completeness, a completeness that comes from seeing with understanding, and you have felt its completeness? It is a matter of seeing with your heart and loving with your mind. It's related to the wisdom that tells us "to love is to know and to know is to love." For vision is not simply a question of satisfying our intellect. Vision implies a contentment of the heart that accompanies understanding with our minds.

The beatific vision allows us to see all that flows out of God in His love for us. What bliss it must be to see in awe, wonder, and contemplation all that can be seen in Goodness, all that can be seen and experienced in Love, all that can fill us with Beauty. The list of things to be seen, to be known and understood, is endless.

> ...our spirit does not desire to contain, but to be contained in you, and even in knowing, rather to be known by your heart. When all wisdom collapses, it is not unknowing that we experience, but rather the truth that all wisdom is secured in you. The wave of the world boils up boldly, but then its impetus overshoots itself and turns to spray, and casts itself, widely dispersed, upon your shore in spent adoration. How I thank you, Lord, that you resolved the painful wilderness of the world only by dissolving it into the blessed wilderness of your love, and that everything conflicting and raging within us is melted together in the crucible of your Creator's might. I thank you that everything in us which is ambiguous and which, therefore, gleams seductively, is reconciled in you and beams with the redemption that makes two into one. You transfigure enigma and replace it with mystery. Everything, sin included, is to you raw material and building stones. Through your atonement you take each being to yourself and, without destroying its reality, you confer upon it a new being.
> **Hans Urs von Balthasar**

83

For me it would be bliss to gaze into Christ's eyes and experience His love for me, a love in which He would see me, and in which I would see my self, in full forgiveness. In such an ecstatic state I would no longer experience shame, no longer see my sins, no longer see my self as having rejected His love and His will for me.

How much of our time, energy, and resources do we expend on achieving bodily perfection? How much time, energy, and resources have we not expended on striving for spiritual perfection? And as for our relationships with others? Clearly, major overhauls are called for. In the ecstasy of heaven, our relationships with others will come to us with perfectly natural ease. All things will be reconstituted in Christ, along with all relationships. Since we are relational beings, we are who we are because of our relationships with others. To have our relationships reconstituted in heaven's perfection must be blissful beyond what mere words can describe.

Some of the worst afflictions that people suffer have to do with self-punishment, even self-hatred. Feelings of inferiority, inadequacy, unattractiveness, and rejection well up in so many of us. What bliss it will be, what happiness, to be free of all such thoughts and feelings! Imagine what it would be like to be happy with yourself, to be satisfied and content with who you are, how you look, and with how others see you and relate to you. That, I think, will be one of the great joys of heaven.

We need to be careful here and remain faithful to the fundamental dynamic that constitutes our relationship with God. God offers, we respond. This means that if our relational life with others is going to be reconstituted, it will happen only when we freely respond to what God offers us. He won't reconstitute us and present us with that gift; He will, however, work with us. Again, everything rests on the truth that we cooperate, of our own free choice, with God.

Our intuitions and our moments of more lucid thoughtfulness bring us to the conclusion that in all probability we are purpose-built, deliberately fashioned, made by God to know and to love Him and others. A little whisper tempts us with the notion that we can't prove that. What sort of proofs would you have for that proposition? Even the most solid scientific statements are not invested with absolute certitude.

Without needing any proof we are all quite aware of the obvious, namely that we have a limitless hunger and capacity to know and to love. There is never enough of either to satisfy our basic drive for more, more to know and more to love. We also have powerful intuitions with which we can know and love apart from sensory data, and beyond our DNA and instinctual urges that are programmed into our physiological constitutions.

Like metal shavings under the influence of a magnet, our lives are organized around knowing and loving. And our energies are such that there is much we know through loving, and conversely much we love through knowing.

Isn't there a happiness that lies beyond endorphins, dopamine, temporary narcosis, and other chemical reactions to a few physical stimuli? Who has ever found happiness in the body's reactions to chemicals or drugs?

85

Heaven's Recovery

We spend so much of our lives dealing with loss, dealing with the emotional and spiritual after-effects of loss. We deal with the loss of those whom we have loved, our parents, spouses, children, and friends. We deal with the loss of our mental and physical powers as we age, or as a result of terrible accidents.

Lost opportunities assault our memories. We spend so much time thinking about what we might have been and what we could have become, along with coping with who and what we really are. Realism replaces wishful thinking and our emotional side tells us that it is a loss.

> Amazing grace! (how sweet the sound)
> That sav'd a wretch like me!
> I once was lost, but now am found,
> Was blind, but now I see.
>
> 'Twas grace that taught my heart to fear,
> And grace my fears reliev'd;
> How precious did that grace appear,
> The hour I first believ'd!
>
> Thro' many dangers, toils and snares,
> I have already come;
> 'Tis grace has brought me safe thus far,
> And grace will lead me home.
>
> The Lord has promis'd good to me,
> His word my hope secures;
> He will my shield and portion be,
> As long as life endures.
> **John Newton**, *Olney* Hymns

The loss of our hopes and dreams certainly beset us, but perhaps the most terrible loss of all is the loss of our values and our ideals. Can we pass them on to our children? Will our own children accept our values and ideals? If they will not, or cannot, the emotional suffering we endure can hardly be calculated.

All of us have been unfaithful to some degree at times, and when that happens people we love and admire lose faith in us. They can no longer believe in us, at least for a period of time. The spouse who has been unfaithful brings more than anger, sadness, and disappointment to his or her mate; the infidelity brings a loss in reliance and trust. No matter how many times we state our good intentions and our "firm purpose of amendment," the acidity of loss of faith continues to eat away at hearts and souls. It puts a person in a hellish sort of isolation. When we break faith with others, a mortal blow is struck at our closest relationships.

Try to imagine the happiness that will be ours when in heaven we recover all we have lost. We must remember always that the main mission of Christ Jesus is to return to His Father those who were lost, and all else that we lost because of our sins. Those who have known recovery in this life have a taste of that joyful banquet. The joy in heaven over the return of what has been lost must be a joy beyond which any mere human words can convey.

Heaven's Contentment

Heaven is that realm wherein God governs and we don't. That which God wants us to do is, in heaven, all-pervasive. How will the self-willed be able to survive there? What will happen to those who are filled with their autonomous selves? Perhaps those "who simply cannot be told" will not be able to endure heaven. Once again we come upon the notion that we determine our own destinies. God offers; if we don't respond then we damn ourselves in our own hell of rejection.

What happens when you realize what it is that God wants of you and you do not choose to comply? Examine the dynamics. Isn't it true that you immediately challenge the perception of God's will, claim that the messenger is misinformed, or that something is wrong with the messenger, all because the message doesn't conform with your expectations of what God's will should or would be? In heaven all of those rationalizations, denials, and avoidance techniques will be useless, for God's wishes will be immediately (without mediation) present to you. Then what will you do?

Will it be in heaven that love will triumph, that I will love God's will, that I will love all others whom God has created, and that I will love them all as God loves them? I hope so, for then, and only then, will I love in full contentment and peace.

In the funeral liturgy we pray, "Eternal rest grant unto them, O Lord...." Rest? If God is anything He is Activity, always creating, always redeeming, always sanctifying, always loving. He is forever engaged. It's hard to imagine a heaven of complacency, inactivity, and noninvolvement.

(St. Paul tells us) "Now we see through a glass, darkly; but then face to face." This vision is reserved as the reward of our faith; and of it the Apostle John also says, "When He shall appear, we shall be like Him, for we shall see Him as He is." By "the face" of God we are to understand His manifestation, and not a part of the body similar to that which in our bodies we call by that name.
St. Augustine, *City of God,* Book XXII, Chapter 29, "Of the Beatific Vision"

Being in His image and likeness, there will probably be a great deal for us to do when we're in heaven.

So, rest? Rest from what? Rest from anxiety; rest from the fear of loneliness; rest from hungering and thirsting for love and acceptance; rest from our guilty consciences; rest from our terrible self-punishing thoughts and feelings about ourselves. In heaven we will be resurrected into a new and higher life, fully reconstituted in our very being and in our total personality. Our selves will, by God's grace, be totally new, new in body and soul, new in our relationships with others. Gone will be the fear of loneliness and rejection, the fear of loss and pain.

Fear controls most of us most of the time. Imagine the peace, the rest, the serenity, and the contentment of living in total freedom from any fears whatsoever. Imagine resting in the peace of being free from anger, gluttony, pride, sloth, envy, greed and lust. What bliss!

Dante's "Paradiso" suggests it is vision that gives us bliss. It is what the soul sees, contemplates, and enters into that gives us complete happiness, contentment, and peace. Our souls long to belong but will nevertheless be at peace in the certitude that we do in fact belong to the One who is Love, the One who has in Himself an infinite desire to belong totally to you and totally to me.

The story of the Tower of Babel is the story of pagans attempting to please, placate, and build their own way to a remote and distant God. Underdeveloped prayer often finds us begging, imploring, and crawling in a groveling manner back to God. Underdeveloped prayer seeks to overcome God's

SOJOURNS IN THE PARALLEL WORLD

We live our lives of human passions,
cruelties, dreams, concepts,
crimes and the exercise of virtue
in and beside a world devoid
of our preoccupations,
free from apprehension – though affected,
certainly, by our actions. A world
parallel to our own though overlapping.
We call it 'Nature;' only reluctantly
admitting ourselves to be 'Nature' too.
Whenever we lose track of our own obsessions,
our self-concerns, because we drift for a minute,
an hour even, of pure (almost pure)
response to that insouciant life:
cloud, bird, fox, the flow of light, the dancing
pilgrimage of water, vast stillness
of spellbound ephemerae on a lit windowpane,
animal voices, mineral hum, wind
conversing with rain, ocean with rock, stuttering
of fire to coal – then something tethered
in us, hobbled like a donkey on its patch
of gnawed grass and thistles, breaks free.
No one discovers
just where we've been, when we're caught up
again
into our own sphere (where we must
return, indeed, to evolve our destinies) but we
have changed, a little.
   Denise Levertov, *Sands of the Well*

anger, get His attention, and inform Him of all that's wrong in us and in our world in the hope that He will do something about it. But that isn't real prayer. Real prayer is simply being in His presence, accepting His love for us, content in His immediate love.

"When you pray," Jesus instructs us, "do not pray as the pagans do," thinking that many words will get God's attention and move Him to take pity on us. God doesn't pity us, He loves us. He has redeemed us in the blood of His only Son and sanctified us in His Holy Spirit. There's no pity in that.

My prayer, therefore, should lead me to get out of God's way! He is coming into our world. He is coming to you and to me. He is coming to share His love and His life with me in my life forever. My prayer should open the way for that to happen, remove all that blocks His coming to me, all that prevents His abiding in me. My prayer should enable, not hinder. It should seek His agenda, not mine. It should tell me of His wishes, not mine. It should center on His desires, not my wants. Do we really feel that God is seeking us out in order to condemn us?

When we try to imagine what we will be doing in heaven we need to remember the real question: What will we be doing with God? God doesn't do whatever He does all by Himself any more than He exists all by Himself. The reality of our lives is found in the relationships we have with God.

Isn't there a sort of blissful peace in that? Isn't there a lovely sense of rest and peace in accomplishing His purposes rather than making sure our agendas, projects, and purposes are well served?

Those who write about heaven consistently speak in terms of our "seeing," specifically seeing God face to face. The "seeing" is more than vision, for the writers go on to speak of "understanding" and "knowing." This "seeing" takes us into the depths of the One who is other, it takes us into the heart of God. There is an intimate oneness in knowing the one we love and being known by the one we love.

God comes to us in His Word, in His Light, and in His Spirit of Wisdom, Understanding and Knowledge. Heavenly bliss, we must deduce, must be understood within those contexts.

Is There a Hell?

The world's greatest artists and photographers know how to reveal beauty in the art of contrast. Light is "seen" in contrast to surrounding darkness. Contrasts and "high" lights bring to us the awareness of loveliness and beauty. Artists and photographers know that contrasting light and darkness reveal the beauty of what is in the light. Perhaps we should here follow their lead by contrasting heaven and hell.

It used to be that beautiful photographs were printed from negative images. In the same way it is helpful, I think, for us to heighten our awareness of the evidence of heaven by looking at the evidence of hell. Some descriptive words may be helpful, descriptions of what we are living in and what we could be living in.

Hell is the absence of what is good. Sin is the disfigurement of what is good and beautiful; hell is the total absence of what is good and therefore beautiful, what is beautiful and therefore good.

Heaven	Hell
Rest	Fear
Peace	Anxiety & Worry
Fulfillment	Emptiness
Contentment	Loss
Awe	Disgust
Wonder	Contempt
Innocence	Shame
Meaning	Triviality
Ecstasy	Meaninglessness
Blessedness	Hopelessness
Tranquility	Struggle
Acceptance	Rejection

Hell is living forever in your own hatred of your self and in the fear-based rejection of being infinitely loved. It is living in the hatred of not being independent and in the knowledge that you must depend upon God. For the omnipotent self, the everlasting loss of your own autonomy is a horrible suffering.

"Fear not," Jesus kept telling us. In the New Testament the opposite of faith is not doubt, it is fear. When fear is replaced by faith, the "loss" of giving your self away in love to your Lover is ecstasy. Living forever in the awareness that in order to be happy you must depend upon others and upon God is painful only to the prideful.

93

Lucifer's exquisite pain is in hating God for loving others, particularly the human men and women He created. Lucifer's pain is his awareness that God decides whom He loves and the extent of His love for them, that God's love is out of control, particularly Lucifer's control. Legend has it that Lucifer became enraged when he saw the length to which God would go in order to redeem men and women from their sins. The paradigm is found in the spiritual condition of the elder brother who, seeing his father pouring out his love for his prodigal son, entered into his own hellish inner rage. It is the father's prodigality that causes the elder son to suffer in his own self-created hell.

> From that time on, Jesus began to show his disciples that he must go to Jerusalem and suffer greatly from the elders, the chief priests, and the scribes, and be killed and on the third day be raised.
> Then Peter took him aside and began to rebuke him, "God forbid, Lord! No such thing shall ever happen to you."
> He turned and said to Peter, "Get behind me, Satan! You are an obstacle to me. You are thinking not as God does, but as human beings do."
> **Matthew 16:21-23**

Heaven is filled with joy, especially the joy that all share over one repentant sinner. "There is more joy in heaven," Jesus declared, "over the return of just one repentant sinner" (Luke 15:7). What a joy it is to experience the fact that God has come in search of you and has found you. You don't have to go in search of Him, He comes for you.

What joy must come to those who recognize that it is God who justifies: we don't have to. It is God who sanctifies, not us. It is God who brings justice and mercy

94

together, we can't. What joy it must be to be relieved of such grave responsibilities and to recognize that it is God who does these things, and does them perfectly. We get a glimpse of it in the return of the prodigal son and see him once again in his father's all-embracing arms, the arms of the father who went out to get him and bring him back into his home.

I often marvel at the time and energy expended by so many in vainly attempting to declare who is damned and who is saved. How do we know? That's God's job, not ours. Instead of figuring out who is excommunicated and who is damned wouldn't we be more about our Father's business if we were more the prodigal son and less the elder brother?

Could it be that the Catholic notion of Purgatory is correct? Could it be that God offers us more time right here in this life so that we might, using His graces, purge ourselves of our stonyhearted intolerance of others? That God gives us one gigantic opportunity with His grace to purge ourselves of all prideful notions by which we judge ourselves and others? Perhaps we are living here and now in our purgatories so that, when we die, we will take what we have made of ourselves in this life and offer our chastened selves to God as we enter the next life. We must remember that we are already living in eternal time and that death is, however significant, only one event in the eternal time in which we are already living.

Let us keep in mind that God is just, and justice always calls for us to suffer the consequences of our decisions. God is not vengeful, nor is He punishing in the sense of retaliation or vindictiveness. God's punishments are always medicinal. They are evocative; they call for our responses in the form of repentance and contrition; they require us to take responsibility and be accountable for our own decisions and the actions that followed those decisions. Purgatory, then, is yet another chance for us, a chance to get things right with God by getting things right in our hearts and souls. Purgatory is where justice and mercy kiss.

Heaven? Purgatory? Hell? They are states of being, not places. They are descriptions of how we exist in our relational lives with those around us. They are descriptions of the status of our souls, states of being for which we are responsible. We are in these states according to the quality and character of our responses to God's eternal, constant, and unchanging love for us.

As to who is forever living in heaven or hell, that is not for us to decide. Too many of us waste time and energy in taking over God's job. God and God alone definitively judges, we don't.

One final contrast should be noted, which is perhaps the most critical of all: the contrast between life and death. Perhaps I should phrase it as seeing life in the context of death. Certainly during recent centuries our human lives have been lived in the context of death. The contrasting images have been inescapable.

As believers we know that death is but the gateway we pass through in order to enter eternal life. What will we take with us into that eternal life? What will adorn our characters and souls? What will be the treasures with which we begin eternal life?

Pope John Paul II spoke of this often. In one of his noonday allocutions he said: "More than ever, today's world has a need to rediscover the meaning of life and death, in the perspective of eternal life. Outside that perspective," he said, "modern culture, born to exalt man and his dignity, is paradoxically transformed into a culture of death, because without the horizon of God he finds himself a prisoner in the world, overwhelmed by fear, and, unfortunately, gives way to multiple personal and collective pathologies."

Heaven? Hell? Where are you headed? The question goes deeper than good intentions or good wishes. It deals with the very real patterns of our behavior, the actual choices we have made. And how do you know you're headed for the proper heaven? Hell, after all, is the eternal dwelling place of the misguided and self-deluded.

The way to heaven is found in each day's present. What would your life be like if you began each day with a focus on what your life is all about? If you had vision and purpose in what you were doing, in how you would relate to people in your life that day? If you began each day in God's presence, in the vision and purpose of His Christ, you would find calmness, steadiness, and the ability to deal with life's ever-encroaching chaos and unexpected trials. Keeping your eyes fixed on God, and having a vision of what heaven is all about, gives you the vision and the serenity of knowing that you fit in God's grand scheme of things. If you are able to do this you will not be far from the kingdom; you might even find yourself on the front porch of heaven.

* * * * * *

PRAYER

O Father, you well know the longings I have deep within my heart and soul. My life has been a struggle to belong, to find love, to give my heart away totally to others who might have me. But none have known me as you have known me, and none have loved me as you have loved me. "My heart will not rest until it rests in Thee."

* * * * * *

QUESTONS

Describe heaven as you hope it might be.
Describe hell as you think it might be.
What will people be like in heaven?
Do you think you will be surprised by who you find in heaven?

① free - freedom from fear, Anxiety, doubt, etc, etc — Rest, Peace, Joy.

② Hell is what we make ourselves, when we try to go it alone — fear, doubt, anxiety, stress, etc enters in — that is Hell.

③ We will be the creations that God made — we will return Home & be whole.

④ Yes! because we think we know from

HALLOWED BE THY NAME...

"Primary Wonder"

Days pass when I forget the mystery.
Problems insoluble and problems offering
their own ignored solutions
jostle for my attention, they crowd its antechamber
along with a host of diversions, my courtiers,
wearing
their colored clothes; cap and bells.

                             And then

Once more the quiet mystery
is present to me, the throng's clamor
recedes: the mystery
that there is anything, anything at all,
let alone cosmos, joy, memory, everything,
rather than void: and that, O Lord,
Creator, Hallowed One, You still,
Hour by hour sustain it.

Denise Levertov, *The Stream & the Sapphire*

I do not blithely undertake writing about the ineffable holiness of God, realizing full well the danger of diminishing with mere human words God's awe-inspiring Being. Fearing even the remotest possibility of idolatry, our Jewish elder brothers and sisters in the faith are forbidden to speak or even write the name of God. It

Judging people here on earth +
God will Surprise us, of that
< I'm sure >

would be unthinkable for them, an unspeakable blasphemy, to even imagine that God would demean Himself by coming to us as one of us. But that is precisely the point that divides us.

Idols are fashioned by human work, and idolatry is a terrible sin against God's grandeur and exclusive right to the fullness of our faith. Terrible consequences result from our idolatries, consequences that beset us even unto this day.

An idol, however, is not the same as an icon. Christ Jesus is the Icon of God, not an icon made of wood and paint and gold, but by the power of God's Holy Spirit made of human flesh and blood, fashioned from the Blessed Virgin Mary's humanity. She was made holy in order that the Holy would be made of her. In the words of the great English poet Wordsworth, she is "our tainted human nature's solitary boast."

While recognizing the limiting constrictions and inadequacies of human words (particularly my own), we should now reflect on the meaning and content of the Lord's Prayer with respect to its praise in recognition of God's holiness. Of course Jesus included praising God's holiness in the great prayer He taught us. We need to honor the holiness of God no matter how pitifully inadequate we may be in doing so. For it is precisely our inadequacies that Jesus takes, as he did five measly barley loaves and two fish, and makes them infinitely bountiful. God is forever taking insignificant little things and making them infinitely significant.

What dare we say about His holiness? The Prophet
Daniel said this:

May you be blessed, Lord, God of our ancestors,
be praised and extolled for ever.
Blessed be your glorious and holy name,
praised and extolled forever.
May you be blessed in the Temple of your sacred
glory,
exalted and glorified above all for ever:
blessed on the throne of your kingdom,
praised and exalted above all else forever.
Blessed, you fathomer of the great depths,
*   enthroned on the cherubs,*
praised and glorified above all else forever;
blessed in the vault of heaven,
exalted and glorified above all else forever.
All things the Lord has made, bless the Lord:
Give glory and eternal praise to him.
                    Daniel 3:52-57

The Presence

Walk with me now into affluent Modern Man's Temple
of Gods and Goddesses. Isn't the façade beautiful? Aren't
the Corinthian columns magnificent? Guido, our guide,
bids us walk along the interior of this pantheon. We pause
at gorgeous, creamy statues cut from Carrara marble,
standing bigger than life on their impressive pedestals.
They represent the gods and goddesses to which we give

ourselves -- fame, fortune, beauty, power, sex, money, indolence, sloth, jealousy, hatred, gluttony, and pride, each one of them capturing the thoughts and fantasies of many people in our day.

Standing in the middle is a gigantic statue that towers over all others. We notice that the eyes of all the other gods and goddesses are discreetly directed toward this central dominating figure. Cut into the stone pedestal we find the words: "The Glory of the Imperial Self." The evoked feeling makes me uncomfortable.

Departing from this temple, located on a hill high above the city below, we descend into the whirl of this world and come upon a little church located at the head of a small street's intersection with our main boulevard. Guido takes us inside. I find myself bathed in the soft rays of colorful hues that come from beautiful images of holy men and women depicted in the little church's old, stained-glass windows.

Looking around I find warm and inviting statues of men and women who peacefully gaze down at us. Flickering flames of votive candles bathe everything in soft lights. Faint whiffs of incense waft by, mingled in with the smells of burning beeswax. There is Something here that was not in the temple high on the hill above us, a near palpable Presence.

My eyes take me to the apse of the church. Hanging above us in the central spot of the church is a crucifix. It is beautiful, although at one point in time long ago it was a hideous instrument of Roman execution. The Man hanging on it was one like us but at the same time not just like us. He hung there not so much in death as He did in rest. There was something profoundly serene and peaceful about him, more the peace that follows something that is finished rather than destroyed.

I did not feel the need to kneel in the pantheon but I needed to kneel here. I was aware of a Presence, a nearness that both surrounded me and yet was within me. I became aware of a stirring deep within, a movement, if you will. Someone was close. Someone wanted to draw me near. It was almost as if I was at home, not the home in which my mother and father loved me and raised me, but my real home.

Here I knew I belonged.

He let me go through my usual litany of sorrow for sins; he let me rattle on about all of my failures, all of my neglect, all of the things I did and didn't do. Then when I became weary of talking about me and all that I had done and not done, I began to realize that He wanted me to simply tell Him that I loved Him. All He wanted to hear from me was that underneath all of the ash and debris of my sins and failures I really did love Him. He wanted me to tell Him that I wanted Him to love me. The Holy One wants to transform us with His love.

People, Places, and Things

Everything is touched by God. Perhaps it would be better to say that everything touches God; whatever is in being intersects with God's being. Since we cannot have come into being from nothing, we must have come into being from a Cause. Since nothing has Existence in itself, everything is held in being by the One who is Being itself. "I Am who I Am," said God in response to Moses' question. God is Being it its wholeness, in its holiness.

> ### Great Spirit Prayer
>
> Oh, Great Spirit, whose voice I hear in the wind,
> Whose breath gives life to all the world.
> Hear me; I need your strength and wisdom.
> Let me walk in beauty, and make my eyes ever behold
> the red and purple sunset.
> Make my hands respect the things you have made
> and my ears sharp to hear your voice.
> Make me wise so that I may understand the things you
> have taught my people.
> Help me to remain calm and strong in the face of all
> that comes towards me.
> Let me learn the lessons you have hidden in every leaf
> and rock.
> Help me seek pure thoughts and act with the intention
> of helping others.
> Help me find compassion without empathy
> overwhelming me.
> I seek strength, not to be greater than my brother, but
> to fight my greatest enemy
> Myself.
> Make me always ready to come to you with clean
> hands and straight eyes.
> So when life fades, as the fading sunset, my spirit may
> come to you without shame.
> **A Native American Prayer**

Spring water carries within it the spring from whence it came. So also anything that exists carries within it the Existence from which it came. This tells us that anything that exists carries within it its original blessing. All

104

people, no matter how evil, depraved, or disgusting, carry within them God's original love, even Lucifer himself! Lucifer could be in heaven tomorrow if he renounced his pride, repented in genuine contrition and sorrow, and threw himself upon God's love, as did the prodigal son. He won't, of course. But he still carries within his being the blessed existence from whence he came.

Native Americans recognized the Presence and the holiness of God nearly everywhere, not only in humans but also in the animals, birds, waters, and trees among which they lived. They named Him the Great Spirit and were ever conscious of His presence. These natives had no churches or temples, no ordered liturgies, no priestly class. Yet they worshipped. They worshipped everywhere and in all significant events and activities. Their cult was in their culture.

In their prayers and traditions they often spoke of the covenant between the Great Spirit and all life, a covenant extending to the animals and birds as well as to men and women. While they were aware that animals were not conscious of themselves and that humans were a higher form of life, they nevertheless gave enormous respect to all living creatures, even when they found it necessary to kill fish, animals, and birds for human food in order to sustain the "great circle of life" among living human creatures.

What do you revere as holy, hallowed, and sacred? Who do you regard as holy? From time to time while reading a magazine, or a newspaper, or while watching television I wonder what we as a people revere as holy, if anything.

105

I'm saddened to conclude that it seems our culture is hollowing the name of God, not hallowing it. So often the very word "God" has been reduced to being an epithet, an exclamation point, or used only as a curse.

Would you recognize holiness if you saw it? Many do not. Even the people of Jesus' hometown, Nazareth, did not. "Isn't he just a carpenter?" they asked. "Don't we know who he is?" And Jesus could not work any miracles there. Think of what they missed! What he could have done there! "He was amazed at their lack of faith," St. Mark reports (6:6).

Although seemingly strange, Pontius Pilate and especially his wife, both unbelievers, were aware of Jesus' holiness. But Pilate, the Roman governor who ruled by fear, ended up being ruled by fear of the mob and had Christ put to death by crucifixion (Matthew 27:20-26; Mark 15:2-15). This raises another question: Even if we are aware of holiness, will we act on it?

All things are being redeemed in Christ, the world and all that's in it, not just souls. Christianity is not a spiritualist religion in the sense that only what is spiritual matters. It is rather a realist religion,

> He has let us know the mystery of his purpose, the hidden plan he so kindly made in Christ from the beginning to act upon when times had run their course to the end: that he would bring everything together under Christ, as head, everything in the heavens and everything on earth.
> **Ephesians 1:9-10**

recognizing that what is material is likewise being redeemed, bought back for God, along with the spiritual.

The sad fact is that humans have ravaged the world's resources, stripped it of trees and minerals simply for

106

profit and for our own selfish purposes, leaving the refuse for our children and their children's children. We have failed to remember that we are only stewards of God's creation, not owners of what we plat out for ourselves.

As believers and followers of Christ we need to pay much more attention to what environmentalists are telling us. But we need to look beyond the consequences they are predicting and develop a theology of environmentalism. A good beginning can be found in the Book of Genesis, along with a closer look at what Jesus was teaching us about stewardship. We need to stop treating the world as if it were ours and start treating the world as God's.

We should pay attention, also, to the teachings, beliefs and practices of Native Americans, for they held the earth, the waters, the animals and birds, and all that is found in nature, as sacred. They recognized that the earth and all it encompasses is the gift of the Great Spirit to them. They even recognized the Presence of the Great Spirit inside themselves. Do we?

A hymn that was sung in the early Church of the Apostles, and one quoted by St. Paul in his letter to the Colossians (Colossians 1:15-20), goes right to the point:

> *"He is the image of the unseen God*
> *and the first-born of all creation,*
> *for in him were created*
> *all things in heaven and on earth:*
> *everything visible and everything invisible,*
> *Thrones, Dominations, Sovereignties, Powers –*
> *all things were created through him and for him.*

Before anything was created, he existed,
and he holds all things in unity.
Now the Church is his body,
he is its head".

To desacralize, to desecrate, is commonplace today. I see much in my religious field of vision that has been either trivialized by Christians or trashed by others who have little or no faith. In our day the vulgar is time and again marketed to us, while the sublime, except in rare instances, is kept at a distance, reserved only for museums and churches, which we enter only with infrequent curiosity. It's so much easier to bring down than to build up. We can slide when we go down; we must work to go up.

After this we say, "Hallowed be Thy name;" not that we wish for God that He may be hallowed by our prayers, but that we beseech of Him that His name may be hallowed in us. But by whom is God sanctified, since He Himself sanctifies? Well, because He says, "Be ye holy, even as I am holy," we ask and entreat, that we who were sanctified in baptism may continue in that which we have begun to be.
St. Cyprian, d.258
Treatise IV. *On the Lord's Prayer,* 12.

Does God have a "home," a sanctuary or a tabernacle in our world? In our hearts? To be sure, we have built temples and shrines, and made holy places for God, or at least places in which we try to experience God's presence and offer ourselves to God. Some things we call holy, recognizing that they are dedicated to God. But the holiness of God is found more profoundly in persons, persons He made and destined to be in His image and likeness. The holiness of persons is more significant than the holiness of things or places.

But what has God built? God has uttered His Word, has fathered-forth His Presence and that expression of His Presence, His name, in seeking a home among us. Christians recognize God's presence in the Mystical Body of Christ, a body made up of billions upon billions of cells, a body composed of human flesh, a body composed of you and me and all of those who have ever been, or will be, baptized and confirmed. This means that God's "home" among us isn't found in a particular place, but in a home that is everywhere and anywhere we are gathered in His name. "The foxes," Jesus said, "have their dens and the birds of the air their nests. But the Son of Man has nowhere to lay His head" (Matthew 8:20). He is always moving amongst us.

The holy is the transcendent. What is transcendent can be smeared by human touch, tarnished by our expressions of what is transcendent. Mercifully the transcendent is beyond human manipulation. Truth, Goodness, Justice, Wisdom, and Beauty are Transcendentals that measure our works, we don't measure them. We have, however, nearly always stained them by misusing and mistreating them.

We even managed to crucify God's self-expression, His Word made flesh. The way to the cross was opened by a human judge, Pontius Pilate, who exclaimed "Truth? What is truth?" Once that transcendental was knocked down it logically followed that Justice would be the next to fall.

109

But in the end the Transcendentals always come back up out of the graves we fashion for them, rolling back the stones of the tombs in which we attempt to confine them. For the truth is that every time this world's illuminati have declared "God is dead!" He has come roaring back from the grave to encounter us anew in His Church.

Praying "hallowed by Thy name" adds nothing to God, or His grandeur. But praying those words does confront our willful human pride with a greater reality to which we must yield. For God is holy in His being, ineffable, mysterious, sacred, immeasurable, untouchable, and limitless -- beyond the reach of our minds. It is that last quality that is an affront to human pride, "beyond the reach of our minds." Such a Being, human pride declares, does not exist. It is impermissible to our egos, an affront, an insult to our lust to control everything in our own self-declared omnipotence. A suspicion immediately becomes present in our hearts when we come upon the mysterious, the awesome from another dimension. Our rationalizations are immediately drafted into service as we war against the unknowable, the holy, which perhaps accounts for our modern reduction of human life to an entity we can control. Birth, life, and death can no longer be tolerated as holy mysteries but must be subjected to human technological control.

The boundary between this world and the world that is holy is frighteningly close to us. We cross over that boundary every time we love. We "pass over" into God's world whenever we die to ourselves and, stripped of everything, hand ourselves over to Love. Perhaps that's why we have crucifixes with a human body on them, and perhaps that is why crucifixes make us feel uncomfortable.

Some of my deepest experiences of being present to God's holiness and awe-inspiring transcendence have occurred when participating in the Divine Liturgies of the great Eastern Churches. The stupendous

> We are not God. We are simply the image of God and our task is gradually to discover that image and set it free.
> **Michael Quoist**

mystery of God's divinity enfolding us has touched my soul in these liturgies. One cannot simply recognize the symbols in these liturgies but rather one has to enter in to them. It's not simply a question of seeing these symbols and understanding what they mean, for these Mysteries are by their very nature incomprehensible. It is a matter of surrendering one's self into them and allowing one's self to be swept up in them, swept up into the One in whom God meets man, the One in whom God presents Himself to us. What can our response be other than to fall flat on our faces in awe and adoration of God's loving condescension in actually seeking out our love for him?

The sacred music of the Russian Orthodox Church is likewise powerful; it infuses itself into the inner core of our being and carries us aloft into the realms of a higher world, the world in which the Risen One, having gathered us all into His being, presents us and our world to His Father in heaven.

Our Lady of Gethsemani monastery in Kentucky is another place that is "out of this world" while being very much in it, as Thomas Merton revealed to us. Any number

111

of churches, cathedrals, and shrines are places in which to experience holiness. So, too, the Grand Canyon, the mountains and meadows, and the lakes and rivers of our earth.

Above all, holiness is best revealed in people, a certain few who have surrendered themselves into God's love and providence, and with whom we too can enter into the heart of God. The Communion of Saints is not some distant abstraction, it is a present reality. The souls of Mother Theresa, Joan of Arc, Francis of Assisi, Thomas More, Elizabeth Seaton, John Paul II, and countless others, both famous and obscure, have touched us.

Holiness is fearsomely close to us; it is not necessarily found behind the walls of a monastery or cloistered convent. The insistent call to be wholly for others, wholly for God, to heal that which is unwholesome and become whole, is a call to holiness we continually resist.

Heal, Whole, Holy

A young Vietnamese student came to America to study at a university. He was a delicate young man (at least by external appearances), sensitive and quiet serene, a reflective type of person. A professor asked him to give his opinion about what was wrong here in the United States. The young Vietnamese man responded by telling the story of a farmer who was working in his fields when a man came galloping up on a horse. The farmer asked the rider where he was going. As the horse galloped away the rider shouted back, "I don't know. Ask the horse!"

We are like that rider, out of control. Events dominate us rather than the other way around. Many of us lack a basic sense of control; perhaps, as a society, we reflect this basic deficiency. A typical response to this lack of control is to try to increase our domination through technology, political coalitions, money, repression, and whatever else gives us the illusion of power over others. A quick look at our news media makes this abundantly clear.

Yet the real type of power that we need is genuine contact with reality, a difficult task given all of the cosmetic denials that overlay it. "Where do we find truth?" we ask. "Is there such a thing as truth?" "What do you mean by reality?" Our defensive protections are so thick that we are barely able to remain in touch with our own selves.

The resulting cost is that we are out of control. A joint perception of truth, a communal, shared understanding of reality, and the joy of shared discovery, is possible. Our problem is that we just don't seem to know how to achieve that spiritual communion, we even fear it. But as any recovering addict will tell you, we gain control by turning control over to our Higher Power. Overcoming the fear of doing just that is the big obstacle.

A phrase often heard in recovery groups is, "Let go, and let God." Finding the critical touchstone of humility, relinquishing our fierce (and isolating) independence, and handing over our defiant selves into the care of God, is the fabled Ring of Power that will set us free. In other words, healing is found in the quest for holiness.

113

We live fractured lives, in dislocation with each other in an incomplete world. But the fact that our world is incomplete is a gift to us from God. He has invested us with the enormous dignity of working with Him to bring creation to completeness, wholeness. What faith He has in us! What dreams and hopes He has for us! We are His cooperators, coworkers in bringing His world and our lives into completeness, wholeness, and therefore holiness.

The word religion comes from *re-ligio*; we are to re-ligament our fractured humanity and dislocated union and bring it back into a holistic body. Isn't that what Ezekiel was talking about when he gave us his oracle of the dry bones lying out there in the desert, fractured and torn apart? (See Ezekiel 37.)

The work of Christ is to make us whole again, to bring us to share in a holistic common union, a Holy Communion, whereby in Him we are made into His Holy Mystical Body and brought back in Him to our heavenly Father. Everything we do that is consonant with that work is holy, Christ-like, God-like.

What could give us greater happiness? When I was a young boy my mother told me "Happiness is something to do, someone to love, and something to hope for." Who can be happy if they are not living a life of dedication, if their lives without purpose and without meaning?

I have stood in wonder before men and women who are living lives full of love even in the face of love that is not returned. Who doesn't know of friends who are living with spouses and children who simply take them for granted, ignore them, or are openly hostile toward them, and still they stay, and still they love? Such is the stuff of holiness, it seems to me.

Holiness is all around us. It is found in mothers and fathers who care for self-centered and uncaring children. It is found in lives lived in the face of terminal illness, or in mental derangement and emotional depression. It is found in lives lived in the face of death, both physical death and in relationships now cold and dead that were once alive and vibrant.

Holiness is found in lives lived in hope and in the hope shared with those around us. Isn't it true that the greatest gift Christians with genuine spirituality can give to others is the gift of hope? Such a gift is grounded in the mystery of Christ's suffering, crucifixion, and resurrection. The core of a Christian's gift to the world is his or her share of living in the resurrection, living in the hours that follow the emptiness of loss.

Saintly persons are those living in dedicated lives, lives dedicated to bringing the love of Christ along with His values and vision of life to every person they encounter, along with bringing Christ's ways into every situation in which they find themselves. Such persons live in happiness, a happiness that spills into the hearts and souls of all those around them. There is something immensely attractive about them. Those who know them wonder about how they do it, what mysterious characteristic do these people possess, regardless of their station in life, that makes them love and act as they do with everyone they encounter?

Sanctity exists deep within us; we are endowed with it by our Creator. Our task, our work, is to purge, to sculpt and chip away, all that disguises and disfigures our sanctity and to reveal our true identity, the identity in which God sees us and to which God calls us individually, by name. That can be done only by working with God; we cannot do it on our own.

What's in a Name?

We did not name God. God, rather, gave us His name, declared it to us. We give something a name when we recognize its essential nature, what makes it be what it is. For instance, we name certain things "chair". Such an object can be made out of stone, fabricated with man-made material, or made in many other ways. But when we identify it, we call it a chair because it is, in its nature, not a table, a ladder, or anything else. It is uniquely and exclusively a chair.

> Then Moses said to God, 'I am to go, then, to the sons of Israel and say to them, 'The God of your fathers has sent me to you'. But if they ask me what his name is, what am I to tell them? "And God said to Moses, 'I Am who I Am'. This, he added, is what you must say to the sons of Israel: 'I Am has sent me to you.'"
> **Exodus 3:13-15**

Taking the name of God in vain is not simply using it as a curse or an epithet. On a deeper level it is presumption, or assumption. When we think we know God or what kind of a God God is, we are being futile and foolishly arrogant. Pride, the root and ground of all sin, is again at work here.

116

You and I have experienced those wonderful moments when parents choose a name for their newborn child. It is a special time. Indeed, it is a sacred time. For in the giving of a name one recognizes the inner reality of the human being named. The name is not really something imposed from external reality; the name reveals who the person is, it recognizes the inner reality of the person bearing the name.

There is something God-like in the act of naming. An inner essence is being recognized; something of the person's essence is being externalized in the giving of a name. Thus it is that in certain religious orders new members are given new names. God changed Abram's name to Abraham and Jesus, acting as only God would, changed Simon's name to Peter and Saul's name to Paul. Their being was altered. There was an existential change. This is the deeper reality, the grace of God within, of Baptism and of ordination into Christ's Priesthood.

> So from the soil Yahweh God fashioned all the wild beasts and all the birds of heaven. These he brought to the man to see what he would call them; each one was to bear the name the man would give it.
> **Genesis 2:19-20**

All that exists shares in God's existence. He is the First Cause, as we have said, the Prime Mover, the One in whom all that is, is. While God is intelligible, God remains incomprehensible. All that we know about God through our senses is derivative.

The name of God informs us of His inner being. A name, therefore, is a symbol that opens up a mystery to be revealed to us, a mystery at the level of being. A sign is

117

something that controls us, signs such as "Stop," "Yield," and "No Admittance." A symbol, however, invites us to look into the deeper reality of what is symbolized. The Statue of Liberty, for instance, is a symbol. Christ's cross is a symbol, and a kiss is a symbol. They present a reality for us to enter into; they do not dominate, manipulate, or control us. Symbols are not merely signs, then, because symbols free us, they do not control us.

God's name is holy, wholly other and wholly distinct from what we can manipulate or control by our human knowledge. We can only apprehend God in His being; we cannot comprehend Him. There is a saying advising us "knowledge is power." This perhaps explains why pious Jews do not even utter or write the name of God. This is why they find statues and depictions of God as idolatrous. Humans idolize what they want to dominate and control. The thirst for knowledge can be a seductive lust to know and control solely in our human power. Comprehension subjects people, places, and things to human techniques, offering them up to our technology god. This is why mysteries, along with Transcendentals, remain intelligible but at the same time incomprehensible.

When you whisper your lover's name you capture her heart. "Oh, Anne," you murmur, "you are so wonderful!" She is open to you when you do that. You have a sort of mysterious power over her. That's why magicians and "seers" believe that using the name of the one they conjure up commands their presence. Love and reverence are the most insistent of calls.

118

What father or mother does not become totally available to their children when they call out "daddy" or "mommy"? When a person is lovingly sought, or called for, he or she becomes vulnerable. Can we possibly imagine how "powerless" our Almighty Father becomes when He hears us call out His name with our hearts full of awe and wonder over His love for us?

God calls us by name in order that we might call Him by name. For when we hear someone speak our name we become (or should become) totally present to him or her. Imagine that your telephone rang and a voice on the other end announced, "This is the White House. The President of the United States would like to speak with you." Then a new voice comes on, that of the president, and addresses you by your own name. How would you feel? Would you not be totally attentive to him?

When you hear your name spoken with respect and affection, a powerful spell of closeness and intimacy comes over you. Do you imagine it is any different with God when we call him "Abba," "Papa," "Father"?

PRAYER

I cannot understand why it is that you love me anyway, even though I am disgusting, twisted and deformed. How can you possibly love me when my "outer self" is so ugly and repulsive? How can you possibly re-create me when I don't want to be touched, don't want to be loved, and flee from your outstretched arms? I fear your terrible love and so I must nail your outstretched hands to your cross so they cannot touch me, so they cannot embrace me. Stay on your cross, Lord, so I do not have to change.

O Lord Jesus, I need your wholeness. I need your completeness. I need your power. Help me to want your power enough to not only ask for it but to accept it from your loving hand. Your love is terrible – it terrifies me. Your love would force me to give up those pitiful things to which I cling as my self-proclaimed "needs." I want to give them up. I want you to redeem and sanctify me; I want to be filled with your Spirit so that in His beauty my soul will be lovely and desirable in your eyes. Fill me with your Spirit now, because I can never do that by myself.

* * * * * *

QUESTIONS

What does holiness mean for you?
Is it idolatry to respect holy things? To use them as
"visual aids" that reveal the presence of God within them?
Do you know of people who could be described as
   "saintly," and if so, why?
What does the "Name" of God bring to your
   consciousness?
When the bible speaks of the "Name of God", what is
   being brought to us?

① Living Jesus's teaching —
Loving as He loved,
forgiving as He forgave —
Being Compassionate
to all his Children — Rich or Poor,

② No, I believe they help us as
human beings to focus on
Jesus, God Our Father, etc.
We need visual aids
Sometimes to help us see?

③ They are the people that
go about doing what is right
& not concerned about the
Consequences + not wanting
to be recognized —

④ Presence

⑤ His omnipresence, his power +
his Love for us!!

Part 2

Prayers of Submission

THY KINGDOM COME...

Filled with the Holy Spirit, Jesus left the Jordan and was led by the Spirit through the wilderness, being tempted there by the devil for forty days. During that time he ate nothing and at the end he was hungry. Then the devil said to him, "If you are the Son of God, tell this stone to turn into a loaf." But Jesus replied, "Scripture says: Man does not live on bread alone."

Then leading him to a height, the devil showed him in a moment of time all the kingdoms of the world and said to him, "I will give you all this power and the glory of these kingdoms, for it has been committed to me and I give it to anyone I choose. Worship me, then, and it shall all be yours." But Jesus answered him, "Scripture says: You must worship the Lord your God, and serve him alone."

Then he led him to Jerusalem and made him stand on the parapet of the Temple. "If you are the Son of God,' he said to him 'throw yourself down from here, for Scripture says: He will put his angels in charge of you to guard you, and again: They will hold you up on their hands in case you hurt your foot against a stone." But Jesus answered him,
"It has been said: You must not put the Lord your God to the test." Having exhausted all these ways of tempting him, the devil left him, to return at the appointed time.

Luke 4:1-8

Our Problem with Kings and Kingdoms

Imagine God sending His only-begotten Son to us as a Cosmic Warrior, a Prince at the head of an army of bionic soldiers equipped with laser guns and an overwhelming array of weapons beyond anything we could imagine. Imagine Him subjecting us to His rule in a newly established kingdom.

If we were to invent a Divine Being, fashioning him in our own image and likeness, we would likely imagine him coming to us in such a scenario. The reality, however, is just the reverse. God's Son arrived in a stable built to house animals, and for a crib He had a feeding trough. It was much like the arrival of E.T. in Steven Spielberg's famous movie. When I watched that movie the parallel struck me. I saw E.T. as J.C., a Christ figure. The story line of E.T.'s arrival, his time with us, and his departure, presents an eerie analogue to Christ's.

E.T, the Extra-Terrestrial, arrives among us surrounded in mysterious light. Children find him in a shed in back of the main house. Children are fascinated with him, not threatened, while adults are fearful of him and threatened. They are so threatened that officials seek to apprehend and arrest him.

E.T.'s message is love; his search is for acceptance. Eventually, however, he is caught and as he is dying he asks his followers, innocent children, to turn on their "heart lights." They do and E.T. comes back from death into life.

He speaks of "going home" and invites his followers to come with him. They, of course, do not understand and do not "go home" with him. He ascends in the heavens promising to return to them, inviting them to follow in his way until he returns.

And what about God's kingdom? Do I really want to live in His kingdom? As a U.S. citizen I live in a free society. I am able to be autonomous, independent, and can make up my own mind. Why would I want to live under a ruling king?

Christ Jesus is a king like no other king ever known in human history. When we think deeply about what the term "Christ the King" means, our thoughts are going to be inadequate because our models have been limited. Earthly kings rarely reflect His type of kingship, but they are paradigms despite falling far short of His kingship or His kingdom.

It is difficult for us to grasp Jesus' vision because we do not live in a kingdom and hardly know what living in a real kingdom is like. Most modern monarchies have parliaments and elected representatives as members of their majesties' governments. They are radically different from the kingdoms of ancient times.

Two notions about earthly kings are important for us today. The first is that the entire populace is summed up in and represented by the king. The nation's existence is found in the king, and all of the subjects' lives are interdependent with the king and grounded in the king's life. They owe him total loyalty and obedience. He, in turn, owes them his very life in protecting them from their enemies. He owes them his life in securing for them peace and justice. Between a king and his subjects there is a set of mutual obligations.

The second notion is that there is no compromise. The king's will is sovereign and supreme, to be accepted without question.

Politics has been described as "the art of compromise, the art of making possible things probable." If that is true, then there is no room for democratic politics in a kingdom. No compromise is necessary between king and subjects because the king's mind and will are sovereign and supreme. The king may seek the advice of trusted advisors, but in the end there is little, if any, room for argument and debate as to the courses of action to be taken. The controlling will is that of the king.

So when it comes to giving my ultimate allegiance, is my citizenship limited to living in a humanly constructed democracy, republic, or kingdom, or do I recognize the fact that I have a dual citizenship? Whatever my national citizenship may be, by baptism I have another citizenship and live under the dominion of God.

> For us, our homeland is in heaven, and from heaven comes the saviour we are waiting for, the Lord Jesus Christ...
> **Philippians 3:20**

Christ is my king because He is the expression of God, God's love and God's will for me. I want Him to be my king because I don't want God to compromise one bit in His love for me, or in what He wants to give me, or the kind of world in which He wants me to live. I much prefer that He remain King for me. My best interests are in doing what He wants done. Be that as it may, God cannot compromise His love for us in any way. His "yes" for us exists in His very being

> I swear by God's truth, there is no Yes and No about what we say to you. This Son of God, the Christ Jesus we proclaimed to you...was never Yes and No: with him it was always Yes, and however many the promises God made, the Yes to them all is in him.
> **2 Corinthians 1:18-20**

and is the everlasting love He gives us in Jesus Christ.

Jesus and the Kingdom

Jesus is quoted as speaking of God's kingdom 107 times in the Gospels, an astonishing number considering the relatively few quotes of Jesus recorded in the Bible. Therefore, it must be a matter of great importance both to Him and to me. What, then, would it look like? What would it be about? What kind of a kingdom is Christ portraying for us?

It is not a political, legal, or social entity, which is why separating Church and State is a good idea, while separating faith-based values from our culture is not. Its delineation is beyond our categories, beyond our specifications. It is made real (realized) in our human hearts, in our human attitudes, in our human ways of relating to each other, all of which reveal here on earth the kingdom as it is in heaven. We need to begin where Jesus began, in those moments when He inaugurated His mission here on earth.

He came to Nazara, where he had been brought up, and went into the synagogue on the Sabbath day as he usually did. He stood up to read, and they handed him the scroll of the prophet Isaiah. Unrolling the scroll he found the place where it is written:

"The Spirit of the Lord has been given to me, for he has anointed me. He has sent me to bring the good news to the poor, to proclaim liberty to captives and to the blind new sight, to set the downtrodden free, to proclaim the Lord's year of favour."

He then rolled up the scroll, gave it back to the assistant and sat down. And all eyes in the synagogue were fixed on him. Then he began to speak to them, "This text is being fulfilled today even as you listen." And he won the approval of all, and they were astonished by the gracious words that came from him lips.

They said, "This is Joseph's son, surely?" But he replied, "No doubt you will quote me the saying, 'Physician, heal yourself' and tell me, 'We have heard all that happened in Capernaum, do the same here in your own countryside." And he went on, "I tell you solemnly, no prophet is ever accepted in his own country.

"There were many widows in Israel, I can assure you, in Elijah's day, when heaven remained shut for three years and six months and a great famine raged throughout the land, but Elijah was not sent to any one of these: he was sent to a widow at Zarephath, a Sidonian town. And in the prophet Elisha's time there were many lepers in Israel, but none of these was cured, except the Syrian, Naaman."

Luke 4:16-30

This was Jesus' inaugural address and like all such addresses it set forth His mission and purpose, His vision of what He would be all about. For those of us who identify ourselves as Christians, it likewise gives us our own mission and purpose as citizens of His kingdom.

Most important, we hold a citizenship that is higher than that of belonging to our particular nation.

So you are no longer aliens or foreign visitors: you are citizens like all the saints, and part of God's household. You are part of a building that has the apostles and prophets for its foundations, and Christ Jesus himself for its main cornerstone. As every structure is aligned on him, all grow into one holy temple in the Lord; and you too, in him, are being built into a house where God lives, in the Spirit."

Ephesians 2:19-22

We belong together with each other in Christ's kingdom, that social order for which He labored with His life to establish in our hearts and souls. To make God's kingdom real for us Christ Jesus sacrificed His life in order that it be founded and brought to fruitfulness here on our earth as it is in heaven.

Can we imagine living in a society in which there is no partisanship, no setting of one group over and against another, a non-adversarial system of justice, and a non-stratified economic order in which there are no winners and no losers? These ideals conjure up such a lovely picture that our imaginations are taxed when it comes to realizing, making real, such a social order. One knows how difficult idealism really is and how rare it is to encounter sincere and genuine idealists, making their ideas reality. Nevertheless Jesus challenges us with His vision of an ideal kingdom. He calls us to work with Him for it.

> The Quaddish
>
> Exalted and hallowed by His great Name in the world which He created according to His will, may He establish His kingdom in our lifetime and in your days, and in the lifetime of the whole household of Israel, speedily and at a near time.
>
> First Century Synagogue Prayer

A lawyer asks Jesus what He believes is the first and most controlling of all the commandments. Jesus answers by reciting the Shema, a prayer that the lawyer, Jesus, and every other faithful Jew would recite from memory every day: *"Listen, Israel: Yahweh your God is the one Yahweh. You shall love Yahweh your God with all your heart, with all your soul, with all your strength"* (Deuteronomy 6:4-5). Thereupon Jesus immediately joins it to another commandment: *"You must love your neighbor as yourself"* (Leviticus 19:18).

When the lawyer happily expresses agreement along with understanding, Jesus says to him: "You are not far from the kingdom of God." In his Gospel St. Mark adds that no one dared to ask Jesus any more questions. Perhaps they no longer dared because the closer God's will comes to us the more insistent is its demand that we live accordingly. Pleading ignorance of God's will allows us to go on living in delusional denial.

The expression "kingdom of God" appears more than 150 times in the New Testament. The concept has multiple meanings because all human relationships have multiple levels and characteristics. The kingdom is, in fact, the sum total of our relationships with those around us, with none of the relationships exactly the same all the time. Furthermore, we are dealing with God's entrance into our human condition, our time, our history, and into our relationships with those around us. Therefore, mystery is inevitable, definition impossible. Only description will do.

God enters our time, our space, and even our human nature to present Himself to us with His offer of love. He has to communicate with us humanly, it's the only meeting ground available upon which we can encounter Him and receive His self-expression and offer of shared life with us. He has to use human metaphors, symbols, and analogues. If God doesn't communicate with us humanly His only alternative is inhumanly... and that won't work.

God offers; we respond. While God is omnipotent, omnipresent, omniscient, and without limits in His being or activity He is, after having made His offer of love, as powerless as any lover. In a lover's powerlessness He simply awaits our response. The humility, meekness, and tenderness are as profound as they are astonishing. It is the mystery of God's condescension toward us. In order that He might by loved by us He first had to love us and then forgive us. Only then would we be able to love Him in return.

St. Matthew reports the words of Jesus telling us of the kingdom in metaphors: the kingdom of God is like a wheat field with good wheat and darnel in it (13:24); like a tiny little mustard seed that grows into something big (13:31); like a little bit of yeast in a mass of dough (13:33); like a buried and

> There follows this prayer, Thy kingdom come. We ask that the kingdom of God may be set forth for us, even as we also ask that His name may be sanctified in us. For when does God not reign, or when does that begin with Him which both always has been, and never ceases to be? We pray that our kingdom, which has been promised us by God, may come, which has been acquired by the blood and passion of Christ; that we who are first are His subjects in the world, may hereafter reign with Christ when He reigns, as He himself promises and says, "Come, ye blessed of my Father, receive the kingdom which has been prepared for you from the beginning of the world." **St. Cyprian**, d.258, Treatise IV, On the Lord's Prayer, 13.

hidden treasure (13:44); like a priceless pearl for which the merchant searches (13:45); like a fisherman's dragnet (13:47).

God is at work in ordering all things, but in the eyes of the worldly God's activities are hidden, dismissed by worldly sophisticates as "insignificant" or "irrelevant." Yet at all times God is at work planting, nurturing and then, with our cooperation, bringing His work to fruition. To see that we need inner vision, an insight that sees through the lens of faith. Without this faith we are blind and cannot see the extraordinary within the ordinary.

There appears to be no urgency on God's part. He doesn't seem to be in any hurry. In God's eternity there is no urge for instant gratification. He is patient, tender, gentle, and restrained. Lovers are like that; they treat the ones they love the same way, waiting, always patiently for a freely chosen, un-coerced response.

The fullness of our response will be known (and made real) only at the end of our own temporal lives and at the end of time when God's kingdom is fully established here on earth. Still, truly, each one of us is "not far from the kingdom of God" because

> Christ has no body now but yours, no hands but y ours, no feet but yours.
> Yours are the eyes through which Christ's compassion must look out on the world.
> Yours are the feet with which He is to go about doing good.
> Yours are the hands with which He is to bless us now.
> **St. Teresa** of Avila

God is more proximate to us than we can possibly know or imagine. The consequences of our own freely made choices either to neglect God or to respond to His love are weighted with the gravity of infinity. They bear infinite consequences in the everlasting life that awaits us.

134

When we pray "thy kingdom come" we are charging ourselves with the responsibility of revealing God's kingdom in the network of our relationships with those around us, be they close or distant. To be sure, we want God to bring His kingdom here on earth. What often eludes us is the realization that He is going to do it through us. He is not going to do it for us. Because He is going to make His kingdom real through us, we must be in a close relationship with Him. It is a joint venture we are entering into, a partnership that requires us to bring all of our spiritual and natural human powers to bear.

The Spirit enabled Jesus to perfectly and fully realize the kingdom of God in Himself by accepting His Father's infinite love, by responding to that love in total trust and obedience, and by loving His neighbors (us) even unto death as a criminal on a cross. When we pray "thy kingdom come" in the Lord's Prayer we ask that God's Spirit empower us to make those decisions that will reveal His already-established kingdom in our part of the world, the world where we personally and individually act, in the communion in which we live.

Solemnity of Christ the King

This solemnity in the Church's liturgical calendar occurs on the last Sunday of the Church's year and is followed by the first Sunday of Advent, the first Sunday of the Church's next year. Pope Pius XI instituted this Solemnity in 1925 because he was commemorating the sixteen-hundredth anniversary of the Council of Nicea. This Ecumenical Council was of the utmost importance in that it was an exaltation of Christ's nature and purpose in coming to us. Along with other exaltations of Christ, Christ the King

Father, all powerful and ever living God, we do well always and everywhere to give you thanks.

You anointed Jesus Christ, your only Son, with the oil of gladness, as the eternal priest universal king.

As priest he offered his life on the altar of the cross,

And redeemed the human race by this one perfect sacrifice of peace.

As king he claims dominion over all creation, that he may present to you, his almighty Father, an eternal and universal kingdom:

   a kingdom of truth and life,

   a kingdom of holiness and grace,

   a kingdom of justice, love and peace.

Preface for the Mass of Christ the King

Sunday presents us with images not of this world. He whose beginning among us will be celebrated at the end of Advent is now seen as having an unending reign as Sovereign of the Universe at the end of temporal time.

Images of a monarchy, images of solemn ritual, especially royal weddings -- along with their elegance and the posturing of the powerful -- fascinate us. Is it because we want to give ourselves over to a Great Cause? Is the burden of freedom with its duty of responsibility too weighty for us to carry? Do we want to make others responsible and thereby absolve ourselves of responsibility? Freedom, after all, is a cross to carry

Being an Icon of *The* Icon

Are Christ's concerns my concerns? Are my concerns Christ's concerns? The essence of spirituality is to configure my efforts and my attitudes to His, to be "icons" that reveal His convictions and vision, His teachings and truths, His heart and Spirit to those around me. If His kingdom is to be revealed

136

on earth as it is in heaven then Christ's desires, love, energies, efforts, and concerns must be mine. Otherwise I will simply bury the talents He has given me and end up being an unprofitable servant.

Christ our King will provide us with peace and security and justice and mercy. He gives these to us as they are in heaven, calling us to make them real on earth as analogues to their heavenly reality. He gives them to us in a way that this world cannot give them. God our Father in His Christ offers us His peace and security, His justice and mercy.

Can heaven be brought to earth? God thinks so! When we are baptized and confirmed into His Christ, God our Father calls us to that mission and purpose. We need to realize that when we ask God to bring His kingdom here "on earth as it is in heaven" we are in fact presenting our time, talent, and treasure to God in order that He might use our gifts in accomplishing His purposes. In asking God that He do this we are charging ourselves with tasks, things to do in cooperation with God our Father.

In the Mass for Christ the King we pray:

As king he claims dominion over all creation, that he may present to you, his almighty Father, an eternal and universal kingdom:
  a kingdom of truth and life,
  a kingdom of holiness and grace,
  a kingdom of justice, love and peace.

Those are our marching orders. To be sure, Christ has established the Kingdom of God. But His kingdom here on earth is much like a fetus, it lies hidden within our humanity. Our task is to nurture it and bring it forth into our real world. We are to realize it, make it real, in our relationships with others.

> Keep your Church alert in faith to the signs of the times and eager to accept the challenges of the gospel.
> Open our hearts to the needs of all humanity, so that sharing their grief and anguish, their joy and hope, we may faithfully bring them the good news of salvation and advance together on the way to your kingdom.
> **Eucharistic Prayer**

Some people think that religion is all about making us "nice." We go to church, they think, in order to be shaped and formed so that we will be polite, considerate, and kind, and so that we will be tolerant of others. Such people send their children to parochial schools so they will learn discipline, self-control, and how to get along with everyone else. This being so, they tell me "it doesn't make any difference about what religion one might have. They all teach basically the same thing. It's all about being disciplined into tolerant politeness."

This type of thinking is sentimental religion. It is reductionism. It's a way of avoiding the cost of discipleship and the demands of living in the way, the truth and the life of Jesus Christ. Christ hanging on the cross is not a pretty picture; there is a human body on it challenging us to see that sin has its costs and love has its demands.

What, then, of the Kingdom of God? Was Jesus only about forming us to be nice? We need to notice that His kingdom of truth, life, holiness, grace, justice, love, and peace is far more profound than establishing our own personal courtesies.

Nor, on the other hand, is the kingdom a theocracy composed of subjects who are required only to give automatic submission. Our Father, after all, has given us the stupendous dignity of free will; He wants to be freely chosen in love. He calls us to co-operate with

138

Him in bringing the world to completion, completion in that vision He had when He created it and us in the first place. In our Father's loving vision for us, more than simple submission is involved.

What should we leave up to God, and what should we do by ourselves? The Christian answer cannot choose between these because we are called to both. As the saying goes, "We pray as if everything depended upon God, and we work as if everything depended upon us." The effort is cooperative.

Christ on Trial

There are those who think of Christ as simply another holy man, a holy man among many holy men and women who have walked the face of this earth. But was Christ Jesus simply one among many great religious leaders? The answer is found in the evidence, and the evidence is His works, His accomplishments, and His acts.

Others claim that Christ's life and acts are not credibly reported. Such claims echo those of the Pharisees thereby taking us into a legalistic analysis of proofs and evidence, and the credibility of the evidence and proofs. This leads into an endless maze in which each response serves only as fodder to generate even more questions. The motivation is to generate doubt through confusion, a favorite technique of defense attorneys in criminal trials in which convictions must be decided on bases that are "beyond a reasonable doubt." But what, then, do we mean by the word "reasonable"? This is the question that must be answered when we

> Plurality is not to be assumed without necessity.
> **William of Ockham,** *Quadlibeta,* Book V, (c. 1324)

examine the life of Christ. Are the events reported by eyewitnesses to His ministry probable? Or do we require a proof positive, so positive that it is the only possible answer?

Here it is appropriate for us to ask ourselves whether or not our own lives give credible evidence that the Father is at work through us, with us, and in us. When you realize that God, Christ, the Church and even Christianity are on trial and that you play an important role in the assessments of critics, then perhaps you will see why your personal and private prayer is so necessary. For without your own individual times of prayer you may not follow Christ by actually doing what your Father in heaven intends for you to do.

Loving others is to love with committed openness, openness to what they can become. Loving others means calling them to be all that's best within them; it's giving them the call and the freedom to be more than they are now; it's helping them to see and respond to the best that's within them. Loving means being open to goodness, truth, and beauty wherever it is found, even in the most defective of those around us. Love calls to the hidden goodness deep within criminals, addicts, and outcasts. Love reveals the truth that God has not and will not abandon anyone. We all belong to Him regardless of our state or condition in life.

Christendom or Christianity?

There are those who fear that perhaps some Christians seek to restore the medieval idea of a Universal Christendom established by God to govern the entire world. For those who adhere to conspiracy theories no amount of evidence to the contrary would ever be sufficient. The real danger to the modern democratic state is found in relativism, not in a theocracy. In one of his allocutions Pope John Paul II said:

> *If Christians must "recognize the legitimacy of differing points of view about the organization of worldly affairs," they are also called to reject, as injurious to democratic life, a conception of pluralism that reflects moral relativism. Democracy must be based on the true and solid foundation of non-negotiable ethical principles, which are the underpinning of life in society.*
>
> *... a kind of cultural relativism exists today, evident in the conceptualization and defense of an ethical pluralism, which sanctions the decadence and disintegration of reason and the principles of the natural moral law. Furthermore, it is not unusual to hear the opinion expressed in the public sphere that such ethical pluralism is the very condition for democracy.*

Relativism's result? Legislators claim they are respecting freedom of choice by enacting laws that ignore the principles of natural ethics and surrender the field to those who, with Pontius Pilate, ask "Truth? What is truth?" We are presently experiencing the resulting chaos, a chaos generated in a nihilistic philosophy that allows each

...today we do not trust that we are being told the truth by politicians, our doctors, business executives, even the clergy and above all by the media. We are drowning in information, but we do not know whom to believe.
Fr. Timothy Radcliff, former Master General of Dominicans.

personal autarchy to declare what is be accepted as true and what is not.

If we cannot understand certain things to be true, and hold to a shared understanding of them in common, then there is no glue left to hold us together in any community, family, or society. Truth becomes simply a matter of personal opinion or taste. Thomas Jefferson, along with the other founders of our American democratic republic, recognized the potential for this void. This is why Jefferson and his colleagues deemed it essential to have an enlightened as well as a moral electorate for the protection and preservation of our Republic.

Politics (the enactment of policies), law, and morality are inextricably linked to each other. Each discipline endeavors to present what is good behavior and what is bad, to reward good behavior and to punish bad behavior. The question immediately arises: "Who determines what is good and what is bad? By what norm do we judge what is good and what is bad?" Surely religion should have a voice in that on-going debate. To silence religion is to force upon us secular answers to these questions. Secularism becomes our established "religion."

Presently we are in a great national debate over the issue of when it is that human life is "endowed by our Creator" with unalienable rights. Some question our nation's foundational assertion that a divine Creator in fact endows us with rights. They tell us that only Congress and the courts can grant or deny basic human rights. Should these people succeed, they will extinguish the light in which we find the certitude of our moral and legal rights. The decision of the Supreme Court in the Dred Scott case in 1857 is still with us and the issue has yet to be resolved. Unborn persons are yet our slaves.

Where Is the Kingdom?

If Jesus Christ was truly the Messiah, why is there no peace on earth? If He were the real Messiah, many argue, we would not be living in a world filled with pain, loss, and suffering. We hear many say, "My life is nothing but drudgery; I am filled with sadness, tired of dealing with the mess other people have made of this world. Life is an unbearable burden. Will it ever end? Is there a God out there who cares what happens to us, or are we helpless pawns on some cosmic chessboard, only accidentally born?"

If God is so good, they ask, why does He allow us to experience pain, loss, terrible depression, and various disasters? Why does a good and loving God allow wars to happen, babies to die, and people to suffer? We have all heard these questions many times. Some of the published answers by media-designated "Christian representatives" have been embarrassingly simple-minded, fear-based, and just plain wrong-headed. I have yet to hear a response based on the notion that God loves us so much that He gives us the dignity and freedom to choose. And in our freedom of choice we suffer the consequences of our choices along with the choices of others. Perhaps the more insidious deadly cause is found in our non-choices, in our indifference, and in the way we ignore God, His love, and His will for us.

Suffice it here to say that God has chosen to put us into an incomplete world, living in our own personal incomplete lives. But by His grace we have the enormous dignity to be His co-operators, to work with Him while investing our own love and determination into the task of bringing ourselves and our world into completion and wholeness. This is a great gift, an act of faith that God has made in us. We can be who He dreams we can be, if we work with Him, if we place ourselves in His loving presence and allow His power to enter into us. That can happen only in a world and in personal lives that challenge each one of us in our own way.

There are huge forces at work on us, both natural and supernatural. We wrestle, says St. Paul, with "angels, principalities, powers and spiritual forces on high." And we wrestle with our own egos, while trying to put down the demons that beset us deep within our hearts and souls.

There are demons against which we struggle, forces of evil that are outside us, cosmic and worldwide, as well as forces that are personal and deep within us. There are those who are uncomfortable with public accusations of evil. The use of the term "demons" discomforts many, perhaps thinking that it smacks of voodoo, witchcraft, and medievalism. If we are in denial, however, then how can we mobilize our efforts to rid the world, ourselves, and those around us of what besets us? How will we, living in denial, rid ourselves and our world of the demonic?

The time comes when we simply have to put aside questions of "why?" and take action. At some point the need to deal with all that threatens our peace and well-being becomes more important than theorizing over external causes. Then, too, perhaps the road to happiness lies in setting ourselves to the task of freeing others from all that besets them rather than thinking only about our own misfortunes and lack of happiness. That is what St. Paul urges us to do.

To be sure there are times when a good hard look at

ourselves is necessary. Call it a moral inventory, if you will. What elements in my life cause my own unhappiness and which bring unhappiness to those around me? Where do I start? Do any of my inner demons have their roots in such timeless human failings as pride, anger, envy, gluttony, lust, avarice, sloth, or self-centeredness?

How can I bring health, happiness, and good news to those around me if I do not live with those qualities within me? I cannot give to others what I do not have myself. If I am to better the lives of those around me then I need to identify and cast out my own demons so that I might better live in the power of God and then share His exorcising power with those around me.

If we do nothing, if we give up the struggle to grow spiritually and grow in the love and power of God, then all that will be left for us is to moan and groan about life and all its unfairness.

The Good News of Jesus Christ is that God has chosen not to remain isolated in His nice, safe, cozy heaven. God chose to get Himself mixed up in our miserable humanity and therein to release His power and love within our humanity so that His kingdom might come here on earth as it is in heaven. Jesus, the Son of God, knew what it was like to live among the sick, the suffering, and the oppressed in a land held in subjugation by the princes and powers of this world, namely the occupying army and governors of Imperial Rome. The Good News is that He has given us the power to deal with all that subjects us to evil.

The Good News of Jesus Christ is the news that God is casting out evil and establishing His kingdom here among us. The challenging news is that God is accomplishing all of that within us when we respond to Him, when we submit ourselves to His will, when we choose to work with Him, collaborate with Him, co-operate with Him. We must surrender our autonomous selves into the love and care of God, for without Him we can do nothing. Without Him we are poor and weak. Without Him we will be subjected to the imperial power of majority opinions, political action groups, and the other human power brokers of this world. With His Presence within us we are richly endowed and full of strength. Then we can face the world and all that life hurls at us.

To be sure there are times when each of us simply sits back and demands that God do it all for us. To be sure there are times when we are exhausted, depressed, and seemingly beaten down. But, then, so was Jesus. The question put to us every day is: "Will I be controlled by sin, by evil, by all that is demonic around me? Will I allow life to entomb me?"

The stones of our tombs have been, by God's power, rolled back. He unbinds us and cries out to us: "Come forth! Rise from whatever is death-dealing, rise and be victims no longer. Walk in the glorious freedom of the sons and daughters of God."

Job suffered, the saints suffered, the righteous have suffered, Jesus Christ suffered, Mary suffered. And we suffer. The question is: What are we going to do about it? What are you going to do about it in your own heart and soul, and what are you going to do about it when it comes to removing suffering, loss, and evil from the lives of others? Are you passive-dependent, or are you actively decisive?

If we do nothing, then indeed life will be uncaring, threatening, and overpowering. If we do nothing we will have nothing left to do but complain and shake our fists at God. On the other hand, if we enter deeply into the life and Spirit of Jesus Christ then we shall have the power to face any and all evils, internal and external. Then life's challenge will be an opportunity; then all that confronts us will become promises. Rising off our mats, no longer crippled, we will have the wherewithal to cast out the worst of demons and reveal the presence of God's kingdom here on earth as it is in heaven.

Evidently the Christian vision for the kingdom of God here on earth is entirely different from any earthly models we may have had, or may yet have, of what God's kingdom here on earth would be like, or where it would be found.

The keys to His kingdom are found in the Beatitudes. With them we gain entrance, entrance into a world unknown to the sophisticates of our day, futilely wielding their worldly power while accomplishing little that will last throughout the ages to come and into eternity.

* * * * * * *

PRAYER

*O Father, I want Christ to be my King,
and you to be my Father. Help me to be a
part of Jesus' work; help me in Him to
reveal your Kingdom here on earth as it is
in heaven. I cannot "bring" it, for you
have in your Christ already established it.
I can only realize it and reveal its reality to
those around me. Help me to be decisive.
Lord Jesus, today in each and every
thing I think, say and I do...let it be you.
Help me to actively engage my heart and
soul, my body and energies in this cosmic*

work of Christ Jesus, your Son and our
Lord, who lives and reigns with you and
the Holy Spirit, God, forever and ever.
Amen.

* * * * * * *

QUESTIONS

Does religious thought have a voice in making the
  policies that shape and govern our public order?
When Jesus speaks of "the kingdom," what does that
  mean to you? What is the kingdom?
How do you interpret Revelation 11:19, 12:1-10?
How can you be a part in revealing God's kingdom here
  on earth?

THY WILL BE DONE...

God wills us free, man wills us slaves,
I will as God wills, God's will be done.
Daniel Bliss (1740-1806)

Surrendering to God

Picture yourself, for a moment now, next to someone you dearly love, someone you want to be with all of the time, someone who has captured your heart. Hear yourself say, "I love you. I'm here for you. What would you like me to do for you? I'll do anything you ask." In the moment you expressed such devotion you would be truly intimate with your beloved.

Now picture yourself saying those words to the one you love every day, first thing in the morning or last thing at night. Picture yourself saying those words each and every day of your life. What do you suppose would happen in your relationship with that person you love so much?

Our Father in heaven wants to hear those words come from our hearts each and every day of our lives. He wants to hear them from us consistently, regularly, and continually, when times are good and when times are bad, whether we face a huge problem or are experiencing profound joy. It's the persistence, the regularity, and the consistency that proves we are not just mouthing words but instead are living out our love. Love, as we all know, demands constant renewal. Without that, love grows cold.

Committing ourselves to God in this way is a prayer we must constantly live out. The quality of our prayer, the kind of conversation we have with Jesus, doesn't depend on its length. It is persistence and daily constancy that counts, not the long, windy words we pile into our prayers.

The whole point of spirituality is to be available to God. "Thy will be done" is the most important part of any prayer.

> *And going on a little further he fell on his face and prayed. "My Father," he said, "if it is possible, let this cup pass me by. Nevertheless, let it be as you, not I, would have it"*
> Matthew 26:39

This passage calls to mind a picture many of us have seen, Christ in the Garden of Gethsemani suffering in agony, sitting beside a skull-shaped rock (Golgotha awaits Him), His hands folded, resting on the rock in prayer. He is looking heavenward and saying, "...not my will, but thine be done." He was about to move from the rock to the hard place, the cross upon which He would be nailed and die. I often recall this scene when life is cruel and I must repeat those words.

When we pray "Thy will be done" and really mean it, a sense of loss wells up deep within us, a loss of personal power. We experience a sense of diminishment, a loss of control over our lives. Like Jesus in His prayer, we are challenged as we, too, must relinquish our sense of power and control over what is happening to us.

Adam and Eve's fundamental sin was grounded in the quest for power, power over life. In seeking freedom from God's will, a major control issue becomes operative. Perhaps this is the most difficult petition in the Lord's Prayer because it requires that we yield our independence over to God in interdependency.

We pray this prayer so superficially, so very facilely hurrying over it without much thought. The more we penetrate into the meaning, however, found in its words and phrases, the more we realize how very demanding this prayer really is. God has great expectations of us; love has its demands, imperatives that impinge on the Imperial Self.

Self-Determination: Our Prideful Defiance

Although affirmation of what is the very best in us is good, even godly, a self-determination that sets our own selves over and against the wishes and needs of those around us is a bad thing. Our problem is distinguishing between self-affirmation and self-determination, and sometimes the distinction is easily blurred. For instance, ask yourself: Do I love to give, or do I love to receive? Do I love in order to receive in return? The main issue here is once again control. How often do I give gifts, my friendship, or my love to another with the hidden assumption that I'll receive in like kind back from that person? While it is true that "It is more blessed to give than to receive" (Acts 20:35), it is likewise paradoxically true that sometimes it is more blessed, more God-like, to receive than to give. To genuinely receive authentic love, one must humbly wait for it to be freely given devoid of any sense of obligation. No one is obliged to love us, to be our friend, or to give us anything at all.

Power and control. They're so much a part of eveything we think, say, and do. The desire to hold power and to gain control, particularly over others, seems to be deeply rooted in our subconscious attitudes and drives, the wellsprings of our decisions. That drive is in our DNA coding, our bones, our origins. How quickly it surfaces in babies and young children! How soon the "war of wills" breaks out! It is the original sin. Just as the needle on a compass seeks true north, so our decisions and actions seek control over our lives and the decisions of others around us.

Adam and Eve wanted to be like God, to wield unfettered power over self, to be self-actuating, self-affirming, independent, and autonomous beings. Isn't independence a good thing? Isn't it virtuous? God-like? That was their mistaken concept of God. They viewed God through the prism of power. God is all-powerful and the serpent seduced them into thinking that they, too, could be omnipotent and all knowing: "...your eyes will be opened and you will be like gods," he whispered (Genesis 3:5).

God, on the other hand, is totally other-directed, self-emptying, self-giving, interdependent. The icon, the revelation of who He is, can be seen as God the Son hanging naked and powerless on His cross. It's the sign of death, death to self in order to bring life for others.

> I know all about you: how you are neither cold nor hot. I wish you were one or the other, but since you are neither, but only lukewarm, I will spit you out of my mouth.
> Revelation 3:15-16

While it is true that God is our loving (even tender!) Father who loves us unconditionally, He nevertheless has expectations of us, great expectations. He wants us to be as passionately in love for others, as He is. Lovers, after all, do have expectations. To love is to want to see the best in the other and to seek the best for the other. The opposite of love, therefore, is sterile and bland indifference, not anger. Indifference is uncaring; it says that what another person thinks, says, or does is of no consequence.

Are we willing to meet His expectations, to yield to His purposes, to accede to His plans? Lucifer, the Archangel whose name means "Light Bearer," was not. He allowed his soul to be filled with an inordinate pride, a self-

152

determination that took the form of defiance toward God Himself.

Abraham, Moses, the saints, and our Blessed Mother Mary, lived with a "Yes" to God in their souls. Somehow they were able to see that the best within them, their self-affirmation, was to be found together with God, not just in themselves.

Submission to God

I believe this dying to self-determination is the root cause of fewer and fewer young men becoming priests. The determining factors are not the lack of sexual intimacies, the inability to experience the joys and beauties of marriage, or the vow of celibacy. I believe the most important factor is the total relinquishment of control over one's life. One of the main fears about joining the priesthood is that a young man must hand over this ability to decide for himself what he will do with his life. This is something far more profoundly fundamental than celibacy. To be ordained a priest of God in Jesus Christ is to die to self-determination. Perhaps this inability to cede control explains why marriage is likewise on the decline.

Upon ordination, one freely chooses to hand over one's will and radically loses one's life. In the Rite of Ordination, immediately preceding the bishop's "laying on of hands," the candidates for priesthood prostrate themselves on the floor of the cathedral in front of the altar of sacrifice and lie there, as if dead. They are

> Lord, teach me to be generous;
> Teach me to serve You as You deserve;
> To give and not to count the cost,
> To fight and not to heed the wounds,
> To toil and not to look for rest,
> To labor and not to ask for reward
> Save that of knowing I am doing your will.
> **St. Ignatius of Loyola**

153

drowned in another baptism, that of the Holy Spirit, while the Litany of the Saints washes over them. It is a powerful, meaningful symbol of the candidate's death to his former way of life.

I'm afraid, however, that what is not seen so clearly is the death to his ability to make crucial life-decisions for himself. He rises to be ordained without any further ability to decide what will happen to him. He rises to a new life that is totally and completely in the will of God which he finds in obedience to the Church and her bishops. Where he will live, with whom he will reside, and how long he will remain in any particular assignment are decisions he cannot make for himself. His life is no longer his, it is God's. In the romanticism of the moment and in the splendorous beauty of the ancient Rite of Ordination the awful truth slips out of the ordinand's thinking; it is absent from the fantasies of the future that fill his mind.

Years later I came into full relization of what had happened to me when I was ordained a priest. All that I had dreamed of achieving died when I was ordained. It was all there on the cathedral floor where I had lain flat on my face in the posture of death. What I had hoped for no longer ultimately mattered. What the Church wanted of me now controlled my decision making and still does, even in my "retirement." And as for my dreams of achievement? They no longer matter because what God has given me has far exceeded my fondest hopes!

We all profess that we want to do God's will. The problem we have is determining what it is. How can we find it and know it?

The question of knowing God's will for us must necessarily be placed in the context of today's new order and culture that surrounds us as questioners. All religions are facing a shared problem, namely how to re-present their offerings to modern minds which insist upon fashioning all thought, along with their spirituality and religion, to suit their own desired wants and personal preferences. Salvation is thus replaced by autonomous self-development. "Rugged individualism" has evolved into autarchy; each individual is his or her own universe in revolt against any and all limiting commitments. The result is the perceived unraveling of social order, the fragmentation of community, the ignoring of our Common Good, and the disintegraton of the nuclear family.

It seems that everything today must be individualized and personalized. We enter our world much like we enter a shopping mall. We push our shopping carts through canyons of over-stacked aisles while selecting what is suitable for us. We buy only what we want. When we enter our churches we carry with us that same attitude and vision of reality. We'll "buy" only what is suitable for us to take with us when we pass back through the front doors and out into the world again. It's not what we give that seems to matter, it's what we get.

Catholics and other Christians want their beliefs to be authenticated by God. Their suspicions about self-authentication are understandable given the extensive experience the Christian tradition has had with human self-deceptions. We therefore look to the Son of Man to authenticate our relational responses to God. We look to the Son of Man to find our knowledge of the will of God. In particular, Catholic spirituality grounds itself in the mind and response of Jesus Christ in His life, passion, and death. Having done that we await God's response in Christ's resurrection. It is in Christ's resurrection that we are once again fully God's children in His New Creation. We call it the Paschal Mystery. All Catholic spirituality begins and ends in it.

What is God saying to us? We need to discern God's will by listening to the traditions, the accumulated wisdom, and the history of others, and ask them to help us authenticate what we think God's will really is for us. Contextual understanding of the Word of God and the revelation of God derived through nature likewise requires us to give our attention to the communal and contextual comprehension of our faith community.

In the process of determining God's will for us it is important to remember that the Teaching Ministry of the Church provides us with insights that we may not be able to discern on our own. For example, studying Scripture in a Bible study program can be very valauable because the group can focus on the shared understanding of a passage provided by the Church. The scriptural scholarship of the Church, after all, reaches back over 2,000 years. If this discipline is not observed a Bible study session can simply devolve into a series of individual and personal faith-sharing declarations. Although there is nothing wrong with faith sharing or individual interpretations of Scripture, there is something askew when an individual understanding is presented as the teaching of the whole faith community, or is presented as the teaching of the Church.

In order to know God's will one must interpret the words of Christ and read any Bible passage in context with other passages in the Bible and other people who are skilled in interpreting God's Word. One must understand Christ's words in a comprehensive historical context, which requires time and effort. Taking a single passage in isolation and then generalizing it will likely lead to misunderstanding of God's will.

I cannot save myself; it is God who saves me, God who justifies, God who sanctifies, God who removes my defects of character -- but only with my cooperation. Oh, to be sure, there are a few miracles in which God saves

All that is hidden, all that is plain, I have come to know, instructed by Wisdom who designed them all. For within her is a spirit intelligent, holy, unique, manifold, subtle, active, incisive, unsullied, lucid, invulnerable, benevolent, sharp, irresistible, beneficent, loving to man, steadfast, dependable, unperturbed, almighty, all-surveying, penetrating all intelligent, pure and most subtle spirits; for Wisdom is quicker to move than any motion; she is so pure, she pervades and permeates all things.

She is a breath of the power of God, pure emanation of the glory of the Almighty; hence nothing impure can find a way into her. She is a reflection of the eternal light, untarnished mirror of God's active power, image of his goodness.

Although alone, she can do all; herself unchanging, she makes all things new. In each generation she passes into holy souls, she makes them friends of God and prophets; for God loves only the man who lives with Wisdom. She is indeed more splendid than the sun, she outshines all the constellations; compared with light, she takes first place, for light must yield to night, but over Wisdom evil can never triumph. She deploys her strength from one end of the earth to the others, ordering all things for good.
Wisdom 7:21-8:1

people in spite of themselves, but those cases are rare. Again, God wants to be loved by those who respond to His offer freely. Those who choose to fully accept Him and surrender to Him requite His love, as opposed to reluctant lovers who keep power and control to themselves.

Yielding to the will of God gives us access to His power. This connects us to His mighty power, a power that can give our crazy, unmanageable lives the opportunity to be refashioned into lives that are orderly. "Wholesome," "whole," "heal," and "holy" are all related to one root word, one fundamental reality. To be healed is to be made whole once again, the fundamental first step toward living life in wholesomeness, which is the essence of living in holiness.

What Is God's Will for Me?

People have asked me many times to identify what God's will is for them. To answer this we need to take a look at how we expect God to answer our prayers. All too often we're looking for God's answers in terms of a series of specific plans and things to do. We want God to give us techniques and strategic plans, thereby attempting to see God's enlightenment in terms of technological responses.

It is the will of God that we choose the good, the better, or the best, never what is evil. It is not God's will that we choose anything evil in the name of good. The end never justifies the choice of evil means to attain a goal, no matter how good that goal may be. As obvious as this should be, we nonetheless choose what we want to do over the goodness of God's will. What we want is not necessarily what we need; what we want to do is not necessarily what we need to do.

> Prayer is not asking. Prayer is putting oneself in the hands of God, at his disposition, and listening to his voice in the depths of our heart.
> **Mother Teresa** of Calcutta

It is the will of God that we be responsible for our own decisions and live with their consequences. Many find this notion to be troublesome, and it leads them into difficulties in their relationship with God, feeling that God is responsible for everything that happens.

When we pray to our Father saying, "Thy will be done," we should understand that we are asking for God's will to be done on earth, today, in our life, in our decisions, in all that we think, say, and do. We're asking God for the inspiration and strength to conform our decisions to His will, His purposes, His efforts. We're praying: "Thy will be done in my marriage, thy will be done for my children and in how I treat them, thy will be done in my work, in

158

my business, in health, in war, in poverty, and in all my dealings with others. Thy will be done in my spirit, thy will be done in how I treat you, my Father in heaven."

In our attempts at changing and improving our lives, we often stop all forward motion when we arrive at simply knowing what it is we must do. Left undone is actually doing what we know should be done. Knowledge alone never saves. Simple recognition of the truth is never enough. Knowing the will of God for us is one thing, actually doing it is quite another. One can have earned a doctorate in theology and still lose one's soul.

Consider, for instance, people who are in high governmental office, or others who hold privileged places in the Church, in education, or in corportate leadership positions. How many have impressive academic credentials and yet have acted in ways that even children know are wrong? Knowledge must be accompanied by moral decisiveness to carry us forward through life in answer to our prayer, "Thy will be done."

We need to live in hope, a hope that is based on a power greater than ourselves, a power that is available to work with us and through us, not simply for us. "Father, thy will be done, not mine" was the ultimate prayer of Jesus upon which He added His decisions to act.

What is God's will for me? What does God want me to do? That's the question to which so many of us want an easy answer. The answer is found only in prayer, and the highest form of prayer is conversation with God. It means presenting God with what's on our minds. We come to him "where we're at" and offer ourselves to him in the condition in which we find ourselves. If we're in a mess, well... so be it. We offer him our messed-up selves. If we're in good shape, energized, full of vigor, and ready to take on whatever is in front of us, well, so be it. We offer Him our energized selves.

159

Doing God's will requires effort, and effort requires discipline. Being Christ's disciple is not effortless. Reason must be exercised. Will-power must be developed, which requires effort just as muscular development requires sweat and pain applied against resistance.

Will-power, the energy to choose rightly, results from disciplined exercise, which is why St. Ignatius of Loyola gave us his "Spiritual Exercises." Ask any athlete or accomplished musician or artist about practice and discipline. Skill and facility always result from such efforts, from practice and repeated patterns that are not easy. This is why the word disciple is derived from the word discipline.

> These are the very things that God has revealed to us through the Spirit, for the Spirit reaches the depths. Of everything, even the depths of God. After all, the depths of a man can only be known by his own spirit, not by any other man, and in the same way the depths of God can only be known by the Spirit of God. Now instead of the spirit of the world, we have received the Spirit that comes from God, to teach us to understand the gifts that he has given us. Therefore we teach, not in the way in which philosophy is taught, but in the way that the Spirit teaches us: we teach spiritual things spiritually. An unspiritual person is one who does not accept anything of the Spirit of God: he sees it all as nonsense; it is beyond his understanding because it can only be understood by means of the Spirit. A spiritual man, on the other hand, is able to judge the value of everything, and his own value is not to be judged by other men. As scripture says: Who can know the mind of the Lord, so who can teach him? But we are those who have the mind of Christ.
> **1 Corinthians** 2:10 - 16

But what does God have to say? Half of prayer is admitting to God that we know what's happening in our hearts and souls. The other half is listening, trying to determine what God wants of us. That may be in the form of centering prayer, meditative prayer, reflective prayer, or other forms of prayer. The common element in all types of prayer, however, is making ourselves fully available to the divine action.

160

In the end, we reach the point where we do our best to become conscious of God's Spirit. The things of the spirit are the things of the mind and heart, the qualities of knowing and loving. A spiritual person takes those qualities to the heights, and is humbly and submissively available to God's Holy Spirit. Spiritual things can only be seen and apprehended spiritually.

Times of reflection and contemplation are required so that we may "have eyes that see and ears that hear." We need to correct our vision so that we see things as God sees them, not as we see them. Only the spiritual can discern what is of the Spirit. And the gifts of the Spirit are always the answer to our prayers. "How much more will our heavenly Father give us the gifts of the Spirit," Jesus proclaims.

We, the worldly, look for answers in our world. God, the Holy One, gives us our answers in the spiritual world, always and infallibly. They are there waiting for us in an infinite savings account. But if we never make any deposits or withdrawals from that account, how will we ever know they are there?

"Thy will be done" is not simply a nice, pious wish or sentiment. "Thy will be done" is in the depths an act of submission. It is surrender, something so alien to our egos.

Why do I do what I do? Why do I choose things that deep down I know I should not? I've tried to help hundreds of people wrestle with those questions. Often they believe they are helpless victims of past events in which the decisions of other people have irreparably damaged them. They feel they must do what they do because they are victims of what others have done to them.

You and I may not be called to that sort of passive acceptance. Jesus Christ is risen from the dead, victim no longer. He lived, died, and rose from the dead in order that we may walk in the glorious freedom of the sons and daughters of God. It is our Father's will that we live and move and have our being in that victory of His resurrected Christ. Why, then, should we allow ourselves to live in victimhood? Dr. Martin Luther King, Jr. had a good theological grasp of this truth. He believed that no matter what others may do to us, we should not afflict ourselves with attitudes of passive victimhood, and we should rise up against all that holds us in that state of being.

God Offers, We Respond

Too many of us go through life as if we are sleepwalking. We live unreflective lives in which we look only outward. We live as if we have no souls. We live as if we have an infinite amount of time to eventually "make ourselves better" and so prepare ourselves to meet God, if we allow ourselves to grant there is a God. How absurd! It is God who makes us holy, we don't.

Is my identity the result of what my Imperial Self has declared me to be? If so, then the person I am is nothing in comparison to who God wants me to be and what God wants me to be. This is why we hear Jesus saying so many times that we must "die to our selves," put our egotistical self to death. In recovery groups you will often hear the phrase, "Let go and let God." The ultimate pattern is Jesus dying on the cross, then handing His human self over to His Father and allowing it to be put to death only to discover His "new" self in His resurrection, that self that was always with the Father in the first place.

This journey into the unknown, this "leap of faith," fills us with fear. Perhaps this is the fear Jesus speaks of so frequently when He continually tells us, "Fear not, I am with you." He knows, of course, how fearsome death is.

You cannot read the Gospel accounts of His passion and death without realizing that.

Yet we have the security of knowing that He has gone before us through death's passage into the sort of life God our Father intends us to have and intended for us in the first place in the Garden of Eden. Every great spiritual mystic tells us of that fear, that dark night of the soul, that terrifying confrontation when we face death and then, with Jesus, freely choose to enter into it so as to pass through it. Our Imperial Self does not easily surrender, however. Nor does our inner ego allow us to pass through life in "the glorious freedom of the sons and daughters of God." We don't "make ourselves better." It is God who justifies us; God who sanctifies us; God who makes us worthy; God who redeems us. We are utterly powerless to do those things on our own.

> He is the image of the unseen God and the first-born of all creation, for in him were created all things in heaven and on earth: everything visible and everything invisible, Thrones, Dominations, Sovereignties, Powers – all things were created through him and for him. Before anything was created, he existed, and he holds all things in unity. Now the Church is his body, he is its head.
>
> As he is the Beginning, he was first to be born from the dead, so that he should be first in every way; because God wanted all perfection to be found in him and all things to be reconciled through him and for him, when he made peace by his death on the cross.
>
> **Colossians 1:15-20**

But how can God do those things for us if we let ourselves be carried along in the whitewater of life's rapids and waterfalls? And if we are loaded down with resentments and bitterness toward others, loaded down with anger and the lust to get even, we will surely be swamped and drown, deprived forever of the breath of God's Holy Spirit, the One whose creative breath fashioned us out of the slime of the earth.

Many people claim that outside forces govern them. A "spin" is put upon events so they are choreographed to the claim that "I am a victim of what others have done to me," or what fate has given me. Some even assert that it is God's will that we should suffer, that God is "testing" us by cruelly inflicting pain to see how we will respond. I am uncomfortable with such thinking; it makes God out to be cruel. Cruelties and pain do not come from God. Their source is elsewhere.

Making God responsible for human choices is a form of escapism and denial. If such a view is true then I am absolved from taking responsibility for what I think, say, and do. I can live in irresponsible denial and not be accountable for my own decisions and actions.

There are people who sincerely believe that their careers, relationships, and lives are determined by the alignment of the moon, planets, and stars. Astrology, crystals, and New Age beliefs control their destinies. Others place their fate in notions of predestination, believing they are merely actors on a vast stage who can only play out the roles assigned to them. For them, "free will" really is not free. All of our choices are determined by fate, the forces of the universe, or even by God himself. Determinism, it seems to me, is a way of escaping from our responsibilities, our ability to respond.

If we pray the Lord's Prayer with sincerity and faith then we believe that God has created the sun, moon, and stars and that He sets them in motion. He is their creator. We are not governed by His creations but rather by His grace, love, and call to us to let Him, and Him alone, be our Father, our destiny, and our direction in which we make our choices in response to His loving offers to us. Even more, He has invested us with a dignity which is beyond what many of us are ready to believe, namely the dignity of joining with Him and co-operating with Him to bring His creation to completion.

Convictions vs. Feelings

In the course of my years as a priest I have come to know how much others (and me, too) are ruled by feelings. How many decisions we make based on feelings! How many courses of action we follow based on feelings!

Please don't misunderstand me, feelings are good. They are God's gifts to us. But ungoverned they can become fickle little tyrants that point their pistols at our foreheads and dictate the course we will steer our ship. Then, when disaster strikes, they disappear and leave us in misery, with nothing but their wreckage surrounding us. Just ask yourself: "How much misery, how much pain and suffering do I live in because I acted without thought, without foresightful consideration... because I acted only on my feelings?"

Feelings are not necessarily bad. After all, lovers talk about their feelings all of the time, as do friends. And feelings are more than just charming. They are signals of what lies deep within us, down where the spirits roam. We ignore them at our peril. Suppressing them can result in great damage. No. Feelings are terribly important. But we should understand their role and locate them in their proper place.

To live happy and successful lives, to live in God's love, to live in accordance with His will and purpose for us, we simply must make our decisions and act on our convictions, not our feelings. Are not pride, anger, greed, sloth, lust, gluttony, and envy based more on feelings than on thoughtful considerations? How many temptations would be overcome if we gave them more thought instead of yielding to their seductively good feelings?

We began this chapter with a consideration that Adam and Eve's fundamental sin was grounded upon the quest for power, power over life. The terrifying truth is that to be truly pro-life one must relinquish power over self and power over others' lives. God gives Himself to us in powerlessness. One of life's hardest tasks is to do the same for others. What freedom it is to be free from self! Perhaps that's why God is so utterly and infinitely free.

Understanding God's will is not the goal. To understand God's will is to understand God Himself, which is impossible for finite creatures. All we can do is receive God's will for us and then act accordingly. We will never comprehend God's will with complete understanding. Living while doing God's will brings peace, contentment, a "sense of rightness" to our actions, and above all, freedom.

Obedience to God's will liberates us from the tyranny of Self. Most of the time we tyrannize our very selves, judging our selves by impossible standards. So often we feel incapable of doing good, feeling that we are in the grip of evil. Even St. Paul complained about this. Nevertheless, no matter how we feel about our selves, God's will is that we live in the freedom of His sons and

> The Law, of course, as we all know, is spiritual; but I am unspiritual; I have been sold as a slave to sin. I cannot understand my own behaviors. I fail to carry out the things I want to do, and I find myself doing the very things I hate. When I act against my own will, that means I have a self that acknowledges that the Law is good, and so the thing behaving in that way is not my self but sin living in me. The fact is, I know of nothing good living in me – living, that is, in my unspiritual self – for though the will to do what is good is in me, the performance is not, with the result that instead of doing the good things I want to do, I carry out the sinful things I do not want. When I act against my will, then, it is not my true self doing it, but sin which lives in me.
> **Romans 7:14-20**

daughters; God's will is that we live in the freedom to choose what is good, and act upon what is good.

Our Tyrant Self holds us in captivity, continually seducing us with thoughts of exclusive self-interest. So often, however, self-interest leads us to selfishness and egoism. These, in turn, lead to nothing but misery, misery for others along with misery in our own hearts and souls. Certain forms of self-interest are healthy and good, but our Tyrant Self is not interested in them.

There are times when we fear and resist God's will, thinking perhaps that His will for us, what He wants of us, will somehow deprive us of pleasure, and work against our interests. The Father of Lies may whisper in your ear that God wants you to suffer, to deny you pleasure and happiness. All such suggestions are lies. God is never delighted when you experience pain or loss.

On the other hand, however, you cannot love others and care for others and not experience pain. God the Son in loving us experienced horrible pain and loss. Whenever such things come to us we have a choice. We can either blame God or we can take them as opportunities to join Him in His loving redemption, join ourselves into Christ's suffering for the redemption of the world.

> It makes me happy to suffer for you, as I am suffering now, and in my own body to do what I can to make up all that has still to be undergone by Christ for the sake of his body, the Church.
> **Colossians 1:24**

The truth is that God is always in favor of your interests. He wants you to be happy, to love others, and enjoy life in fulfillment and happiness. His will is that you live in truth, beauty, goodness, justice, and peace. God created us to live in the Garden of Paradise; He has never taken back or renounced that purpose and desire. His original plan remains.

167

The biggest problem many people have with God is that He allows us to choose, to choose what is bad for us and what brings harm to others. He allows us to suffer the consequences of our free-will choices. Why, they ask, didn't God create a world wherein we couldn't choose to do those things that bring harm to ourselves and harm to others? Because Love always invites: it does not manipulate and control.

To add to it, God calls us to change; He calls us to repent of our sins, to be sorry for them, and to change our ways. It is we who have to enter into repentance and conversion, not God. This galls human pride. God doesn't change us; rather He calls us to exert the effort and the discipline to change. We want God to do it for us. He wants us to do it for Him, to do it for love.

Too much effort? It is easier to call God into account rather than ourselves. We avoid blame that way. We exonerate ourselves and thus avoid all that nasty work that is needed for us to change our attitudes and our ways of relating to others.

Where can I find God's will for me? There are many fonts from which this "living water" springs: from nature; from the tradition and experience of the Church as expressed in her teachings; and from the hearts and wisdom of others around me, particularly those whom we know to be spiritual, those who are close to Christ and live in His way, His truth, and His life. We find God's will expressed in sacred Scripture, His holy Word for us. We find God's will for us deep within ourselves when we pray and are truly open to His presence deep within our hearts and souls.

There is one more extremely important and sacred source from which we can receive God's will for us, our own conscience. It is a sacred and holy space, one that the

Catholic Church reveres. Consider, if you will, the following:

Truth, however, is to be sought after in a manner proper to the dignity of the human person and his social nature. The inquiry is to be free, carried on with the aid of teaching or instruction, communication and dialogue, in the course of which men explain to one another the truth they have discovered, or think they have discovered, in order thus to assist one another in the quest for truth. Moreover, as the truth is discovered, it is by a personal assent that men are to adhere to it.

On his part, man perceives and acknowledges the imperatives of the divine law through the mediation of conscience. In all his activity a man is bound to follow his conscience in order that he may come to God, the end and purpose of life. It follows that he is not to be forced to act in a manner contrary to his conscience. Nor, on the other hand, is he to be restrained from acting in accordance with his conscience, especially in matters religious. The reason is that the exercise of religion, of its very nature, consists before all else in those internal, voluntary and free acts whereby man sets the course of his life directly toward God. No merely human power can either command or prohibit acts of this kind. [Paragraph 3]

Declaration on Religious Freedom,
Dignitatus Humanae, Second Vatican Council

** * * * * *

PRAYER

Dear Father in heaven, fill me with your Holy Spirit. Inspire me to seek and to know your holy will for me. I do not need to understand your will and purposes; I need only know what you want of me as best I can know it.

And even when I do not, I know that in seeking your will I am in fact doing your will, no matter what may result.

Keep me honest. Relieve me of my own delusions. Release me from my many forms of avoidance and denial. Remove my blindness, heal my crippled heart and soul, and roll the stone back that imprisons me with the weight of this world. Call me forth in the glorious freedom of the sons and daughters of God.

And, dear Father, if it pleases you, allow me to accomplish your works, your tasks, those things for which you created me, so that in my own poor way I may reveal to all those around me your Kingdom here on earth as it is in heaven.

* * * * * *

QUESTIONS:

What do I withhold from God's will? Am I the victim of
"fate" or do I still have effective, free will choices?
What in my life do I allow to be under the control of
"urges," "needs," and "desires"?
Do I actually and freely choose to do God's will, or do I
simply "go along with it" in passive compliance?
"What is God's will for me?" is a problem we all must
face. Where and how do I look for answers to that
question?

① Myself

② No, I have free choice to do his
will or not;

③ I try to control those urges +
needs + desires - I get better
as I get older;

④ I freely choose

⑤ I ask to be open to his word
+ He will let me know, until
then I wait patiently;

ON EARTH AS IT IS IN HEAVEN...

"God's Grandeur"

The world is charged with the grandeur of God.
It will flame out, like shining from shook foil;
It gathers to a greatness, like the ooze of oil
Crushed. Why do men then now not reck his rod?
Generations have trod, have trod, have trod;
And all is seared with trade; bleared, smeared with toil;
And wears man's smudge and shares man's smell; the soil
Is bare now, nor can foot feel, being shod.

And, for all this, nature is never spent;
There lives the dearest freshness deep down things;
And though the last lights off the black West went
Oh, morning, at the brown brink eastward, springs --
Because the Holy Ghost over the bent
World broods with warm breast and with ah! bright
wings.

Gerard Manley Hopkins

St. John states it theologically in the prologue to his Gospel:

In the beginning was the Word:
and the Word was with God
and the Word was God.
He was with God in the beginning.
Through him all things came to be,
not one thing had its being but through him.
All that came to be had life in him
and that life was the light of men,
a light that shines in the dark,

172

a light that darkness could not overpower...
The Word was the true light
that enlightens all men;
and he was coming into the world.
He was in the world
that had its being through him,
and the world did not know him.
John 1:1-5,9-10

The Letter to the Colossians gives it to us in the form of a liturgical hymn:

He is the image of the unseen God
and the first-born of all creation,
for in him were created
all things in heaven and on earth:
everything visible and everything invisible,
Thrones, Dominations, Sovereignties, Powers –
all things were created through him and for him.
Before anything was created, he existed,
and he holds all things in unity.
Now the Church is his body,
He is its head.
As he is the Beginning,
he was first to be born from the dead,
so that he should be first in every way;
because God wanted all perfection
to be found in him
and all things to be reconciled through him and for him,
everything in heaven and everything on earth,
when he made peace
by his death on the cross.
Paul to the Colossians, 1:15-20

The Book of Revelation caps it off:

Then I saw a new heaven and a new earth;
the first heaven and the first earth had disappeared now,
and there was no longer any sea.
I saw the holy city, and the new Jerusalem,
coming down from God out of heaven,
as beautiful as a bride all dressed for her husband.
Then I heard a loud voice call from the throne, "You see this
city?
Here God lives among men. He will make his home among
them;
they shall be his people, and he will be their God;
his name is God-with-them. He will wipe away all tears from
their eyes; there will be no more death, and no more
mourning or sadness.
The world of the past has gone."
Then the One sitting on the throne spoke:
"Now I am making the whole of creation new."
Revelation 21:1-5

God's Presence in our World

God's expression of Himself is seen and apprehended in all of His creation, in mountains, rivers, and forests, in sunrises and sunsets, in the seas and mighty rivers, in the skies with the sun and moon, planets and stars. His creating presence remains in them; indeed His Being abides in them, but creation in its totality is not God. We are not pantheists; we know that the sum of all creation is not God. But creation in all of its components, like Michelangelo's

> Yet in fact he is not far from any of us, since it is in him that we live, and move, and exist...
> **Acts** 17:27-28

statue of David, reveals the spirit and creating presence of its Creator. To claim "everything is God" is to be a pantheist. To claim "God is present to everything and His presence is found in everything" is to be a Christian.

Above all, God reveals Himself in men and women, in their nature, in who they are. Being persons and by His design, men and

> God made the angels to show him splendor - as he made animals for innocence and plants for their simplicity. But Man he made to serve him wittily, in the tangle of his mind!
> St. Thomas More in Robert Bolt's
> **A Man For All Seasons**

women are in the image and likeness of the God of Persons, the One who is constituted in and by Persons.

Christ Jesus came from above, from His Father; in Him the supernatural was joined into the natural. Not only did He become a man, He entered into our entire human breed.

God's Word comes to us in Light, a Light that illumines past human history, what we are doing now, and what we should be doing in the future. Old Testament events are seen in light of Christ; in His Light we

> He has put all things under his feet, and made him, as the ruler of everything, the head of the Church; which is his body, the fullness of him who fills the whole creation.
> **Ephesians 1:22-23**

see their meaning and purpose. The Star of Bethlehem led learned and wise kings, powers in this world; that star, that heavenly light, brought them to the Light of the World.

In this light we can see how God was preparing for His entrance into our world and into our humanity, personal and collective. All events are centered in Christ. All meaning is found in Him. All purposefulness is oriented in Him. When that light's beam is directed upon past events it reveals God at work preparing for the entrance of the Light of the World into our human history. Like a beam from a lighthouse, the present and the future are illuminated. The course of our present decisions and actions are likewise seen in God's light.

Powerful examples of seeing past events in God's Light are afforded us in the prophets of the Jewish Testament. Christ, the Light of the World, gives us insight into our human history and allows us to understand ancient "seers" in a unique way. Consider, for instance, the prophet Isaiah. As Christians we see his prophesies concerning the "Suffering Servant" in a light that has profound meaning for us because of the life of Christ. (See Isaiah 52:13-53:9)

In Good Friday's liturgy, when we hear the Gospel accounts of Christ's passion, death, and resurrection, and then hear these words from the prophet Isaiah, we come into a personal encounter with what was formerly historical and abstract. Christians see and interpret other Old Testament passages and prophesies in a similar vein.

Christianity is more than creed and code of conduct. It is a religion, not a philosophy. It involves our personal commitment to a Person, expressed in a type of marriage covenant. We believe in a Person and love a Person. To be sure, we have statements of belief and we have the Church's authentic teachings. But everything found in the Church, every component in the life of the Church, and most of all in its liturgy, points us toward and carries us to a Person, the Son of God and Son of Man, Christ Jesus living among us and present to us. In Him we live, and move, and have our being.

The modern mind rebels against absolute commitments. The rate of divorce is perhaps indicative of the fear of losing personal autonomy. "Religion shopping" is another symptom. We prefer to pick and choose, to buy only what we want to buy, to retain self-sufficiency. Wouldn't it be nice if Christianity were only a set of creedal statements? Then we could fashion them as we pleased.

As Christians we are not surrendering ourselves into the hands of a first-century Jew. We are summoned by God's expression of Himself, by God's Word made flesh, by God the Son to belong, and

> Birds afloat in air's current,
> sacred breath? No, not breath of God,
> it seems, but God
> the air enveloping the whole
> globe of being.
> It's we who breathe, in, out, in, the sacred,
> leaves astir, our wings
> rising, ruffled — but only the saints
> take flight. We cower
> in cliff-crevice or edge out gingerly
> on branches close to the nest. The wind
> marks the passage of holy ones riding
> that ocean of air. Slowly their wake
> reaches us, rock us.
> But storm or still,
> numb or poised in attention,
> we inhale, exhale, inhale,
> encompassed, encompassed.
> **Denise Levertov**, *Sands of the Well*, "In Whom We Live and Move and Have Our Being."

belong totally, to Him as a present, living reality, not simply a historical figure. The implication is too much for many to bear; it means that He can come into contact with us and encounter us as a Person, personally in our lives. Why can He do this? Because He is God!

Furthermore, He encounters us in mysteries and signs, holy things that are beyond our human standards for measurements and proofs, in ways that are far beyond human control, preserved and protected from our human smudge and smear. But God not only accomplishes His plan via these means, He also actuates His purposeful love in them. For it is through them, with them, and in them that He joins the natural into the supernatural, conjoining our humanity into Christ's divinity.

Christianity is a historical religion to be sure, but it is more than that. Accepting Christ as our Friend and Savior likewise involves God revealing Himself to us, opening

His heart to us, allowing Himself to be "known" in our hearts and minds.

God not only rearranged our humanity, He likewise rearranged human history in His Incarnation. Earth is joined to heaven as God brings heaven to our earth. All things are reconstituted in Christ. Everything is directed to Him by God the Father in order that, infused into His Incarnate reality, all might be redeemed (bought back) for the Father, the One from whom they originated. Nothing compelled God to do all of this, nothing except love.

God's loving providence sustains all things in their being. God's creating presence remains within them, holding them in their beauty as God conceived them before the mountains were raised, the seas were filled, and the planets thrown into their orbits. Moreover, God's Incarnation sanctifies them. They have a certain holiness simply in their being.

In our prideful human arrogance, however, we think we own land, animals, the earth's resources, and we have even claimed ownership of other human beings. Sadly, we often do not see our fellow humans as holy, as reflections of God.

Jesus called us to realize (to make real) His kingdom here on earth. It was to be a present reality, one based on His Father's kingdom as it is in heaven. This was to be an ideation, an idea created in His Father's creation, a creation in which we might live while responding to His dream for us. His Father has a dream; He dreams of what we can be, not just what we are now. Christ's expectation is the same. He has great expectations of us.

Too often people do not want to take responsibility to become what God imagines them to be. Instead, they use the cop-out question: "Why didn't God make this world free of suffering, free of pain, free of misery?" Evidently, they think God should be held responsible for the mess we have made of things. What they miss in their sentiment is that in order to hold God accountable and responsible for our choices, God would have had to create us without our powers of free will. Without free will, however, we would be creatures, not human beings.

There are certain things God "cannot" do. He cannot make a square circle. He must make either a square or a circle, respecting the nature of each in their being. Nor can God make an "un-free" human being. Our very nature in being human is that we be free, free to choose. Therein lies the source of our pain; therein lies the root cause of all that is wrong in the world.

A young man shared a story with me once that demonstrates the power of free will. He and his brother were once in a horrific fistfight in their home, battering each other and wrecking things as they fought. Suddenly, as one was about to deliver a terrible blow, the other brother stopped, dropping his arms and opening his fists. He looked his brother in the eye and declared, "You can't hurt me, I love you!" His brother stood there frozen and immobilized. The war was over, and they fell into each other's arms in a long, loving hug.

The brother who declared his love told me this story. It illustrates the unbelievable strength and courage needed to make God's presence, power, and love incarnate in our world. Souls such as Mother Teresa of Calcutta exemplify that for us.

I believe that God's presence still abides with us in spite of all the carnage caused by human sinfulness. The crucifix tells me so. Some theologians tell us that human works really "availeth nothing." I respectfully disagree. In the Incarnation, God's presence has become present in our fallen nature. "For God so loved the world that He gave His only Son, so that everyone who believes in him might not perish but might have eternal life" (John 3:16).

God's Presence and Our Response

Here you will encounter the crossroads, the central reality of following in the way, the truth, and the life to which Jesus calls you. For at the heart of the matter, the stuff of religion is entering into that point where God's Presence intersects with your own life.

To become conscious of the serenity and peace of being in God's Presence you must surrender to His loving will for you, personally. You "win" by surrendering to Him. Immediately you will feel a rebellion rising within you. You will feel the tension rising between doing what you want to do and the urge to do what God offers you. It's the original battle. Yet to find that for which your soul longs you must follow the central teaching of Jesus and do what your Father calls you to do. It is likewise the call of Mary: "Do whatever He tells you."

We must see spiritual things spiritually; see things from a perspective that is beyond what our world offers. A major "control issue" presents itself. We want power over our lives and over the people, places, and things in our lives so that we can "get" that for which we long. The paradox, however, is that we win by surrendering, surrendering ourselves into the care of God.

The kingdom of heaven comes to us on earth when we work together to reveal Justice, Peace, Beauty, Mercy, Truth, Goodness, and Compassion. When we somehow and in diverse ways cause the great Transcendentals to become more present in our world, we thereby fulfill our prayer that God's kingdom may come upon us on earth as it is in heaven.

The chasm between heaven and earth has been spanned. Christ Jesus stands in both. In Him we are pontiffs, "bridge builders," who can carry earth to heaven and bring heaven to earth. The supernatural becomes present deep within the natural. Deep down nothing is totally "secular"; everything is touched by God's Incarnation.

> Moses said to the people:
> "...if only you obey the voice of Yahweh your God, keeping those commandments and laws of his that are written in the Book of this Law, and if you return to Yahweh your God with all your heart and soul."
> "For this Law that I enjoin on you today is not beyond your strength or beyond your reach. It is not in heaven, so that you need to wonder, 'Who will go up to heaven for us and bring it down to us, so that we may hear it and keep it?' Nor is it beyond the seas, so that you need to wonder, 'Who will cross the seas for us and bring it back to us, so that we may hear it and keep it?' No, the Word is very near to you, it is in your mouth and in your heart for your observance."
> **Deuteronomy** 30:10-14

What is natural is seen with natural eyes and understood with natural reason. What is supernatural is seen with spiritual eyes and understood with reason infused with faith. What is supernatural cannot be measured by the scientific method or manipulated by technology. It is beyond our artful human techniques, however helpful science and technology can be in assisting us to see and understand the world around us.

Poetry, music, and art have an inner, subjective power that enables us to escape the bondage of this world. The Transcendentals can do likewise, giving us direction, vision, and purpose in our lifetime journey of discovery. They assist us in seeking and finding the extraordinary in the ordinary. Does Justice exist, or do only fools look for it? Goodness? Beauty? Truth?

> Every Christian, especially the Christian priest, must be a witness. To be a witness consists in being a living mystery. It means to live in such a way that one's life would not make sense if God did not exist.
> **Emmanuel Cardinal Suhard** in *Priests Among Men.*

181

Cynics and Stoics have despaired of such concepts and think we are foolish to believe they even exist. For them, Christianity is nonsense and philosophical Idealism is little more than a useful tool.

The way we respond to reality, to Truth, Justice, Goodness, and Beauty, is at the crux of the matter. Do we question with the intention of questing, with the intention of seeking? Or do we question with the intention of ridiculing and destroying? Jesus leads us in the Way of questing, seeking and eventually finding.

> We are not on earth as museum-keepers, but to cultivate a flourishing garden of life and to prepare for a glorious future.
> **Pope John XXIII**

The Gospels are loaded with questions posed by genuine seekers.

> *One of the scribes who had listened to them debating and had observed how well Jesus had answered them, now came up and put a question to him, "Which is the first of all the commandments?" Jesus replied, "This is the first: Listen, Israel, the Lord our God is the one Lord, and you must love the Lord your God with all your heart, with all your soul, with all your mind and with all your strength. The second is this: You must love your neighbour as yourself. There is no other commandment greater than these." The scribe said to him, "Well spoken, Master; what you have said is true: that he is the one and there is no other. To love him with all your heart, with all your understanding and strength, and to love your neighbour as yourself, this is far more important than any holocaust or sacrifice." Jesus, seeing how*

wisely he had spoken, said, "You are not far
from the kingdom of God."
Mark 12:28-34

The Parts of the Lord's Prayer

The first three phrases of the Lord's Prayer are declaratory: prayers of praise, adoration, and acclamation. The remaining phrases of the prayer are prayers of submission and petition: prayers in which we seek God's activity, asking Him to act in our lives and in our world.

"On earth as it is in heaven," asks God to act presently, not in some remote future. This phrase asks God for His loving concern now, to intervene directly as we are living out our lives here, not in some place and time removed from our immediate concerns. We want God to act through us and in us as we face tasks that confront us this day.

Pious wishes can delude us into thinking we are doing something when we are not. For example, wishing to quit smoking, or telling ourselves that we will stop drinking, are quite different from taking immediate and decisive action to quit these habits. Concrete steps may require us to seek the help of others or to join support groups. We have to "walk the walk and not just talk the talk."

In God's economy of salvation, our decisions and our actions have infinite value. A cup of cold water given in His love, in His plan, has more volume and more value than all of the oceans combined.

There are those who reject any notions that God uses intermediaries between Himself and us. How, then, would they explain the purpose and function of angels? If there is no "we" in religion, if it is nothing but "me" and God, how can we explain the existence and function of the

Mystical Body of Christ? Indeed, Christ is THE intermediary between His father and us.

If you claim, "I don't need any priest to give me God's forgiveness, I go directly to God," you thereby cancel out half of God's will for us. You may as well say, "I don't need His angels, I don't need His ministers, I don't need the Church, I don't need any intermediary." How, then, do you account for God's use of so many intermediaries? His decision to employ us in making Himself present to those around us and in our world? It is quite evident that God our Father intends for there to be intermediaries.

There is a human body on the cross. It represents not only the Jesus of Nazareth of 2000 years ago, but also His Spirit-filled Mystical Body, the Body in which He lives, suffers, and dies in our humanity every day. The cross has its vertical dimension, our contact with God in His Christ, but also a horizontal dimension, namely Christ's extension of Himself throughout all of our humanity, time,

> It makes me happy to suffer for you, as I am suffering now, and in my own body to do what I can to make up all that has still to be undergone by Christ for the sake of his body, the Church.
> **Colossians 1:24-25**

and space in His Mystical Body, you and I who are baptized and confirmed in His Spirit. God has chosen to have His hands, His human hands, nailed to the cross of our sinful humanity in order to work in us and join all that we do into His redemptive work.

Productivity and Risk Taking

In the scriptural passages chosen for the liturgies at the end of the Church year, we hear Christ Jesus giving His disciples what many hold to be His most important teachings. Thus, in St. Matthew's Gospel, we find Jesus giving His "End Time" discourse, which focuses on being useful servants, productive servants in terms of building up the kingdom He establishes through His life, passion, death, and resurrection.

To understand His teaching we must go back to the beginning, to Genesis, and there recall God's purposeful creations. We, created in His image and likeness, are to be His stewards, to co-work with Him to bring His incomplete creation to completion, into the fullness of His intentions in creating the world and us in the first place.

> *God said, "Let us make man in our own image, in the likeness of ourselves, and let them be masters of the fish of the sea, the birds of heaven, the cattle, all the wild beasts and all the reptiles that crawl upon the earth."*
> *God created man in the image of himself, in the image of God he created him, male and female he created them. God blessed them, saying to them, "Be fruitful, multiply, fill the earth and conquer it."*
> Genesis 1:26-28

The accounts taken from St. Matthew's Gospel during the final weekends of the Church year are found in his 24th and 25th chapters. Christ's teachings in these chapters are His last before He was to enter into Jerusalem and there be crucified. They are His final testament to His disciples, intended to guide them and us in the "already but not yet time," that time between His presence here on earth and His Second Coming at the end of the world. These final teachings, especially three parables, are therefore of great importance. And, when you plumb them in their depths, they are challenging, even menacing and threatening to the complacent, indolent, and comfortably self-centered.

185

The first parable concerns five wise and the five foolish virgins. The foolish ones did not look ahead and make provision for the coming of the bridegroom. They were guilty of the sin of presumption, presuming that in their lack of oil for their lamps the wise ones would provide for them. Their even greater presumption was that once they finally arrived at banquet the bridegroom would let them, along with the others who had prepared themselves, into the wedding feast. They found the door slammed in their faces.

In the second parable Jesus teaches about a servant who lacked courage and who, being fear-driven, was consequently unproductive, excusing himself by accusing his master of being a hard man. This servant, like the foolish virgins, was looking for an excuse. He was in a state of denial, denying his own responsibilities, blaming his master for his own lack of productivity.

The third parable is about other "do-nothings" who were unproductive, and who found themselves on the outside because they ignored and failed to use all that God had given them. In Christ Jesus, God has given us enormous treasures and talents. We have a powerful currency, the powers that God has given us, and He expects us to employ them to accomplish His work, to reveal His kingdom, and to bring our world into completion according to His plans and purposes.

Christ is interested in productivity. He isn't looking for passive-dependent persons to follow Him. He wants risk-takers to be His post-Ascension agents here on earth. He wants spiritual entrepreneurs to be His followers and to vivify His Church. Doesn't it strike you that the parables of Jesus center on farming, fishing, and business activities? They all involve risk taking.

Remember the man who found the pearl of great price and then risked all of his net worth to acquire it?

Remember the fishing episodes when Jesus asked Peter to throw out his nets yet again even though he had gone through the whole night without catching a single fish? And remember when Jesus came upon a poor little fig tree that produced nothing and was going to annihilate it, but held back when the landscaper asked him to wait a year so he could manure it, tend it, and bring it to bear fruit?

Christianity without courage is Christianity without blood and spirit. God encourages us to jump into life and run the risk of growing. It doesn't take courage to hide in our fear. It takes courage to risk something new.

It helps, now and then, to step back and take the long view.
The Kingdom is not only beyond our efforts,
it is even beyond our vision.
We accomplish in our lifetime only a tiny fraction
of the magnificent enterprise that is God's work.
Nothing we do is complete, which is another way of saying
that the kingdom always lies beyond us.
No statement says all that can be said.
No prayer fully expressed our faith.
No confession brings perfection,
no pastoral visit brings wholeness.
No program accomplished the Church's mission.
No set of goals and objectives includes everything.
That is what we are about.
We plant seeds that one day will grow.
We water seeds already planted,
knowing that they hold future promise.
We lay foundations that need further development.
We provide yeast that produces effects far beyond our capability. We cannot do everything, and there is a sense of liberation in realizing that. This enables us to do something and to do it very well. It may be incomplete, but it is a beginning, a step along the way, an opportunity for the Lord's grace to enter and do the rest.
We may never see the end results,
but that is the difference between the master builder and the worker. We are the workers, not master builders; ministers, not messiahs. We are prophets of a future not our own.
Archbishop **Oscar Romero** (1917-1980)

When we experience economic downturns, when unemployment rates go up and capital investments drop, what do our economists look for? Risk-takers! "Go out and spend," they tell us. "Invest, buy and get the currency changing hands again," they insist. Notice that they are all asking us to have faith, to make faith-based decisions, to act, and act boldly, on faith.

Christ is presenting us with the same challenge when it comes to managing the talents and currency God our Father has given us. He's telling us that faith isn't something we can acquire and then keep all to ourselves in our own little spiritual savings account. And faith isn't something we can hide, clutch, and hold only unto ourselves. It needs to be invested in the lives of others and thereby multiplied. Only then can it possibly bear fruit. Only then can our world be fashioned into a better place.

Turning the other cheek is a profound risk, requiring a tremendous "risk-capital investment," so to speak. The same is true in forgiving seventy-times seven times. One takes great risk when one tells another, "I love you," and "I want to belong to you for the rest of my life." Assuming that others, even your adversaries, are acting in good faith requires a great expenditure of your spiritual capital. Showing compassion and giving tender loving care to those who are anything but loveable, who are self-concerned, self-centered, and grasping, requires an investment of your own risk capital.

Having the courage to be openly Catholic is personally demanding for each one of us. It's not easy to stand up for good priests and defend them in the face of the withering scorn directed at them and our Church these days, especially by the cultured despisers of religion who are regular opinion columnists in the elite media.

Coming to Mass, especially when it's not convenient, requires a risk, one that must be taken in order to increase your own spiritual productivity, not the sort of productivity that benefits just you, but productivity that yields good fruit in the lives of those around you.

We hear a lot of talk these days about accountability, usually about other people who need to be held accountable, such as corporate executives, Wall Street banking and investment house officials, and Roman Catholic bishops. There is no question these people should be called into account. They have been given much and much should be required of them.

It's easy to point to rich, powerful, prominent people and declare that "they should be held accountable." But what about us? Do we realize that we too will face our own Day of Judgment, that our own little world will one day come to an end? What about our own productivity? Are our decisions fear-based or faith-based?

The Scripture readings for the last Sundays of the Church year ought to challenge and even disturb us. While the words of Jesus can comfort the disturbed they likewise should disturb the comfortable. It is true that Jesus is meek and mild, boundlessly compassionate and merciful, and that He loves us unconditionally. It is likewise true that He has great and high expectations of us. After all, God our Father didn't create us to do nothing. It is what He created us to do that ought to occupy our attention, disturb our conscience, and prod us into spiritual productivity.

How else can we reveal God's kingdom here on earth as it is in heaven?

Can we have excellence in our society? Can we have moral excellence here on earth? Must everything be reduced to the lowest common denominator, to the lowest within us, to what is merely common? No! We may be told that such ideas are "elitist," but they are not.

Democracy does not necessarily imply egalitarianism. A democratic society empowers us to develop ourselves to be the best we can be and then to share all that is best within us with others. I believe our recent societal trend toward mediocrity is grounded on a confused failure to distinguish between "equality" and "sameness." Where is it written that everything American must be reduced to the lowest common denominator? Where is it written that we are all supposed to be the same?

God's kingdom here on earth is revealed in the way we treat each other. His kingdom is a social order of relationships, relationships in which we regard others with self-interest. It is in our self-interest to live among others who are the best they can be, who employ their God-given talents as His stewards, who care above all for the poor, the oppressed, and the disadvantaged in the way Jesus did, and with His love.

To accomplish all of this and reveal the presence of God's kingdom here on earth we must live according to the highest of moral standards, we must live Christ's law of love. Simply being well educated is not enough. Some very well educated people have committed some of the world's greatest crimes. Human history certainly testifies to the fact that education and intelligence are no guarantors of morality.

For this reason, the founders of our American republic realized that schooling in morality was just as important as schooling in knowledge. With this awareness the Continental Congress enacted the Northwest Ordinance on July 13, 1787, two years before George Washington was inaugurated as our nation's first president. In this ordinance, article 3 states: "Religion, morality, and knowledge, being necessary to good government and the happiness of mankind, schools and the means of education shall forever be encouraged."

Without an enlightened electorate, an electorate that is both knowledgeable and moral, no nation can long endure.

* * * * * * *

PRAYER

O Father in heaven, thank you for the gift of this day. Help me this day to think of the things you want me to think, to ponder the things you want me to ponder.

Help me to feel what you want me to feel, to consider what you want me to consider, and to judge as you have me judge.

Help me to do the things you want me to do today, and to love as you would have me love.

O Father in heaven, thank you for all of the days of my life. Each one of them was a gift from you.

And thank you especially for the gift of this day. May all that I think, say and do today serve to accomplish your purposes and work to reveal your kingdom here on earth as it is in heaven.

* * * * * * *

QUESTIONS:

What that is of God can we reveal here on earth?
What do the words in the first part of the Declaration of
   Independence mean for us today?
Are our human relationships in fact separate from our
   relationship with God?

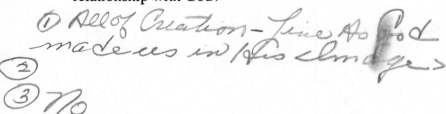

Part 3

Prayers of Petition

GIVE US THIS DAY OUR DAILY BREAD....

The Prayer for Serenity

God, grant me the serenity to accept the things I cannot change, the courage to change the things I can, and the wisdom to know the difference - living one day at a time, enjoying one moment at a time - accepting hardship as a pathway to peace - taking, as Jesus did, this sinful world as it is, not as I would have it - trusting that You will make all things right if I surrender to Your will - so that I may be reasonably happy in this life and supremely happy with You forever in the next. Amen.

Reinhold Niebuhr

The Bread

Luke's presentation of the Lord's Prayer asks for God's Bread of Life, that which nourishes the human soul, each and every day. For what do we ask God each and every day? Or do we simply assume God will give us His gifts, and then take them in vain? In our vanity do we expect God to take care of us without even asking? Without the simplest of prayers?

> I tell you most solemnly, if you do not eat the flesh of the Son of Man and drink his blood, you will not have life in you. Anyone who does eat my flesh and drink my blood has eternal life, and I shall raise him up on the last day. For my flesh is real food and my blood is real drink. He who eats my flesh and drinks my blood lives in me and I live in him.
> John 6:53-56

195

One of the most profound reasons for praying is to thank God for His love for us. For a Christian the highest form of thanking God is to receive His Presence in the Body and Blood of His Christ. God comes to us totally and fully in Christ, His Anointed One in whom He gives Himself to us in love. To receive His gift is to thank Him; there could hardly be a better way to thank Him. When someone loves you, can you think of any better way to thank your lover than to humbly and gratefully receive his or her gift to you? That is why we call the gift of our daily bread The Eucharist, our Thanksgiving to God.

Some Christian preachers teach that God sent His Son Jesus Christ to tell us that He loves us, and that is effectively the sum total of their message. For them, nice, warm feelings about God's love are all there is to religion; its main objective is to offer us reassurances. Hell? Punishment? Sin? Those are nasty topics fanatical right-wingers talk about. In a time when we hear a great deal of bad news about human motives and activities, "feel good" Christianity provides an appealing and comforting message.

> When I allow myself to go deep within and find my deepest hunger I then realize that it is your closeness to me that I want most of all. Draw me closer to you today. For it is that which I need for my daily bread, more than anything else.
> Satisfy my hunger, Father, and help me to love you more and more in all that I think, say and do today.
> **Anonymous**

But while the Gospel at times comforts the disturbed, it also can (and at times should!) disturb the comfortable. The Gospel preached by Jesus and the life He lived was hardly comfortable. To be sure, we are told that God our Father loves us, but then Jesus' life and His teachings go much further and call for action on our part. Our "comfort zones" can be greatly disturbed.

Other Christians teach that God sent His Son Jesus Christ down from heaven to tell us that He loves us and to teach us that certain human actions are right and others are wrong. Furthermore, those actions emanate from internal attitudes that are holy or evil, good or bad. In other words, there are questions dealing with virtues and vices, moral and immoral acts, and that the will of God can be known and must be obeyed. Obedience to God's will and laws results from loving God in return for His love for us. Obedience is, after all, a form of love.

Still other Christians, including Catholics, teach that God sent His Son Jesus Christ down from heaven to tell us that He loves us, to teach us what is good and what is bad, moral and immoral, and to share God's very own life with us, to join our lives into His life!

> By this mingling of water and wine may be become sharers in the divinity of Christ who humbled himself to share our humanity.
> **Ordinary of the Mass:** The Presentation of the Gifts

This encounter occurs in each of the seven sacraments: Baptism, Confirmation, and Eucharist, initiate us into the Triune Life of God; Reconciliation, Matrimony, Holy Orders, and Anointing of the Sick take us more deeply into God's life. All of them are acts of Christ encountering us in His Mystical Body.

For Catholics, the reception of God's life in us is celebrated daily. Each day of the year (Good Friday and Holy Saturday being the only exceptions) Catholics celebrate the Wedding Feast of the Lamb, the Lord's Supper, and receive their Daily Bread, the Bread of Life in Holy Communion. The Mass and Communion constitute the Church; the Sacred Liturgy is the summit and source of the Church's life. The Holy Eucharist is the heart of everything that it means to be Catholic. The Church is never closer to what God intends it to be than when she celebrates the Eucharist, the moment when God gives us His very self, His life and all of His love.

197

This is God's work and God's gift. Some folks mistakenly assume that the Catholic Church is a voluntary association of like-minded individuals who have banded together to share a certain and defined set of teachings and values. That would be a lawyer's definition, or a sociologist's. Those who do not share our faith regard the Church as a socio-political, multinational corporation constructed by human hands and maintained by other men who are bent upon exercising power and control over others who do not belong to their elite priestly class.

A Catholic, however, sees the Church not as a humanly constituted institution but rather as a gift from God, the result of Christ's redeeming work and sacrifice. Catholics see the Church as the opposite of the Tower of Babel, which was a man-made attempt to construct the way to God. It was of human design, constructed on human terms, and resulted from a human agenda. As a consequence, it collapsed. It was not "of God."

> Until Jesus, our Savior, comes again, we proclaim the work of your love, and we offer you the bread of life and the cup of eternal blessing.
> Look with favor on the offering of your Church in which we show forth the paschal sacrifice of Christ entrusted to us. Through the power of your Spirit of love include us now and forever among the members of your Son, whose body and blood we share.
> **Eucharistic Prayer,** Mass for Various Needs and Occasions IV

The Church is "of God." If it depended upon human strength, intelligence, and vision to exist it would have long since collapsed. The fact that it is still around is a sure sign that it is of God. Otherwise there is no rational reason to account for its continued presence through two millennia of human history.

At the core of the Church is God's gift of our Daily Bread, God the Son's greatest gift to us, that food and source of divine energy that sustains us as Christians and gives us access to do what is possible only with God.

Essentially both the Church and the Christian person are mysteries. God gives Himself to them in an act of intimacy and love, "marrying" Himself to us in an everlasting and unbreakable bond in the life of the New Covenant, the sacrificial death and resurrection of Jesus Christ. The purpose of this marriage made in heaven is not simply to save us and rescue us from death and hell as individuals, but to fill us with Christ's saving, healing, forgiving, and sanctifying power for the sake of others. Like the Christ we receive in our Daily Bread, we live "for others" (or we ought to).

There is no love without some self-interest. We love God because we want to spend eternity in heaven, in His presence and love. God wants to be loved. And God wants to love. He wants to experience that joy and happiness. We do too. We want to enjoy the happiness and beauty of loving and being loved. There is a form of self-interest in that. Paradoxically, it takes the giving away of our self, the setting aside of selfishness, in order to get what we want. In other words, there is "good" self-interest as well as "bad" self-interest whenever we love.

Our Daily Bread gives us the remarkable and total gift of sanctifying grace. It empowers us to do things that are impossible for men and women but are quite possible for God. Without our Daily Bread, many people act with natural grace, and live naturally graceful

> There is a spiritual food also which the faithful know, which ye too will know, when ye shall receive it at the altar of God. This also is "daily Bread," necessary only for this life. For shall we receive the Eucharist when we shall have come to Christ Himself, and begun to reign with Him forever? So then the Eucharist is our daily bread; but let us in such wise receive it, that we be not refreshed in our bodies only, but in our souls. For the virtue which is apprehended there, is unity, that gathered together into His body, and made His members, we may be what we receive. Then will it be indeed our daily bread.
> **St. Augustine**, Sermons (51-60) On Selected Lessons of the New Testament

lives. They are pleasant, moral, dedicated, self-sacrificing citizens who generously share their time, talent, and treasure for the sake of others. Still, for them, Christ remains only an interesting and historical figure, another religious "Good Guy" among an array of religious "Good Guys" who have lived among us throughout human history. With sanctifying grace, something quite different from natural grace, we act in and with the Spirit-filled gloriously resurrected Christ, the world's Messiah. This puts our lives and actions in a transcendent dimension.

God the Son came to forgive us our sins, reconcile us with His Father, and fill us with God's Holy Spirit. It was the mission of Christ Jesus to "hand over His spirit" to us, and He did this when dying on His cross. St. John reports: "...and bowing his head he gave up his spirit (19:30).

The first thing He did when He rose from the dead was to go to His apostles, breathe on them, and say: "Receive the Holy Spirit..." (John 20:22). Sending the Holy Sprit was His Pentecost gift to us when He established His Church. All of this is accomplished in a unique way when we receive the Bread of Life, our Daily Bread. In it, God's very own life is fused into ours.

The gift of our Daily Bread, the Spirit-filled Body and Blood of Christ, subsumes us into His powerful redeeming presence in our world. If we are in the state of sanctifying grace, when we act, Christ acts. This is the Bread of Life we need in order to be living in life eternal while at the same time still on this earth, being in the world but not of the world.

We need our sustenance, our nourishment, the Bread of Life, the life of God in Christ. Our Father gives it to us daily, in our daily Masses, in the Eucharist that is always there for us, waiting for us to come and be nourished.

The New Testament presents us with quite a list of roles that Christ could model for us, and they are attractive:

- Christ the Leader -- We follow in His footsteps
- Christ the Master -- The One whom we obey
- Christ the Role Model -- The One whom we imitate
- Christ the Teacher -- The One from whom we learn
- Christ the Savior -- The One who rescues us
- Christ the Physician -- The One who heals us
- Christ the Hero -- The interesting historical figure whom we admire

All of these attributes have two components in common: (1) you can say the same things about Buddha or Mohammed or any other great religious leader; and (2) all of these descriptions keep Christ at a nice, safe distance from our souls -- they all keep Him outside, out there, back then.

John's Gospel account makes a claim that cannot be found in the life or times or teaching of any other great religious leader or heroic person. He refers to Christ living IN us, abiding (making His home) in us, making His divinity one with our humanity. How can this be, questioned His disciples? In response, Jesus declared, "I am the living bread come down from heaven. If anyone eats this bread, he will live forever. This bread is my flesh, for the life of the world" (John 6:51). Clearly, this was just too much for some of

> On the night he was betrayed our Lord Jesus Christ took bread, and when he had given thanks, he broke it and gave it to his disciples and said: "Take, eat: this is my body." He took the cup, gave thanks and said: "Take, drink: this is my blood." Since Christ himself has declared the bread to be his body, who can have any further doubt? Since he himself has said quite categorically, *This is my blood*, who would dare to question it and say that it is not his blood?
> **The Jerusalem Catechesis, Cat.22**, Mystagogia 4, 1, 3-6, 9. PG33

His disciples, and they turned their backs on Him and departed from His company.

And what did Jesus do? Did He rush after them, tap them on the shoulder and tell them that His words were only poetic, merely symbolic, and not to be taken literally? Did He beg them to come back? No, He did not! He let them go on their own self-declared way. Christ then turned to those disciples who remained with Him and said: "If you do not eat the flesh of the Son of Man and drink His blood, you have no life in you. My flesh is real food, and my blood real drink" (John 6:55).

This declaration of Jesus Christ puts us at the very core of what it means to be a Catholic Christian. Our Catholic faith is absolutely uncompromising on this doctrine. A medieval pope didn't wake up one morning and declare that we all had to believe it. No, this teaching comes directly from Jesus Christ, in His own words. His apostles and their successors down through the centuries have transmitted it to us. If you want to know what Catholic Holy Communion is all about, read the sixth chapter of St. John's Gospel.

> This petition "Give us today our daily bread" we understand rather in a spiritual sense, for Christ is our bread because he is life and bread of life. "I am the bread of life," he says, and, a little earlier, "The bread is the word of the living God that has come down from heaven." In addition, his body is a kind of bread: "This is my body." Consequently, in asking for daily bread, we are asking to live forever in Christ and never to be separated from his body.
> Tertullian, *On Prayer* 6,2

The core reality of our Church, the central truth of our parish, the quintessential Catholic "thing" is found in this. God in Jesus Christ offers us His very own inner life to be shared, not simply in obedience, or out of a learning experience, or in any merely human activity or function. No, God offers us the invitation to surrender our lives, our wills, and our very selves over into His.

202

God comes to us that way, in powerlessness, in self-surrender, in His handing of Himself over to us. God not only calls us to do so, God Himself does so in order that we might, without fear, do the same and surrender our hearts, minds, wills, bodies, and souls into a living intimacy in Him. The icon of that reality is the crucifix.

This is boldly and repeatedly asserted throughout the New Testament. God's life in Christ intermingles with ours, and ours with His. God has mingled His divinity with our humanity, in order that we might mingle our humanity with His divinity. The eating of His flesh and drinking of His blood is the act of intimacy in which that transaction and that transformation occurs. The bread is transubstantiated that we would be transformed in the Wedding Feast of the Lamb.

We do not use this language when discussing the impact or legacy of other great religious figures. No one has ever thought of saying that about Buddha, Mohammed, Joseph Smith, the Dali Lama, or others you may bring to mind. No one thinks of saying that we should live in Buddha or Mohammed, or that they should live in us. They don't claim it; no one counsels it.

But Jesus Christ claims it, and His Church counsels it. His sharing of His very own life is so complete and so profound that only the most vivid and shocking language can convey the truth of it. He gives us His flesh to eat and His blood to drink, for no other reason than that act of intimacy for which God created human beings in the first place.

The mystery is profound, and my poor words cannot possibly explain it. No one, in fact, can explain it. But anyone can receive it. And for those who do, theirs is life eternal. And life eternal that begins not in some remote and distant future that follows our death, but life eternal that begins now, in the receiving of God's life in His very own flesh and in His very own blood.

There is a beautiful balance in the Christian message. It presents Christ to be followed; it presents Christ as the Master; it presents Christ as the Divine Physician; it presents Christ as the Teacher; it presents Christ as our Lord and Savior. And all of these require our diligent attention and acceptance. But then the Christian Gospel presents Christ as "the living bread" to be eaten, and His blood to be received, that His Body may become part of our bodies, and His blood may mingle with our blood. At this point all external activities and efforts cease and we simply become a part of Him and He becomes a part of us. There, and only there, are our deepest needs met.

Bread for Each Day

When we pray for our Daily Bread we are asking our Father to give us courage, strength, and fortitude to meet the day's challenges. Give us, we ask Him, decisiveness to overcome our sloth, our hesitancy, and our timidity. Give us, Father, the ability to make the right decisions each day, and proper discernment, that we might see clearly what is of God and what is not. Give us the graces and powers necessary to face the trials and tests we meet each day. Our Bread is the Bread of Life, that which nourishes and sustains and strengthens our souls each day. Give us the humility to recognize that without this Bread our souls will starve and eventually die. We cannot successfully meet life's challenges all by ourselves. We need the Presence, the power, and the love of God in order to deal with what the principalities and powers of the world hurl at us each day.

When we pray "Give us this day our daily bread" we must pray with the humility to receive it, to receive that

Food which our Father puts before us today on the Banquet Table of Life, that everyday sustenance that empowers us to act so as to reveal His Presence, power, and love in our world.

The biblical usage of the word "day" is complex and allows for many meanings. Regardless of how we analyze the usage of "day," however, we must always remember that God lives in an eternal Now. In God there is no past or future, there is only His eternal present. He exists in the simple act of being. He is "ising," living in the verb's present tense, active. Christ Jesus brings together our time and eternal time. Our time is chronos time, the movement of things chronologically, by the clock. God's time is Kairos time, present in His Presence to us.

The Lord's Prayer is given to us in three parts, each with its own way of addressing God our Father. In biblical Greek they are written in the aorist tense, the "eternal now and timeless" tense.

Once again Jesus is pointing us toward the Ultimate Moment, the End of Time, the end of the world, the time that brings an end to "this generation." He is ushering in our living in eternity, in God's world, the world of the "living in heaven with God," the One who comes among us in our time in His self-expression, the Word He caused to become incarnate of the Virgin Mary.

When we pray to our Father "Thy kingdom come," we are saying to God, "May your Presence, Power, and Love become present in my life, in our lives, in our faith community's life and in the world community wherein we live, and move, and have our being." The Messianic Banquet and God's Kingdom are present among us, here and now, in the Last Supper that has never stopped, that Supper that continues on presently for us. It may be called "Last" because there is no more time or room for another, and each Mass is simply our re-entry into the Upper

Room to join ourselves into it each day. For it is in our daily participation that Christ Jesus is, by the power of God's Holy Spirit, risen from the dead and reconstituted in His new body, His Mystical Body, in yours and in mine. The Church "makes" the Eucharist present, and the Eucharist makes the Church present.

> If you bestow your bread on the hungry and satisfy the afflicted; Then light shall rise for you in the darkness, and the gloom shall become for you like midday; then the LORD will guide you always and give you plenty even on the parched land. He will renew your strength, and you shall be like a watered garden, like a spring whose water never fails.
> Isaiah 58:10-11

Each day Christ Jesus gives us that bread from His Messianic Banquet, the Living Bread that nourishes us with God's Spirit. Again, this is timeless. When we celebrate the Holy Sacrifice of the Mass we are not repeating what Christ Jesus has already done, we are simply once again entering into the Upper Room, entering into what Christ Jesus is always doing, namely uniting us into Himself and taking us in Him back home to our heavenly Father.

> For it is through Him, with Him, and in Him, that all honor and glory are yours, Almighty Father, forever and ever. Amen.
> Canon of the Mass, final doxology.

Our Bread

Was Jesus teaching His disciples how to pray as a group, perhaps liturgically, or was He teaching them how to pray individually and privately? I believe His purpose was twofold.

Jesus taught His disciples who, as a group, were the first community of faith. They approached Him with the request to be taught how to pray. *Our* is the operative

206

word that runs throughout the prayer. Hence we pray, "give us this day our daily bread."

When I pray this prayer am I asking our Father to give me this day my daily bread? Is that the underlying attitude of my prayer? Actually I should be praying for all of us, for every member of our faith community, asking God to give us the bread we need for our bodies and souls, asking above all for the Bread of Life.

To be sure, God hears our prayers for what we personally and individually need. Spiritually we are all on welfare, we are not self-sufficient. We pray from a sense of want and need. But at the same time we are impelled to pray for what we as a family, a faith-community, and a nation, all need. I ought not neglect prayers for others, and I ought not neglect what they need.

> And I tell you, ask and you will receive; seek and you will find; knock and the door will be opened to you. For everyone who asks, receives; and the one who seeks, finds; and to the one who knocks, the door will be opened.
> What father among you would hand his son a snake when he asks for a fish? Or hand him a scorpion when he asks for an egg? If you then, who are wicked, know how to give good gifts to your children, how much more will the Father in heaven give the holy Spirit to those who ask him?
> **Luke. 11:9-13**

"Want" and "need" are, of course, two different things. We need to have spiritual powers of discernment in order to distinguish between our desires and necessities. To recognize the answers to our prayers we must have "eyes to see and ears to hear" our Father's responses. We need the Holy Spirit's gifts of wisdom, understanding, knowledge, counsel, piety, fortitude, and reverence for the Lord.

We ought to likewise consider whether we are praying that God do such-and-such for us, or that He change so-and-so's attitudes and ways of dealing with us. Perhaps we should change our request and instead ask God to be with us, to work with us, to be present within us as we face the persons to whom we relate and the things that face us each day. How often do you find Jesus praying that His Father do things for Him? Doesn't Jesus pray that His Father work through Him, with Him, and in Him? It seems to me that the prayers of Jesus were for the

> Take ye heed, then, to have but one Eucharist. For there is one flesh of our Lord Jesus Christ, and one cup to (show forth) the unity of His blood; one altar; as there is one bishop, along with the presbytery and deacons, my fellow-servants: that so, whatsoever ye do, ye may do it according to [the will of] God.
> I have confidence of you in the Lord, that ye will be of no other mind. Wherefore I write boldly to your love, which is worthy of God, and exhort you to have but one faith, and one [kind of] preaching, and one Eucharist. For there is one flesh of the Lord Jesus Christ; and His blood which was shed for us is one; one loaf also is broken to all the communicants, and one cup is distributed among them all: there is but one altar for the whole Church, and one bishop...
> **St. Ignatius,** The Epistle to the Philadelphians, Chap. IV, "We Have But One Eucharist," etc.

presence, power, and love of His Father to be with Him. How many times do we pray to God with words that say only "give us this, give us that; do this, do that"?

Sometimes we pray as if we're in contractual prayer: "If you do this for me, God, then I'll do what you request." We'll promise Him anything and everything, and we end up delivering to Him nothing in return.

"Give us this day our daily bread." The early Fathers of the Church and our first spiritual writers wrestled with the Greek word used for "bread." They spoke of it as "our daily bread," or "our future bread," or "our necessary bread." Do we want God to give us bread every day? Or give us each day our necessary bread, that which nourishes and strengthens the soul?

Today is the only day that matters. Yesterday is gone forever. The door is closed, bolted, and locked on all of our yesterdays. We can never, ever, go back and enter into yesterday. Tomorrow is only a future promise. Today is the only day that really matters.

Therefore we ask God to "give us the nourishment for our souls that we need today." Give us the Bread of Life. Provide us with the opportunity to receive Holy Communion, the Body and Blood of Christ, the only "bread" that really matters. Give us the bread we need around our family table, the Bread from your altar, so

> The Eucharist is our daily bread. The power belonging to this divine food makes it a bond of union. Its effect is then understood as unity, so that, gathered into his Body and made members of him, we may become what we receive.... This also is our daily bread: the readings you hear each day in church and the hymns you hear and sing. All these are necessities for our pilgrimage.
> **St. Augustine,** *Sermons* 57

that shared in a communion of love we can be your sons and daughters, brothers and sisters to each other in Christ our saving Brother. Give us the meal that makes us your family, with you as our Father, and Mary as our mother, because Christ has made us His brothers and sisters.

So, yes, in receiving His Body and Blood we accept Jesus Christ as our personal Lord and savior. And that's the proper response we should make to anyone who asks us if we have accepted Jesus Christ as our personal Lord and savior. After this acceptance, however, there is another question that needs to be addressed, namely, His Real Presence that comes into us in His flesh and blood, which is real food and real drink, and without which we do not have the Source of life Himself.

May you and I humbly, gratefully, and with true and authentic faith, now receive what He died to give us, namely His living flesh and His living blood in order that His life may co-mingle in ours.

> *Oh, come to the water all you who are thirsty;*
> *though you have no money, come!*

*Buy corn without money, and eat, and, at no
cost, wine and milk.*

*Why spend money on what is not bread,
your wages on what fails to satisfy?*

*Listen, listen to me, and you will have good
things to eat and rich food to enjoy.*

*Pay attention, come to me; listen, and your
soul will live.*

Isaiah 55:1-3

God sent us His Son Jesus Christ not just to live among
us as if He were to live along side of us, but to pour out
His life-giving Spirit into us. Because of Christ Jesus,
God can now live His life within us, live with His Spirit
fused with our own inner spirit.

Whose Life Is It?

Once at a Christmas party I found myself talking with a
woman from a western European country who in recent
years spent a considerable amount of time living here in
America. She was enthusiastically informing me about
how intolerant most devoutly religious people are about
other people's religions. In her own tolerance she had
filled her home with religious artifacts from all sorts of
religions. She told me of her Menorah, her Buddhist
incense, her Native American tokens, and her copies of
the Koran. "They give me such comfort," she told me,
"such peace."

"You've created your own religion," I observed.
Startled and wide-eyed she responded, "Why, yes, of
course I have!" It was as if she was saying, "Yes, of
course, who doesn't?"

After listing all of the comforts she had received from
her eclectic collection I asked her what she had given to

God as a result. The conversation suddenly ended and she was gone, dissolving into the other "Winter Holiday" celebrants. For her, celebrating Christmas was just another way of imposing the Christian religion on others.

Many people feel like they have everything. But these same people also feel as though they are lacking something essential. Is it perhaps a sense that they are not really giving themselves to God?

When we receive from His hands our Daily Bread we are giving something to God. We are giving Him our acknowledgment that we see Him as our heavenly Father. The gift is our awareness that no matter what we have we still need His love, want His love, and give Him praise and thanksgiving for what He gives us. When we receive God's Daily Bread we honor the Giver. Our gift to Him is to recognize that He wants to give us what we need in order to accomplish His work here on earth. We acknowledge and revere the gift of His Son and dispose ourselves to be temples of His Holy Spirit. The wonderful paradox is that in receiving we give. We give our heavenly Father what He longs to receive from us, our hearts and our souls, and His gift (gratia, His grace) to us is His Presence.

Realism is the acceptance of what we are given. Sin is the delusion that allows us to think that we can shape reality to conform to our own wills. In that delusion we end up angry and resentful that others don't do and live as we wish. The only remedy is to live in Jesus' attitude of acceptance, respecting others and "taking them where they're at" as He did.

"Give us this day our daily bread" is a prayer in which I pray to our Father:

Give me the sustenance of resolve; give me the bread of dedication, courage and strength. When faced with choosing to "go along" or to do what is right and good, strengthen my will and my determination to do what you would have me do. I am weak; you are strong. Fill me with your strength so that I might accomplish your purposes and bring your truth and justice in those critical moments when I must decide to act or not act. Help me to be steadfast, courageous and decisive.

Humility

There are times when it is more blessed to receive than to give.

Thirty-eight years ago, just weeks after I was ordained a priest, I was called to the home of a very

> Dear Lord, help me overcome all of my "gimmie" prayers. Help me to ask for what I really need, not just what I think I need, not just my little wants. Help me to want what you want me to have, to be the person you want me to be.
> **Anonymous**

elderly couple to give Holy Communion to the husband who was bedridden and near death.

They were desperately poor. The smells in the house were fetid and overpowering because they evidently did not have enough money for cleaning materials. Nothing had been washed in quite some time.

The old man's wife met me at the door, and holding a lit candle, knelt down because I was carrying the Blessed Sacrament while I passed through to the man's bedroom.

After saying the prayers and giving him Holy Communion I went back through the living room to the front door. Again she was kneeling on the floor and as I paused to give her a blessing, she grasped my hand while kissing it and pressed a five-dollar bill into it. I gently demurred and told her I really didn't need it, that there

212

was no need to pay me to bring the Eucharist to her husband.

As I was making my refusal, God graced me by allowing me to see something in her eyes and in the expression on her face. I realized that my refusal to accept her offering was, in effect, demeaning her. Wasn't her money good enough for me? Was she to be regarded by me as so poor she could give me nothing?

The poor want to give, too. They don't need those who are well off to tell them that they can't give. Was I, her priest, going to tell her that she had nothing to give to God?

By God's good graces my attitude was changed and with heartfelt thanks I received her gift. After all, she wasn't giving me the gift; it was her gift to God through one of His priests. Her action taught me that sometimes it is more blessed to receive than to give. In receiving her offering, I was giving her the recognition of her dignity.

We should not be so glutted with our own treasures that we cannot allow God to give us His mercy. We should not be so proud that we cannot bring ourselves to the Sacrament of Reconciliation and there receive God's tender, loving mercies. We should not be so sated that we cannot allow Him to give Himself to us in Mass and Holy Communion. Or is it that we have more important things to do, more pressing needs and obligations?

Spiritually, we are all on welfare. We are not self-sufficient, nor can we provide for ourselves that which our Father wants to give us. We pray, therefore, in want and in need.

Faith in God's Providence

Prayer is a humble act of faith; we pray trusting that our Father loves us, cares for us, and wants to provide us with what we need, not what we simply want. Faith's sibling is Hope, hope for a better world here on earth, and hope for a wonder-full eternal life with our Father in heaven. This is what we truly need. It is also something we can share with those around us who hunger for a world in which peace, justice, and true community can be realized. Hope is one of the greatest gifts Christians can give to a world that is spiritually bleak and largely without hope, a world in which "eat, drink and be merry, for tomorrow we die" is the operating principle.

When the Israelites were out in the desert for forty years, under the care of Moses, they were to eat enough manna to last only for a day. Each day they were to depend upon God for their portion of life's necessities. Give us, Father, this day and every day, we pray, the Bread of Life. Give us that which will nourish and sustain our spirits, our hearts, and our souls.

Nothing has changed. Each day God wants us to look to Him for wisdom, understanding, courage, strength, and the gifts we need to face life's challenges. Life is at times unfair; the decisions of others cause us pain and loss. With what do we respond? How do we respond? Too often we whine. Too often we reject God's plans and purposes for us, quickly tire of His manna from heaven, reject Moses and the prophets, and ask to return to the fleshpots of Egypt. Experiences in the days of Moses are not just events in ancient times, they are present-day realities.

God wants us to ask. What loving parent does not want his or her children to ask for things? God wants us to look to Him as a loving and providing Father. But He wants us to ask for the things that we should be asking for, not simply the things we desire. Before we begin to pray we need to sort out what we need from what we want. We need to be ruthlessly honest with ourselves and make sure we are not disguising our wants in praying for what we think we need. What we want should be the good things we truly need.

Actually, only God can know what's in the secret recesses of our hearts and souls. He knows what we need better than we do ourselves. We are too duplicitous; we can't be honest enough to distinguish between what we want and what we truly need. God has a much better insight into us than we do.

God has given us everything. He has emptied Himself out to us, putting Himself into our own poverty. What else does He have to give us? Nothing but love! He knows all about giving. Like Abraham, He has given us His only Son. Abraham's son, Isaac, was spared; his life was not taken. God, on the other hand, did not spare His own Son. His life was taken in a most horrible death, death by Roman crucifixion. Abraham gave God his faith; God has given us His Son.

And He has given us His Spirit, His very inner life, being, and existence. He has given over His existence to be shared by us, so that we might live in it. All that He is, God has given us. He knows all about giving.

Isn't it interesting to note that those who have been stripped of everything, those who are poor, know how to give and give generously? They do not give out of their surplus; they give out of their sustenance, what they need to live on. On the other hand, those who have acquired much, who have enormous surpluses, give with conditions attached. They want to see where their money goes. They want it to be used to accomplish their purposes. They don't give, they invest! They invest their money, their wealth, in what pleases them and makes them feel important. Sometimes, maintaining their own feeling of importance is their motivation to give. The poor don't have that luxury.

Poor people know how to give. They give from their heart, not from their investment accounts, or in order to get a tax break. Like God, they have only love to give us. But what a payback that is! Who is the richer, the person of means who gives, or the poor person who receives? And who receives the more valuable gift, the giver or the receiver?

The One who loves, who is Love, wants to give. The compelling urge of love is to give, to give over into union, communion. God who is total love is "driven" to be totally giving, to be total gift. God wouldn't be God unless He exists in giving Himself to us.

> Just as each of our bodies has several parts and each part has a separate function, so all of us, in union with Christ, form one body, and as parts of it we belong to each other. Our gifts differ according to the grace given us. If our gift is prophecy, then use it as your faith suggests; if administration, then use it for administration; if teaching, then use it for teaching. Let the preachers deliver sermons, the almsgivers give freely, the officials be diligent, and those who do works of mercy do them cheerfully.
>
> Do not let your love be a pretence, but sincerely prefer good to evil. Love each other as much as brothers should, and have a profound respect for each other. Work for the Lord with untiring effort and with great earnestness of spirit. If you have hope, this will make you cheerful. Do not give up if trials come; and keep on praying. If any of the saints are in need you must share with them; and you should make hospitality your special care.
>
> Bless those who persecute you: never curse them, bless them. Rejoice with those who rejoice and be sad with those in sorrow. Treat everyone with equal kindness; never be condescending but make real friends with the poor. Do not allow yourself to become self-satisfied.
> **Romans 12:4-16**

Our human problem is the fear of receiving, which is related to the fear of intimacy. There is a deep-seated fear of intimacy within us because intimacy requires that we become vulnerable, to surrender, to lose power and control. Intimacy means we have to admit that we're poor, that we need to receive from the other. Those who fear intimacy fear loss of control.

When we pray "give us this day our daily bread" we are humbly admitting that we are poor and are in need. So when we pray the Lord's Prayer, are we merely mouthing the words, or are we living the reality?

Love implies that we need to learn how to give love, to give away self. To love we must set aside our prideful arrogance, our lust for power, our delusion of superiority.

Individualism was not brought into being by the American cowboy or the Lone Ranger. It has been with us since Cain and Abel. It was a problem St. Paul was compelled to address in many of his epistles to early Christian faith communities. He appealed to them to defer to their shared, common good. Indeed, the Church continually calls upon us to preserve, protect, and defend the Common Good, a repeated subject in many papal encyclicals and pastoral teachings. The narcissistic individualist flees from Christianity and sometimes wars against it. Remember, Lucifer is the greatest narcissist of them all.

Consider your special talents and abilities. Do you feel a deep-down tug in your conscience to share them with those around you, or do you think of them in terms of your own aggrandizement? We all recognize one of the greatest lessons in human living: if we cling to and hoard what we consider to be "ours," we will end up losing that which we clutch. As in so many areas of life, you only get back what you give.

To put it another way, God has gifted each one of us with life. What we do with our lives is our gift to God. What, then, are we going to leave behind at the end of our lives?

Those who sole focus is the acquisition of more "things," those who seek to control others, especially spouses and children, and those who spend their time determining how best to satisfy their own selfish desires are truly "losers"; they are missing love, losing their families, and losing their chance at happiness. Such people seem to have no idea that you receive in turn only what you give.

What type of legacy do people like this leave behind to their children? What do they teach their children about love? What lasting memories and character traits do they pass on to their families?

There are certainly others, and we are fortunate if we know them, who live lives of total love and devotion to their spouses and children. Their only "wealth" is spiritual, and they share the Bible with their children and teach them about the souls of great human beings who made the world a better place. What a legacy they will leave to their children! What gifts they bestow upon them!

We all have hungers, needs, wants, and desires. In our quest for fulfillment, we need above all else God's nourishing love and presence, not only in our selves as individuals, but also in what we give to others and share with them. God our Father, after all, gives us the Bread of Life, so that the hunger in our hearts may find its fulfillment in that which truly nourishes us.

* * * * * *

PRAYER

*Father in heaven, send your powerful
energizing, life-giving Spirit into me. Often
I am held captive by my routine ways. I
can't seem to break out of my old familiar*

218

ways – I am apathetic, lazy, and lack the will to change my comfortable patterns and improve the life of my spirit, my inner self. I need to read more, to take time to reflect and contemplate. I want to be more aware of your will, your Spirit, and accomplish the things that you want me to do. Overcome my comfortable daily routines and with your powerful Spirit move me to better my life, my self and the lives of those around me. Help me to be decisive, not merely wishful. Give me this day my daily Bread.

* * * * * *

Questions:

Among all of your acquisitions, what lasts? Stock portfolios or investments in people? Businesses or families?

From the talents God has given you, what have you made that will be still standing years after your death?

What do you really want God to give you?

FORGIVE US OUR SINS...

We admitted to God, to ourselves, and to another human being, the exact nature of our wrongs.

The Fifth Step of the Twelve Steps of Alcoholics Anonymous

What Is Sin?

Sin is not simply the breaking of a rule or the violation of a law. Sin is found in damaging or destroying our relationships with God or with others. We don't sin against objects or things; we don't sin against rules or regulations. We sin against other persons; we sin against the honor of God, against our Father's plans and purposes for us, His love for us. "Trespasses" and "debts" are legal terms while "sin" is a theological term, which is why I hope that official translations of the Lord's Prayer will one day be changed to "forgive us our sins as we forgive those who sin against us."

If we abuse our environment and misuse nature and the world's resources, which we as humans all hold in common as God's stewards, then we sin against God and others. If we abuse alcohol, drugs, or tobacco our abuse hurts others, not just ourselves. The idea that there are "victimless crimes" or "victimless sins" comes from our own imposed narcissism, our egotistical self-centeredness that brings injury to others. Sin is never private; it always has an impact upon others, and upon God's love.

Laws, rules, and regulations enshrine values that protect other people from our narcissistic and imperialistic imposition of our selves over and against what is due

220

others or due to God. If you thoughtfully examine the Ten Commandments, the Beatitudes, or the thirteenth chapter of St. Paul's Letter to the Corinthians you will see that they all deal with how we relate to others and to God. Holiness is found in our wholesome and holistic relationships with God and with others.

We must also recognize that we can sin against ourselves; we can demean, abuse, or do great, unjustified damage to ourselves. We can abuse our bodies; we can degrade our dignity; we can sell our souls for cheap pottage.

There is a parallel between recovery from sinful repetitions, repeated wrongful and hurtful behavior patterns, and the recovery programs used for those once held captive by other addictions. Those in recovery from alcoholism, drug addiction, sex, gambling, and other addictions have found freedom in working the famous Twelve Steps.

To come to this new freedom the Fifth Step is a major turning point. To successfully "work it," those in recovery must be willing to admit the need to be forgiven for specific sins that they recognize and for which they acknowledge their own personal responsibility. In order to do that, however, they must abandon hope that they will be forgiven in some generalized, non-specific way.

> I acknowledge my transgression, says David. If I admit my fault, then you will pardon it." Let us never assume that if we live good lives we will be without sin; our lives should be praised only when we continue to beg for pardon. But men are hopeless creatures, and the less they concentrate on their own sins, the more interested they become in the sins of others. They seek to criticize, not to correct. Unable to excuse themselves, they are ready to accuse others.
> **St. Augustine**, Sermon 19:2-3

The same principle is operative when Catholics receive the Sacrament of Reconciliation. In "going to confession" they must not only repent in a general sense but must confess specific sins by nature and by frequency. This is not so much for the benefit of the priest-confessor as it is for the benefit of the penitent. Certainly God does not need to be apprised of such information! The penitent, however, needs to come out from behind his or her shield of denial and accept specific responsibility. Responsible people live lives of personal accountability, something that appears to be counter-cultural today.

Our Recognition of Sin

Sin is caused by us, not by others, an observation that is not as evident as it may seem. As soon as we begin to consider our own responsibility for sin a rebellious defiance immediately jumps in to play, that of denying personal responsibility. "The devil made me do it," was Adam and Eve's defending denial.

Today we claim that our parents abused us, or social conditions oppressed us. We shroud ourselves with the mantel of victimhood in order to excuse ourselves and thereby escape responsibility. Any ploy will do; any claim is asserted whether or not it is grounded in reality. Even reality itself is questioned by bringing in the escape hatch of relativism. There are no absolutes, we claim; everything is relative and so the concept of sin is labeled "medieval" and therefore irrelevant to our enlightened modern ways of thinking. "Whatever happened to good and evil? Who cares?"

Sins? What sins? The modern thought process goes something like this: "There are no sins, only psychological maladjustments, or perhaps behaviors that are determined by our genetic codes. The idea of sin is a medieval concept, created by priests who seek only to manipulate and control us with concepts of sin so they can extort guilt money from dull and unintelligent sheep who follow them.

Others ask: Should we admit that we've hurt others? Isn't guilt a liability to our self-image, something to be avoided at all costs? Don't others use guilt as a means of gaining power and control over us? We are told that priests, rabbis, and ministers "use guilt in order to manipulate us and extract guilt money from us." Once again we find the Imperial Self trying to gain control.

Ours is an increasingly secularized society freed by those enlightened from "religious taboos." At the same time, people seeking to resolve even the smallest of conflicts, both legal and moral, in front of civil judges, jam our court dockets. Legal "rights" have replaced moral norms. Even cases involving children fighting in schoolyards have ended up in courts of law.

We return now to the question, "Should we admit that we've hurt others?" After all, there is the question o liability. Lawyers and insurance companies counsel their clients to never admit guilt either directly or indirectly. Losers, you see, are guilty, and the guilty are losers, i.e., legally liable. Liability, responsibility for injury, must be avoided at all costs. Thus lawyers and insurance companies "stonewall" anyone and everyone claiming injury. They protectively surround corporate heads, political leaders, and even Catholic bishops, by counseling them not to admit wrongdoing.

This prevailing attitude needs to be seen for what it is, namely, irresponsibility. Irresponsibility, the deliberate and planned avoidance of responsibility, is not ultimately grounded on foolishness or stupidity; it is grounded upon duplicitous deceptions, clever denials, and upon lies.

In our human attempts to discover how we have made a mess of life and caused our world to be so dislocated, fractured, and broken, the Bible presents us with the story of Adam and Eve. In doing so, the biblical account goes to the root of our troubles, the lie we bought, the lie that claims we are God's equals when it comes to defining good and evil. The Father of Lies, the serpent, seduces us into believing we are not responsible when it comes to the consequences for our wrongful actions. Our first parents immediately got into the avoidance of responsibility game. Like the alcoholic or drug addict, they go into denial, and unreality sets in.

Even in his own defeat the Evil One, Satan, remains defiant, unrepentant, and autonomous. In *Paradise Lost*, John Milton has Satan hurling his defiance at God, saying:

> *What though the field be lost? All is not lost;*
> *th'unconquerable will, and study of revenge,*
> *immortal hate, and courage never to submit or*
> *yield.*

In other words, God can have everything else in the universe except my unyielding soul. Can anything better describe the sin against the Holy Spirit, the unforgivable sin?

Stubbornly remaining in a state of defiant alienation blocks God's disposition to forgive. It negates what Christ made available to us by dying on His cross. Were it not for Christ we would never be in a position to ask for God's forgiveness; the necessary condition for asking would not have been ours. We would have been unjustified in asking, unjustified in even approaching God, so great was our alienation from Him.

What brings us to admit we have been in the wrong, to admit we have sinned? What power do we have to repent, to resolve not to do wrong again, and even to ask for mercy? Being held in straightjackets of our own making we need a Higher Power, a power greater than our selves, to get us out of the quicksand of our own making, with its inexorable downward pull. The reality is that we are imprisoned, no longer free to do good, to easily and freely choose what is decent, right, and good. Are we driven by a "need" to continue on the evil path we have chosen in order to force others to "justify" what we have been doing? Such nonsense!

Humble Admission of Sin

The Bible speaks of our being justified by the suffering, death, and resurrection of Jesus Christ. "In Him we are justified," it says. This means that we are justified in seeking God's forgiveness and receiving it from Him. We cannot justify ourselves; only because of Christ we are justified.

> And all this is from God, who has reconciled us to himself through Christ and given us the ministry of reconciliation, namely, God was reconciling the world to himself in Christ, not counting their trespasses against them and entrusting to us the message of reconciliation.
> **2 Corinthians 5:18-19**

God's gift of the opportunity to repent remains even after our most heinous or disgusting sinning. Sinners though we are, Christ Jesus has forever established our ability to follow in the footsteps of the prodigal son. We are never, because of Christ, excommunicated from God's love for us.

Only one obstacle stands in the way of our being forgiven: our own unwillingness to repent and seek God's forgiveness. When we are unwilling to repent we are sinning against the Holy Spirit; we are saying, in other words, that even God cannot forgive us. That is why "sinning against the Holy Spirit" is an unforgivable sin. This sin remains unforgivable as long as we are held in victimhood by our own pride.

225

The teaching on original sin comes into play here. Lucifer's pride, his "non-servio," is embedded deep within us; it's in our DNA coding, in our genes, in the origins of our human nature. Although it has not totally corrupted us, it has inflicted a mortal wound in us. But we can be healed. "Salus" in Latin means health; salvation is ours in Christ Jesus. His healing power has been made forever available to us. It is so powerful that it can restore us to something beyond our original innocence; it can bring us into holiness, a state of being profoundly more wonderful than mere innocence. For God to love us in our innocence is one thing; for God to love us in our post-sinful holiness is quite another! The Garden of the Resurrection has replaced the Garden of Eden.

Why, then, are we so reluctant to be forgiven? Most likely it is pride. Shame is another matter. Shame is something we feel for being who we are while guilt is something we experience for a deed we have done. Shame should not be in us because we are all justified and made worthy, and are sanctified by the redemptive death and resurrection of the Christ. Shame is totally out of order. It says that Jesus Christ's suffering and death was ineffectual, that it didn't work. God has justified our being; Christ has sanctified our nature. Guilt, however, is something we can remove by our admission and repentance.

What about guilt? Certainly guilt can be very appropriate. Guilt is a teacher because it points out what we should not do. Our present culture declares that we should not feel guilty, which is why the world is filled with abuse, oppression, and hurt. We are simply unwilling to admit that we have things to learn. Guilt offends our sense of individualistic omnipotence, of being totally in charge of ourselves. But is there anything more absurd than that? Ridding ourselves of guilt requires humble admission to another that we have done something wrong.

Love, on the other hand, erases guilt; it obliterates shame. God, the One who is Love itself, is never more God than when He forgives us. Love is truly present when we are forgiven. It is then that we really know we are loved. But if we do not allow God to be God then we live in our own self-imposed isolation and guilt, perhaps even in shame. We live love-less lives.

Sweeping our misdeeds under a rug and childishly attempting to hide them succeeds only in allowing the wound to fester like a hidden cancer within us. What happens to any friendship when you ignore the fact that you have done something to hurt your friend? Don't you feel the need to tell your friend that you are sorry and thereby restore your friendship to its fullness? We should want our friendships to be full and complete, to have integrity. We should want to feel the warmth and caring that comes from the other when we ask for his or her forgiveness. We will not experience that unless and until we ask for the required forgiveness. Wholesome relationships must be whole and complete, not damaged by things left unsaid.

We should feel properly good about ourselves. Feeling bad about ourselves is damaging and crippling, if not destructive. A good self-concept is proper, even necessary, if we are to be vital and effective in our relationships with others. Appearances will not do. Inner wholeness and completeness is necessary. Superficial fixes, as we all know, lead only to superficial results. Only wholesome truthfulness will do.

So what is lacking within us? Courage? Are we fear-ridden? Is it fear that controls us? Perhaps our inner true being, that which lies deep within us, is revealed most clearly by our inability to ask for forgiveness, by our inertia.

It takes a truly strong person to be genuinely humble. Have you ever noticed that some people who have achieved great fame and notoriety are at the same time quite humble? Humility is not a sign of weakness but rather it is a sign of strength, strength of character.

People who are not afraid of asking for forgiveness likewise possess strength of character. Those who feel inferior are often fear-ridden, afraid that others will "see in to them," afraid of revealing the truth that they are not perfect. So they mask themselves in a perfectionism that forces them into a living hell, and often forces those around them to live under their hellish perfectionism.

The bully on the block is not a strong person. The truth is that he has a deep-seated sense of inferiority and so must bash everyone around him into submission in order to mask his weakness. A whole host of other emotionally disordered relationships also find their root causes in moral weaknesses. Arrogance, manipulative and coercive behavior patterns, and misuse of others, are all signs of inner weaknesses in people who are imprisoned in self-imposed inner isolation. Truly, just as heaven begins on earth, so does hell.

Redemption from Sin's Imprisonment

You and I are loved and being forgiven sinners -- that is the Good News of Jesus Christ. As clear and simple as that statement is, we so often fail to grasp it in our denials and defiance. Understanding and plumbing the depth of these truths is perhaps the single and most difficult task we face in our entire lives.

No one is ever excommunicated from that reality. No one is ever excluded from the heart of God. The only barriers between Christ's overflowing Sacred Heart and me are my own self-pitying ego, my own arrogant anger, my own self-centered autonomy, and my own defiant demand that God accept me according to my self-definition and on my terms.

For the woman at Jacob's well (John 4:5-42), life was all out of joint. With her basic relationships distorted and fractured by a series of bad choices, her life was not what it should have been, or could have been. Five times she had been married and all five marriages had ended in failure. She appeared to have given up because at the time she encountered Jesus she was living with a man to whom she was not married.

Jesus knew her better than she knew herself. Not concentrating on her failures and sins, Jesus reached into her soul and began His healing there. He summoned from deep within her the woman she was destined to be from the moment her life began. She became one of God's "new creations."

We, too, experience failure, even catastrophic failure. Such experiences force us to ask: How can we make life work? What makes for a successful life?

Christ Jesus has come to us from His Father's side to show us the way. Saving broken lives and giving us the wherewithal to lead successful lives are why He came to us. What, then, are some principles for successful living?

First, we need to establish a sense of personal responsibility. This can be difficult, living as we do in a "no fault" society. We not only want "no fault" divorces but we continually search for people to whom we can assign responsibility for our failures, even those failures that result from our own free choices.

I am responsible for me. My choices, my actions, are of my own doing. All successful people readily claim this to be true. The genuine Christian lives in daily recognition that he or she has been radically forgiven and loved by God. Baptism initiates us into that consciousness in living. And since we have been so profoundly forgiven by God, we should live every day forgiving those around us, not blaming them.

We are surrounded each and every day by messages that tell us we are entitled to live in pursuit of our own ease and comfort, and that we are answerable to no one other than ourselves. But living a life filled with alibis and scapegoats leads us into disappointment, depression, and underachievement. Examine the life of any truly successful person and ask yourself whether that person lives in such a way. You will see that he or she does not.

Possession of a sense of moral responsibility for one's decisions and their consequences is the starting point of a life that is well lived.

Second, I must have a sense of responsibility to others. When I discover the power and glory that God has put within me, and when I discover my true nature and self, I must share that goodness, that good news, with others. When, at Jesus' invitation, the Samaritan woman at Jacob's well entered into that self-discovery, she ran off to tell her neighbors all about it. She was so consumed by that impulse that she even forgot her water pot and left it there at the well.

We, like that woman, must be eager to share with others the power of God's forgiving love for us. That cannot happen unless and until we forgive ourselves. How can we experience God's forgiveness if we cannot forgive our own selves? How can we love others unless we first begin to love and respect our selves? We must remember that Jesus did not tell us to love our neighbors. No, He told us to love our neighbors as we love our selves. How can we give to others what we ourselves do not have? If I cannot love and respect myself, how can I love and respect others?

A third element in the lives of successful people is a sense of dependence upon God. God, our Higher Power, can add real power to your life and to mine. He can add limitless and inexhaustible dimensions to our lives. Perhaps there is some truth in the old maxim, "faith in God is not a luxury, it is a necessity." The forgiveness of God empowers us. It gives us the power to change ourselves for the better. When we have that power we can share it with others and have a positive impact on their lives.

If you live your life apart from God and are alienated from the forgiving Christ now living in His Mystical Body, the Church, if you cannot go there and search out forgiveness and find a new beginning there, then where can you go? To whom can you turn for such power, the power to change your self and the power to change the lives of those around you?

"I will go to my father and say to him..." is the great moment of liberation for the prodigal son. In the prodigality of his father's forgiving love, the son's existence is radically altered. In his father's arms, he finds himself restored to his original status. He receives a ring, a cloak, and new shoes, all of which signify his status in his father's family. There is joy not only in heaven, but on earth as it is in heaven, joy over the mutual exchange of gifts, the gift of the prodigal son's recognition of the truth and the gift of his father's re-creative love. The boy is a "new creation" because our Father's creative love did not

> 1 – We admitted we were powerless over alcohol -- that our lives had become unmanageable.
> 2 – Came to believe that a Power greater than ourselves could restore us to sanity.
> 3 – Made a decision to turn our will and our lives over to the care of God *as we understood Him.*
> **The Twelve Steps**

231

stop with the world's beginning. God's love is on-going forever.

We should pay particular attention to the prodigal son's awareness that he could not make himself worthy. The belief in self-justification is rampant in our self-help, do-it-yourself culture. The harsh truth is that there are limits on our powers. Technology, science, and human intellectualism are simply ineffective in the face of the re-creative power of forgiving and being forgiven.

Nothing is more deadly to our spiritual life than the belief that we make ourselves worthy. Yet this erroneous idea seems to hinder us from confessing our sins. We operate under the mistaken notion that we make ourselves worthy to go to confession and then receive God's love. The total reverse is true. God already loves us and makes us worthy in the death and resurrection of His Christ, the One who died in order that we might be forgiven and thus sanctified. It is God who saves, we don't.

> Forgiveness is such a problem for us. We want to receive it quickly and cheaply — no questions asked, please. Yet our hope for quick and easy forgiveness is countered by the conditions, terms and demands we place on others for us to forgive them. We make it really cost; they have to dearly pay in order for us to forgive them. This ought to strike terror into our hearts. God has repeatedly and insistently told us that He will use the same measure in forgiving us that we use in forgiving those who have sinned against us. In a sense, we govern God's judgment of us by the judgments we render to others. I don't know about you, but that scares me.
> **Henri Nouwen,** *Forgiveness, Love, and the Eucharist*

On the night before He died, Jesus Christ loved us in total intimacy: "This is my body, take it. This is my blood, mingle it with yours." It was the Wedding Feast of the Lamb in which He bonded Himself to us in a marriage that would never end in any form of divorce.

Immediately thereafter, human pride played its pathetic trump card: Judas betrayed Jesus and Peter denied by oath three times that he even knew Him! Both were looking for a conquering Messiah of their own design. Both thought God could give them a better gift. Both played their part in crucifying Christ.

Then God played His trump card: raising His Christ from the dead. And what was the first thing Christ did? He went to His apostles and said: "Peace be with you. Receive the Holy Spirit. Whose sins you shall forgive, they are forgiven" (John 20:22-23). The nuptials were restored. The New and Everlasting Covenant was put into effect. God came to us in the Garden of the Resurrection in a way infinitely more creative than His coming to us in the Garden of Eden. It was by no accident that Mary Magdalene mistook Christ to be the gardener! Something new had been planted in God's earth, plunged into it by the cross and watered by His blood. The New Creation, born in forgiveness, has been established. The Garden of the Resurrection is more wonder-full than the Garden of Eden.

Isn't His healing and forgiving love, His redeeming forgiveness, the gift that Jesus died to give us? Are we now going to hand it back to Him on a silver platter saying, "thanks... but no thanks"?

Forgiveness Reveals Our Relationship with God

What distinguishes us as Christians is forgiveness. No other major world religion prior to Christianity (or since for that matter) has held forgiveness as its highest value after loving God above all things. It is in forgiving that we are most God-like.

> Amen, I say to you, whatever you bind on earth shall be bound in heaven, and whatever you loose on earth shall be loosed in heaven.
> Matthew 18:18

233

Judaism, from whence Christianity sprung, speaks of repentance and atonement much more than forgiveness. Jews have a certain suspicion of forgiveness because of worry that it may be seen as "selling out" on all their co-religionists who have suffered so much for their beliefs. Where is justice in forgiveness? Isn't there a kind of betrayal involved in letting their oppressors and persecutors "off the hook" so to speak?

Reconciliation with others is also an important Christian concept but is not completely within your control; it involves the other party's free choice to be reconciled. Forgiveness, however, is completely within your control. You can freely forgive people even though they are unaware of your forgiveness, even if they don't want it!

Human justice, like reconciliation, can be outside your ability to control. God, however, in His infinite forgiving, is always just. He is infinitely just because we refuse his forgiveness.

Forgiveness is a working model of our relationship with God. Christ is the icon, the paradigm of our relationship with God, and Christ's entire mission and purpose in life was that of forgiveness and reconciliation.

> From the *Sermon on the Mount* onwards, Jesus insists on *conversion of heart,* reconciliation with one's brother before presenting an offering on the altar, love of enemies, and prayer for persecutors, prayer to the Father in secret, not heaping up empty phrases, prayerful forgiveness from the depths of the heart, purity of heart, and seeking the Kingdom before all else. This...conversion is entirely directed to the Father.
> **Catechism of the Catholic Church,** 2608

Not to forgive is to be held hostage by your past. Those who will not forgive are locked up in the prison cells of their resentments and desires for revenge. They have no freedom.

When you forgive, a gift is given to you, the forgiver. To forgive is to give yourself a gift. Not to forgive is to be held victim by the person you cannot forgive, the one you don't like or love. Not to forgive holds you to someone whom you can't let go, and you become a victim, a victim of your self. Forgiveness is the foundation of freedom. God is infinitely free because He is infinitely forgiving.

Jesus Christ is risen from the dead, victim no longer. And He does not want you to remain a victim. His resurrection is God's gift to you that you might "live in the glorious freedom of the children of God," free of victimhood, forgiven, and therefore empowered to forgive. Love always conquers evil.

Forgiveness is a decision, an act of your free will. And forgiveness isn't just a nice, pious thought. It requires action. You must act, you must decide to forgive and then actually do so.

In refusing forgiveness for those who have sinned against us we prevent God's forgiving power from entering into our part of the world; we prevent God's forgiveness from entering into our hearts and into our relationships with others. When we don't forgive we hold ourselves in bondage.

We need to ask God for forgiveness. Of course He has already forgiven us and He knows our sins better than we do. The reason for asking is not to change God's mind about us. We don't want to change His mind;

> On the evening of that first day of the week, when the doors were locked, where the disciples were, for fear of the Jews, Jesus came and stood in their midst and said to them, "Peace be with you."
> When he had said this, he showed them his hands and his side. The disciples rejoiced when they saw the Lord.
> Jesus said to them again, "Peace be with you. As the Father has sent me, so I send you."
> And when he had said this, he breathed on them and said to them, "Receive the holy Spirit. Whose sins you forgive are forgiven them, and whose sins you retain are retained."
> **John 20:19-23**

235

He already loves us with an infinite love. He has already paid the cost of redemption for our sins, with the passion, suffering, and death of His only Son. The infinite depth and breadth of His love in forgiving us shows how valuable we are in God's eyes. No, we don't ask God for forgiveness to change His heart. We ask for it in order that we might change.

We need to hear ourselves ask God for forgiveness because of what happens to us in the asking. The asking is an antidote to our arrogance, our sense of omnipotence, our taking of God's love (His name) in vain.

Eventually, you are what you pray for. If you pray often enough for forgiveness and sincerely seek God's forgiveness you will become a forgiving person. If you ask God for compassion you will be a compassionate person. If you cry out for justice you will have justice, and be able to be a just person with others. To the extent you seek to live at peace with God you will have the power and the capacity to live in peace with others.

Jesus tells us that our heavenly Father will always answer our prayers. Every prayer will be answered in some way, sometimes in surprising ways, at other times in ways that are hidden from our eyes, but always in God's good time and according to His good purposes. "God may not be on time, but He's never late."

God's Forgiveness

God our Father's forgiveness and reconciliation come to us in Christ Jesus. We have that certitude when we enter a church and kneel before the crucifix. Seeing Him on the cross, what further need have we of proof?

236

What can keep us away from God's forgiving love? Two major forces come to mind.

The first is fear, the fear of depending on God's caring and merciful love. Perhaps, in our reluctance to forgive others we

> What then shall we say to this? If God is for us, who can be against us? He who did not spare his own Son but handed him over for us all, how will he not also give us everything else along with him?
>
> Who will bring a charge against God's chosen ones? It is God who acquits us. Who will condemn? It is Christ Jesus who died, rather, was raised, who also is at the right hand of God, who indeed intercedes for us.
>
> What will separate us from the love of Christ? Will anguish, or distress, or persecution, or famine, or nakedness, or peril, or the sword?
> **Romans 8:31-35**

think God is likewise reluctant. Fear, however, is the opposite of faith. "Fear not," cries Jesus. "Be not afraid. I am with you." Because of Christ Jesus we can have courage, the courage to approach God in full confidence, knowing that because of Jesus Christ nothing can separate us from the love of God.

The second is pride, our egocentric pride. The impulse to admit that we are less than perfect, that we have done wrong, wars against our narcissistic sense of perfection. We may have a fear of admitting guilt, or perhaps we flee from any sense of shame. Whatever the excuse, that original rebellion is ever-present, the original sin that comes down to us from our first parents, that "nakedness" that came to them only after they had sinned. To admit guilt requires that we stand stripped of all our own little ego-protections while we stand naked and exposed for what we are.

When will we ever realize that God loves us in spite of this? We remain loved sinners. And now, clothed in Christ's wedding garment, in our white baptismal robes, we are seen by our Father as He sees His only-begotten Son. We are redeemed sinners who are infinitely loved by our Father.

Forgiveness is at the heart of Christ's mission to us; it was for our forgiveness and reconciliation with Him that God our Father sent His Christ to us. And that is the work of His Church, His work being accomplished now in His resurrection, in His Presence in His Mystical Body, the Church.

To see this we must go to the core of Christ's "hour," His Kairos time among us; we must go into the Paschal Mystery.

> *While they were eating, Jesus took bread, said the blessing, broke it, and giving it to his disciples said, "Take and eat; this is my body." Then he took a cup, gave thanks, and gave it to them, saying, "Drink from it, all of you, for this is my blood of the covenant, which will be shed on behalf of many for the forgiveness of sins."*
> Matthew 26:26-28

> *On the evening of that first day of the week, when the doors were locked, where the disciples were, for fear of the Jews, Jesus came and stood in their midst and said to them, "Peace be with you."*
> *When he had said this, he showed them his hands and his side. The disciples rejoiced when they saw the Lord.*
> *Jesus said to them again, "Peace be with you. As the Father has sent me, so I send you."*
> *And when he had said this, he breathed on them and said to them, "Receive the holy Spirit. Whose sins you forgive are forgiven them, and whose sins you retain are retained."*
> John 20:19-23

Forgiveness -- it was in Christ's heart at the Last Supper; it was on His lips as He died on the cross and said, "Father, forgive them, they know not what they do" (Luke 23:34). It was His great commission to His apostles when He first appeared to them after having been raised by the Spirit from the dead. "Receive the Holy Spirit. For those whose sins you forgive, they are forgiven; for those whose sins you retain, they are retained" (John 20:22-23).

St. John reports Christ's death on the cross by telling us, "and bowing his head He handed over his spirit." It was thus that Pentecost began; it was in giving up His last breath that the breath of God once again created, this time the "new man," in His new creation, the one begun again in His kingdom established by the death and resurrection of His Christ.

> The LORD God formed man out of the clay of the ground and blew into his nostrils the breath of life, and so man became a living being.
> **Genesis 2:7**

Thus the Spirit that raised Jesus from the dead is the Spirit which He, now at His Father's right hand, breathes into His Church, that Mystical Body in which God our Father has made Him now present to us in the length, breadth, height, and depth of God's universe.

God gives Himself to us intimately, in the sacraments of His risen Christ's Mystical Body. He becomes one with us in them.

In the Sacrament of Reconciliation we experience His forgiveness through His priests. God forgives and the priest absolves in His power and in His name, acting only as His agent. The Church understands this to be the

> I will give you the keys to the kingdom of heaven. Whatever you bind on earth shall be bound in heaven; and whatever you loose on earth shall be loosed in heaven.
> **Matthew 16:19**

> Amen, I say to you, whatever you bind on earth shall be bound in heaven, and whatever you loose on earth shall be loosed in heaven.
> **Matthew 18:18**

meaning of the events presented in Matthew 16:19, Matthew 18:18, and especially in the post-resurrection account reported to us in John 20:19ff.

To be sure, God can forgive outside of the sacrament. So why have any of the sacraments? Why have Baptism if God can love us and come to us apart from the sacraments? We have them because they are the actions of Christ Jesus here and now, tangibly presenting Himself, and God's life within Him, to us. For God sent His Christ not just to tell us that He loves us, but also to share His life with us, to join His into ours and ours into His. Actually there is only One Sacrament, Christ Jesus. After His resurrection He encounters us through His Church, His Mystical Body, in seven highly significant and infinitely effective ways. In the sacraments, God's Kairos time merges into our chronos time. The natural is elevated to the supernatural.

> How can sins be rightly remitted unless the very One against whom one has sinned grants the pardon?
> **Irenaeus** in *Against Heresies*

* * * * * * *

PRAYER

O Father, in your infinite, loving forgiveness, help me to receive the freedom you want to give me. Help me to forgive others so that I might be just like you, so that I might live in your love and bring that same love to all those around me, particularly those who have hurt me, those who have done great wrongs against me. Deliver me of crippling resentments and let me live in the freedom of your Resurrected Christ, bringing

your message of hope and deliverance to the
world around me. May your Kingdom be
revealed in your forgiveness of me, and in my
forgiveness of others.

* * * * * * *

QUESTIONS

What does the fifth step of AA's Twelve Steps mean for
me? (The fifth step is: "We admitted to God, to
ourselves, and to another human being the exact nature
of our wrongs.")
If I forgive someone, am I saying what they did was
okay?
If I do not have feelings of forgiveness toward someone,
can I turn that person over to God for forgiveness?

① It humbles me – if I am admitting
that I am weak, if I am not perfect.
But it frees me to try again,
knowing I am forgiven.

② No – But we forgive, so we
can go on w/ our lives – We
leave the judging to God.

③ I think we must forgive,
even if we don't have the
feeling of forgiveness – God will
take care of the rest – As he has
already forgiven all of us.

AS WE FORGIVE THOSE WHO SIN AGAINST US...

To err is human; to forgive, divine.
Alexander Pope

What kind of God is God, and what does He expect of us?

As Christians we believe that God reveals Himself to us in His only begotten Son, Jesus Christ. We begin to find our answers to our questions about God in Christ's gift of His Father's Presence to us, in Christ's way of living, in the truth He speaks to us, and in the way Christ lives his life both among us and within us.

> Do not judge, and you will not be judged; because the judgments you give are the judgments you will get, and the amount you measure out is the amount you will be given. Why do you observe the splinter in your brother's eye and never notice the plank in your own? How dare you say to your brother "let me take the splinter out of your eye", when all the time there is a plank in your own? Hypocrite! Take the plank out of your own eye first, and then you will see clearly enough to take the splinter out of your brother's eye.
> **Matthew 7:1-5**

What, then, are we to think about God's "unconditional" love for us? Just how "unconditional" is it? While God's love and forgiveness are always present to us, their effect is dependent upon our response to Him. God has offered himself to us unconditionally, now He awaits our response. We cannot afford to be facile and think that "God loves me unconditionally, irrespective of what I do."

This raises important questions for you and for me. How do we forgive others? Easily, or with conditions? Do we make others somehow "pay" for our forgiveness?

242

We've all heard the saying, "Be careful what you pray for, you may get it." The ancient Israelites wanted idols and as a consequence found themselves awash in them, in Babylon! They wanted a king, and when God gave them kings they repented of ever having asked him for a king. God allows us to be saved or ruined in what we ask for.

And what do we Americans crave? Just look around: we, too, are awash in what we want, so much so that many of us are sick of our materialistic and shallow quests for pleasure. We know we're made for higher purposes.

If this is true then be careful and thoughtful about this prayer asking God for the power to forgive others. In it you are asking God to measure you by the same standard you use to measure the intentions, attitudes, and actions of others. The operative word here is "AS."

> ...for all who draw the sword will die by the sword.
> Matthew 26:52

This means you want God to forgive you in the same "tone of voice" you use in forgiving others, to the length, breadth, height and depth that you forgive those around you. This fact is so important that Jesus repeated it several times. He really means it. You will be forgiven to the extent and in the manner you forgive others. If this doesn't make you stop and think, nothing else will.

Paralyzed by the bitter memories that continually replay in our minds ("she said this to me" and "he said that") we are immobilized in pain, nailed on the cross of resentments. Christ died to free us from all of that. In every Mass we celebrate the freedom He wants to give us in our Daily bread, the Bread of Life that He hands over to us in the Living Bread, the Holy Communion He died to give us.

The Pharisee and the Tax Collector

St. Luke was a masterful painter of word pictures, a master in presenting the parable depictions Jesus painted for us. Luke's Gospel is filled with outcasts and sinners, the despised who suffered from the contempt of the self-righteous. Read chapters eleven through nineteen of St. Luke's Gospel. There you'll find wonderful vignettes dealing with sinners.

Luke's Gospel recounts a time when Jesus presents us with two men, a Pharisee and a tax collector, who found themselves together in Jerusalem's Temple. I am sure you remember them. The Pharisee stood up in the front justifying himself and claiming to be better than the tax collector, the one huddled in the back of the Temple beating his breast and asking only for God's mercy.

In Luke's nineteenth chapter we read of a chief tax collector named Zacchaeus. This account is not about a character created in a parable, it is a report about someone whom Jesus actually encountered in His life.

Tax collectors were hated, and Jewish tax collectors were the most hated of all. They were puppets of the Romans. They were given a quota of taxes to collect and had at their disposal the power of Roman soldiers to assist them in collecting taxes. All the Romans expected of them was their assigned quota. The tax collectors, however, could collect more than they owed and could unleash the Roman soldiers upon Jews who didn't pay the amounts specified by the Roman authorities.
Furthermore, tax collectors were considered to be traitors by the Jewish people, traitors to their own religion.

Tax collectors were considered by the Jews to be the very worst of all sinners. They were the most despised of all people among the Jews. The particular one in this account, Zacchaeus (Luke 19:2ff), was the head tax collector in Jericho, a very wealthy city that was famous and envied by all for its economic privilege and affluent citizens. Since he was from this city, Zacchaeus was indeed a very wealthy and powerful man.

Perhaps now you may feel the electrifying shock that must have hit the Jews when Jesus called out to him: "Zacchaeus, come down. Hurry, because I am coming to stay in your house." Jesus was going to dine at Zacchaeus' table; He was going to stay in his house! It was unthinkable, and yet true. Not only was Zacchaeus wealthy at the expense of others, he was also friendless. No one would associate with him. No one, that is, until Jesus came down the road. Suddenly he had the greatest friend anyone could ever have.

This story is important for two reasons. One is that the Jews of Jericho completely misjudged Zacchaeus. The second is that, as a result of his encounter with Jesus, Zacchaeus was thoroughly changed. Zacchaeus not only made restitution for any fraud or extortion he had committed, he saw to it that his victims were more than repaid, four times over. He went beyond simple restitution and put those whom he had oppressed into standards of living they had never known before. Simply stated, Zacchaeus responded totally to Christ. As a result he was totally transformed.

What, then, is our response to God's offer to us in Christ?

The first thing for us to examine is just who it is that we are condemning and so harshly judging. By what standards do we judge them and condemn them? And how do you think God judges them? Do we know what's in their hearts and do we know their intentions better than God does?

The second response, the more important one, is to consider how we judge ourselves and try to discover why it is that we apply such rigid and perfectionistic standards to ourselves. Perhaps we have such an idealistic image of ourselves that we set ourselves up with impossible standards to meet. This can have two possible consequences.

One is despair. The other is that we excuse ourselves from prayer, from going to church, or any sense of closeness to God. The Evil One whispers in our ear: "Why bother?"

Despair is a terrible evil. It leads to completely giving up on ourselves. It leads to self-punishing behavior that certainly doesn't please God and forces others to live with a person who is miserable. The others don't deserve that, God doesn't deserve it, and neither do you.

The other effect of rigid self-judgment is to rationalize one's self out of coming to Mass. It provides a convenient excuse for not participating in the sacraments and in the life of the Church. "I am such a terrible sinner," we tell ourselves, "that even God could not forgive me." Therefore I don't need to go to church any more.

Pride and egoism lurk behind such sentiments. Why do we think our miserable little sins can restrain Almighty God and keep Him from giving us His loving mercy and tender forgiveness? What arrogance it is to declare that you are the worst of all sinners, so bad that God Himself stands powerless in front of you.

But just as the Son of God ignored the judgments and opinions of the local populace with regard to Zacchaeus, so also God ignores our judgments and opinions about others, and particularly about ourselves.

Finally, observe that Zacchaeus is much like the prodigal son who lived among the pigs and then came home to find his father to be even more prodigal in forgiveness, while the elder son stood aloof in icy condemnation and furious judgment. The stories of the prodigal son and Zacchaeus are about God's unbounded prodigality in sharing His forgiveness. They are stories about His all-powerful, life-changing love.

Do you find yourself to be "up a tree" and distantly observing Christ as He walks by? If so, be ready to hear Him call out to you and tell you that He wants to come to your house today and stay with you. Hopefully your response will be as holistic as Zacchaeus' response. For it is God who justifies us, we can never succeed in our own self-justification. It is God who sanctifies us; we can never succeed in making ourselves holy. It is God who saves us; we are incapable of saving ourselves.

If you want your life to be changed, give up the self-delusion that you can change your life all by yourself. Only God can change your life. And He can do it just as easily and just as completely as He changed the life of Zacchaeus, that hated and traitorous Jewish tax collector who found holiness in simply and wholeheartedly responding to God's invitation.

Are We Able to Forgive Others?

There is another problem we all face, and it's a big one. Can we forgive others?

To forgive, some think, is weakness. When you forgive you're selling out on your principles, compromising your dignity, and revealing your weakness. "You're a loser," the serpent whispers, "you're giving in. It is weakness to forgive." In forgiving, am I thereby saying that I agree with what the other has done? That I benignly accept the injury done? The truth is that I am not. Forgiveness does not mean acceptance or compliance.

Of all of the spiritual struggles in which we find ourselves, perhaps the strongest demon holding our souls hostage is the one named Unforgiveness. Its grip is steely.

247

It is unrelenting, besetting us daily, and it robs us of peace.

We think we are self-sufficient and all powerful when it comes to managing our lives and ourselves. In fact we are powerless over so very many people and events in our lives. The truth is that we need God's power in all matters, perhaps more so in finding and gaining the freedom to forgive, to forgive others as well as to forgive our selves. Ask yourself whether or not you really have "freedom of choice" when it comes to your ability to forgive others who have wronged you.

Unforgiveness in our hearts keeps the focus on self. It leads to a continual rehearsing of a one-act drama in which I portray myself as victim, rehearsing my lines when I'll finally have the opportunity to put down my wrongdoer.

Only God can forgive sins. And, if we allow Him, God lives His life in our life, not just with us but in our life. He has come to us in His Son, Christ Jesus, to give us new life, for our original life has been lost by our own rebellions against God. All of our sins are "original." They all go back to the origins of our egos, our self-identities, particularly our own self-declared and self-defined identities.

> I tell you solemnly, whatever you bind on earth shall be considered bound in heaven; whatever you loose on earth shall be considered loosed in heaven.
> Matthew 18:18

Can anyone claim that their self-picture has not been substantially shaped by hurt, pain, and suffering, both as victims of these negative emotions and as we have inflicted them upon others? No, of course not. And so it is that the question of forgiveness, and the power to forgive, touches the very core of our being, our existence.

From whence come the courage, the willingness, and the empowerment to forgive? It is ludicrous to claim that these spiritual powers are self-generated, that we can create them and fashion them. No, they are from God, the one who has the power and who empowers us with His healing forgiveness to forgive others. Forgiving is both a human and a divine act. Forgiveness is a gift God implants within us.

Forgiveness is directly connected with the passion, death, and resurrection of Christ Jesus. It is at the very core of His saving grace and power. The moment when God our Father in Christ Jesus gave us the Eucharist, when Christ's "hour" had come, He immediately proceeds into His redemptive death and resurrection. The conferral upon the Apostles of His power to forgive sins occurs immediately after His death and resurrection. Obviously these two stupendous sacraments are intimately connected with each other in what we call the Paschal Mystery, Christ's Passover.

> Unrolling the scroll he found the place where it is written:
> *The spirit of the Lord has been given to me, for he has anointed me. He has sent me to bring the good news to the poor, to proclaim liberty to captives and to the blind new sight, to set the downtrodden free, to proclaim the Lord's year of favor.*
> He then rolled up the scroll, gave it back to the assistant and sat down. And all eyes in the synagogue were fixed on him. Then he began to speak to them, "This text is being fulfilled today even as you listen."
> **Luke** 4:18-21

Both sacraments renew (and perhaps reestablish) our Father's life within us after we have either diminished or lost His life subsequent to our reception of the Sacrament of Baptism. Both give us an intimacy with God beyond any human intimacies we may have experienced. Both give us a union with God beyond and even deeper than that shared by God with Adam and Eve. In this we see that holiness is richer than innocence, for in sanctifying grace holiness fuses into us God's very own life. In the sacraments of Christ's Mystical Body we receive a supernatural existence far beyond any other kind of existence.

It bears continual repeating that the sacraments are the effective actions of God the Son, the Father's Word through whom He has brought and will bring all His creations into existence. Out of the ash and debris caused by our human sins, our Father in Christ brings into being His New Creation. To regard the sacraments as merely poetic actions of human creativity, however lovely, is to completely miss their true nature and thus to lose out on the immense power they can release within you and your life. Christ's sacraments offer us a new life, a free life, a Spirit-filled life, a life of possibilities, a glorious life.

"As We Forgive..."

We need to take a close look now into the underlying strata deep within that little word "as." The best entrance into that is through Matthew 18:21-35, which is a little drama in three acts.

> *Then Peter went up to him and said, "Lord, how often must I forgive my brother if he wrongs me? As often as seven times?" Jesus answered, "Not seven, I tell you, but seventy-seven times."*
> *And so the kingdom of heaven may be compared to a king who decided to settle his accounts with his servants. When the reckoning began, they brought him a man who owed ten thousand talents; but he had no means of paying, so his master gave orders that he should be sold, together with his wife and children and all his possessions, to meet the debt. At this, the servant threw himself down at his master's feet. "Give*

*me time," he said, "and I will pay the whole
sum." And the servant's master felt so sorry for
him that he let him go and cancelled the debt.
Now as this servant went out, he happened to
meet a fellow servant who owed him one
hundred denarii; and he seized him by the throat
and began to throttle him. "Pay what you owe
me" he said. His fellow servant fell at his feet
and implored him, saying, "Give me time and I
will pay you." But the other would not agree; on
the contrary, he had him thrown into prison till
he should pay the debt. His fellow servants were
deeply distressed when they saw what had
happened, and they went to their master and
reported the whole affair to him. Then the master
sent for him. "You wicked servant," he said "I
cancelled all that debt of yours when you
appealed to me. Were you not bound, then, to
have pity on your fellow servant just as I had pity
on you?" And in his anger the master handed
him over to the torturers till he should pay all his
debt. And that is how my heavenly Father will
deal with you unless you each forgive your
brother from your heart.*

Matthew 18:21-35

Act I - Auditing the books.

The amount the servant owed the master was huge; he
asked only for time. More important, however, is the fact
that the debtor did not ask his master for forgiveness, he
asked only for time. He was concerned about observing
the dictates of the law.

The lesson? Self-righteousness remained. The unjust
steward was living in his head, not in his heart. There was
no change of heart, only observance and manipulation of

laws, rules, and regulations. There was no appeal to mercy, or to the heart. Nevertheless the king forgave. But note that he forgave the debt, not the servant.

Act II – Hardness of heart.

The steward runs out to tell his family and friends all about himself and the good thing that happened to him. Filled with his own self he meets his fellow servant and instead of treating him with a changed heart and soul he treats him to the law. He has his fellow servant and debtor thrown into prison. Self-righteousness can turn us into such monsters!

And the lesson? You can be willing to forgive but you cannot actually give forgiveness to someone who has not repented and asked for forgiveness. Even God can't forgive someone with a hard heart, even though He is ready to forgive. It's called "sinning against the Holy Spirit," the only unforgivable sin. It's unforgivable because the sinner does not allow his inner soul to be influenced by the Holy Spirit.

Act III – The law is applied.

Shaken by the obvious injustice of the situation, the other servants inform the king what has happened. The king then acts on behalf of the powerless; he exercises legal judgment and employs the law on their behalf. He subjects the unjust steward to the full force of the law. The one thing the poor and the powerless need is justice. It is their means of equalizing the balance; it is their access to power.

God comes to us looking for change in our hearts, not simply a change in our ways of thinking and acting. Those are externals, not internals.

Forgiveness is liberating, unforgiveness is imprisoning. Forgiveness allows us to walk in the freedom of the sons and daughters of God, no longer as children of the law. Living under the law leads us to "an eye for an eye, a tooth for a tooth." Living under the law leads us to live in the quest for retribution and justice alone without any change in our hearts.

We cling to resentments in the horrible prison of pent-up anger and the lust to "get even." This throws us into victimhood. We feel like we are victims and seek ways to find just compensation, revenge, and retribution. We live under the law.

Jesus Christ is risen from the dead, victim no longer. He is totally free because He is totally forgiving.

"Forgive us our sins as we forgive those who have sinned against us," we pray. *"As" is the controlling word.* We will be forgiven to the length, height and depth that we measure out forgiveness to others. But remember they can only be given forgiveness if they repent, convert their hearts, and actually accept forgiveness. Sadly, with only legalistic motives and conditions in our hearts, the giving of forgiveness is another form (and a disguised form at that) of control over those we think we are forgiving.

There is perhaps no more concrete way to love than by praying for one's enemies. It makes you conscious of the truth that, in God's eyes, you are no more worthy, and no less worthy, of being loved than any other person. And it creates an awareness of profound solidarity with all other human beings. It creates within you a world-embracing compassion and, in increasing measure, provides you with a heart free of the compulsive urge to use coercion and violence. And you will be delighted to discover that you can no longer remain angry with people for whom you have really and truly prayed. You will find that you start speaking differently to them or about them, and that you are actually willing to do good to those who have offended you in some way.

You cannot be resentful of, or angry toward, another for whom you are authentically praying. Such contraries cannot exist in the same soul at the same time. If your soul is filled with resentment, bitterness, and anger toward someone, start praying for that person or persons. Ask God to give them the graces they need the most. You will find your heart and soul are lighter. Keep it up and soon you will find freedom from your addictive resentments.

Whenever you receive the Body and Blood of Jesus Christ in the Eucharist, His love is given to you, the same love that He poured out over the world as He hung upon His cross. It is the love of God for all people of all times and places, all religions and creeds, all races and classes, all tribes and nations, all sinners and saints.

On the cross Jesus has shown us how far God's love goes. It is a love that embraces even those who crucified Him. When Jesus was hanging on His cross, totally broken and stripped of everything, He still prayed for His executioners: "Father, forgive them; they do not know what they are doing." Jesus' love for His enemies knew no bounds. He prayed even for those who were putting Him to death! It is this power from the enemy-loving God that is offered to us in the Eucharist. To forgive our enemies is not naturally within our power. It is a divine gift. That is why it's so important to make the Eucharist the heart and center of your life. It is there that you receive the love that empowers you to take the way that Jesus has taken before you -- a narrow way, a painful way, but the way that gives you true joy and peace and enables you to make the non-violent love of God visible in the world.

The Benefits of Forgiving

Forgiveness releases us from our imprisoning resentments; they lose their grip and melt away. As we have seen, one cannot give true forgiveness and continue to be possessed by lingering resentments. The two opposing spiritual conditions cannot exist in the same soul at the same time.

Forgiveness gives us newness of life. Forgiveness and the resurrection of Christ Jesus are intertwined. The history of our relationship with God as recorded in the Bible is replete with examples of God continually giving us another chance. Forgiveness is

> You see, if a man keeps the whole of the Law, except for one small point at which he fails, he is still guilty of breaking it all. It was the same person who said, "You must not commit adultery" and "you must not kill." Now if you commit murder, you do not have to commit adultery as well to become a breaker of the Law. Talk and behave like people who are going to be judged by the law of freedom, because there will be judgment without mercy for those who have not been merciful themselves; but the merciful need have no fear of judgment.
> **James 2:10-13**

the initiation of another chance, a new life, for the one forgiven. God's Spirit raises us up, as It raised Jesus, into a new and higher life.

If we are offering God a heart filled with unforgiveness then we are setting the terms for our relationship with Him. He will accept that; He accepts our heart and soul in the condition in which we live. We give Him who we are. Scary! It's not that God does not want to forgive us but rather that we are unwilling to live in His loving forgiveness. If we withhold mercy and forgiveness we have in effect jettisoned the whole of the law and the prophets. We have damned ourselves.

255

An unforgiving heart is one that does not accept God's heart, and so is damned to live accordingly in a hell of bitter resentments. Enlarging our hearts allows God to fill them with His even larger loving

> So you should pray like this: "Our Father in heaven, may your name be held holy, your kingdom come, your will be done, on earth as in heaven. Give us today our daily bread; and forgive us our debts, as we have forgiven those who are in debut to us. And do not put us to the test, but save us from the evil one." Yes, if you forgive others their failings, your heavenly Father will forgive you yours; but if your do not forgive others, your Father will not forgive your failings either. Matthew 6:10-15

forgiveness. We are thus empowered to have the capacity to forgive as God forgives. Once again, it is in giving that we receive.

How can a Christian claim to be a Christian unless he or she asks God for forgiveness? And how can a Christian claim to be a follower of Christ unless he or she forgives those who repent and ask for forgiveness? Justice and mercy intersect at the point wherein the sinner realizes the damage done by sin and has a conversion of heart, a conversion that leads him to be as forgiving toward others as God has been forgiving toward him. Which comes first, the forgiveness of God or the forgiveness of others? In the order of causality the forgiveness of God comes first. In our world of effects the forgiveness of others disposes us to be willing to forgive others as we have been forgiven. We are forgiven sinners, and we know it; we are forgiving sinners and thereby witness to Christ Jesus hanging on the cross so that the power of forgiveness can be effected in our world.

We are not automatically saved simply because we call on the name of Jesus. We are not automatically Christian simply because we claim we are Christian. And we are not automatically forgiven simply because we ask for forgiveness.

Everything depends upon how and in what manner we forgive those who have sinned against us. If we would live in God's life, if we would live God-like lives, then we must forgive others as He has forgiven us.

* * * * * * *

PRAYER

O Father, there are so many things in myself that I see in others…and I'm scornful and cannot forgive them for reminding me of my faults, flaws and sins. Help me to love and forgive myself so that I can love and forgive others. Your Son died to forgive us and sanctify us all, so help me see others and my self in his eyes, and to forgive them as He does.

* * * * * *

QUESTIONS

Is forgiveness a decision or is it a feeling? If I feel like I cannot forgive someone can I nevertheless forgive them?

Can we forgive someone when they don't even ask for forgiveness, or want it?

If I forgive someone, am I thereby saying what they did was okay?

Should restitution be a part of forgiveness?

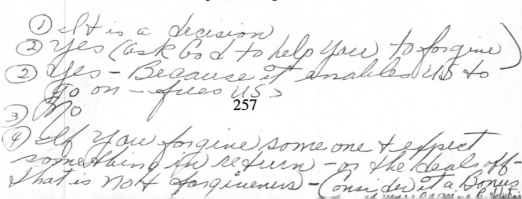

① It is a decision

② Yes (ask God to help you) to forgive

② Yes - Because it enables us to go on - frees us ->

③ No

257

④ If you forgive someone + expect something in return - or the deal off - that is not forgiveness - (consider it a Bonus

LEAD US NOT INTO TEMPTATION...

Yahweh, hear my prayer, let my cry for help reach you; do not hide your face from me when I am in trouble; bend down and listen to me, when I call, be quick to answer me!

Psalm 102

How could a good and loving God lead us into evil? Would an infinitely good and loving God deliberately test us with the occasion of sin? He would not! Rather it is the will of God that we live in wholesomeness, integrity, and peace, the peace of His presence in our lives. It is God's will that we live happily as Jesus

> Never, when you have been tempted, say, "God sent the temptation;" God cannot be tempted to do anything wrong, and He does not tempt anybody. Everyone who is tempted is attracted and seduced by his own wrong desires.
> **James 1:13-14**

reveals to us His Father's will. He wills that we live in justice, peace, fairness, goodness, and holistic wholesomeness, depending all the while upon His providential love. Would He deliberately test us? I don't think so.

We have all heard the expression, "Events cast their shadows before them." Time and again we have examples of God giving us an Old Testament dress rehearsal of New Testament events that will come with Christ. For example, the passage of God's people through the waters of the Red Sea and again through the waters of the river Jordan prefigure our passage through the waters of baptism into the Promised Land of God's domain.

258

One of the most crucial and troubling of Old Testament readings is found in the Book of Genesis, chapter twenty-two. There we find Abraham facing a heart-breaking challenge, to sacrifice his only son Isaac. And what a challenge it was! First of all, God had previously promised Abraham that he would become the father of a people more numerous than the sands of the sea. Yet now it seems that Abraham is to sacrifice his only son, at God's request! Without Isaac, Abraham would be childless. How, then, could God's promise be fulfilled?

We must also remember that the Jews regarded human sacrifice as something horrific. They never practiced human sacrifice. Yet God is asking Abraham to sacrifice his only son?

In the account we find Abraham carrying the knife and Isaac following his father while climbing the mountain carrying wood for the sacrificial fire on his back. The whole thing is almost unbelievable. But it sets the stage for the cosmic drama that will eventually unfold with Jesus Christ climbing Golgotha's hill carrying on his back the wood of the cross upon which He will be sacrificed.

If you visit Rome as a pilgrim you would certainly visit its cathedral, St. John Lateran. It was the original site upon which the early Christians, subsequent to their hiding in the catacombs, built their first public church. It was located on the Lateran hill, one of Rome's seven hills. The popes of the first 1,000 years of Christianity lived and worked there.

When you walk down the nave of St. John Lateran you will find seven stained glass windows on the left side and seven on the right. Those on the left depict Old Testament events; those on the opposite right-hand side depict their New Testament counterparts. Thus the first window on the left side depicts Adam and Eve in the Garden of Paradise and the window opposite depicts Christ's birth.

The window depicting the Hebrews' passage through the Red Sea is juxtaposed with Christ being baptized by John the Baptist in the river Jordan.

There is one set that is particularly striking. The Old Testament side depicts Abraham with his raised hand, gripping the knife, held back by an angel from plunging it into Isaac's heart. Isaac is thereby spared his sacrificial death. The window opposite depicts Christ hanging in death while nailed to His cross. The message is striking. God spared Abraham's precious son Isaac, but God did not spare His most precious gift of all for us, his only Son Jesus Christ. Isaac was not sacrificed; Christ was.

> Now every temptation is not blame-worthy; it may even be praise-worthy, because it furnishes probation. And, for the most part, the human mind cannot attain to self-knowledge otherwise than by making trial of its powers through temptation, by some kind of experimental and not merely verbal self-interrogation; when, if it has acknowledged the gift of God, it is pious, and is consolidated by steadfast grace and not puffed up by vain boasting.
> **St. Augustine**, The City of God, Book XVI, Chapter 32

Abraham's faith in the God of promises allows God to establish His people here on earth. Christ's faith in His Father in heaven, who did not spare Him from death, brings God to raise the humanity of Jesus Christ from the dead in order that our own humanity, joined into Christ's, might be raised from the death of sin into a new and everlasting life in heaven. God's love is more powerful than our evil.

God was aware of Abraham's faith. God did not need to find out what was in Abraham's heart, but Abraham did. The same was true for the Canaanite woman reported by St. Matthew (see Matthew 15:21-28).

Likewise, God is aware of your faith and mine. God knows the struggles we all face, along with the struggles we have in believing. Abraham did not want to sacrifice his son, but nevertheless trusted in God. In His agony

Christ cries out: "My Father, if it is possible, let this cup pass from me; yet, not as I will, but as you will." Therein lies the key: How far will we go in accepting the love of God? How far will we go in believing in God's love for us?

However we may see and understand the promises of God (and we see those promises through our own filters), can we trust the God of promises? Our faith is continually tested by the turmoil of our lives. It is easy for us to believe and to think of ourselves as people of faith when all is going well and we are happy. It's easy to believe, to be people of faith, when we leave Church feeling moved and nourished by what has happened at Mass. But faith is difficult when we are in anguish, when we're suffering loss and pain.

When relationships with others turn sour, when our marriages become bitter and destructive, when our kids push us to the edge of patience and tolerance, when our jobs and careers face termination and loss, when the ones we love face terrible illness, can we still trust in the God of promises? Are we more concerned with the promises of God than we are with the God of promises?

In such times we must cling to the truth that God brings good out of evil. When we turn bitter, do we see through the ash and debris some burning embers of God's love for us? Do we trust that God can cause faith to flame up again within our souls?

As Christians we have a tremendous gift to give to those around us who live in hopelessness. We can give them the gift of hope, the courage of our faith. For we believe that God does in fact bring meaning out of absurdity, order out of chaos, life out of death, and good out of evil. If we do not, then why should we celebrate Easter at all? Why should we believe that every Good Friday is followed by an Easter Sunday?

261

Who Is Testing Us?

The language used in the Bible suggests that God is continually testing us. Personally, I really don't think God plays dirty tricks on us and cruelly tests us. Does God really need to test us? Doesn't He already know ahead of time what's in our hearts and souls?

It is life that tests us. It is our own stubborn willfulness that tests us. It is our own pretentious attitude that tests us. Human sinfulness tests us. I don't think God wastes energy testing us. Rather than viewing life's challenges as "tests" from God, we should see them as opportunities to discover within ourselves depths of faith, love, courage, and hope that we didn't even know we

> Is not the life of man a term of trial upon earth, in which we are daily crying to the Lord, "Deliver us from evil," a man is compelled to endure, even when his sins are forgiven him, although it was the first sin that caused his falling into such misery. And it is in the evils that every one suffers, not in the good things that he enjoys, that he has need of patience.
> **St. Augustine 3**, Tractate CXXIV, Chapter XXI .

had. God knows the depths of our hearts. We don't. Life is made up of our journeys into the power and the glory that God put within us before we were born.

Instead of calling God into question over Abraham's challenge to sacrifice his only son, or questioning God's sacrifice of His only-begotten Son, Jesus Christ, perhaps we should question ourselves. For in the sacrifice of Abraham and in the sacrifice of Christ we find hidden a question we need to answer: What am I willing to sacrifice for God? Do I believe in the God of promises or am I not willing to rely on them and instead cling to what is mine while withholding my love for, and trust in, God our Father?

Questioning God is a form of avoidance and denial. Questioning God allows me to escape from answering the real question: "What am I willing to give up for God?" Am I only willing to offer up a childlike sacrifice, like candy during Lent, or am I willing to sacrifice what I cling to in my heart and keep from God?

It is sin that puts us to the test. Life's unfairness tests us. Should we claim that God is testing us? We even place ourselves into temptation, into occasions of sin. It's hard to imagine God deliberately placing us in an occasion of sin. But clearly the Evil One does. Others take us there. We ourselves do too. To illicitly desire some other person or some thing instead of God is to sink into idolatry. "I am the Lord thy God," states the First Commandment, "thou shalt not have strange gods before me."

Each and every day we are tested by the consequences of the choices of others. Life, in all of its unfairness tests us daily. A dislocated world, a world that is still subject to the random forces of chaos and chance, often impinges itself upon us with the result that our faith and trust in God are tested. Our response to the injuries and evils inflicted upon us by others tests our relationship with God. Will our response to life's unfairness be Christ-like? What would Jesus do in such situations? Asking these questions tests us daily.

"And lead us not into temptation" is translated in the Jerusalem Bible to read, "And do not put us to the test, but save us from the evil one"(see Matthew 6:9-13). In Luke's Gospel, again as presented in the Jerusalem Bible, the phrase is rendered: "And do not put us to the test" (Luke 11:4). Other translations have it as "And subject us not to the trial." It is clear, then, that we need to delve into the content behind those words. For what are we praying?

> Because he himself has been through temptation he is able to help others who are tempted.
> **Hebrews 2:18**

263

"And lead us...." Whenever we pray this prayer do we truly realize that we are asking God to lead us, and if so, are we willing to have Him lead us? For when it comes to temptations, who does the leading? Does God lead, or do we lead ourselves?

However much we are fascinated with any temptation, with all that is so attractive in it, the significant word is lead. Asking our Father to lead us is far more important

> The trials that you have had to bear are no more than people normally have. You can trust God not to let you be tried beyond your strength, and with any trial he will give you a way out of it and the strength to bear it.
> **1 Corinthians** 10:13

and significant than our fascination with the content of the temptation. Regardless of the source of the temptation, or what we are being tempted to do, we are asking that God lead us. It is in His leading that we find deliverance and safety. Moreover, we must ask ourselves if we are more interested in having the temptation diminished or removed than in having God lead us. Are we simply asking for relief, or are we asking for our Father's love? If, like the moth, we are more captivated by the flame than our ability with His help to fly, then we shall be consumed in the fire. It is God's gift in response to our prayer that we are given the ability to fly with His help, no matter where the flame comes from.

Our Father allows us to make the choice to sin or not to sin so that we will, in making the right choices, strengthen our faith and our response to His love for us. In this way God our Father allows us to be tempted.

A temptation is an opportunity. Most opportunities come to us in some form of a crisis. These are opportunities to seek our Father's power and love for us. We must pray that He will help us make the right choices. "'Lead us not' is my prayer for you, Father, to lead me. I want you to lead me." Am I humble enough to let our

264

Father lead me? To allow myself to be led? Or do I think my omnipotent self is strong enough to lead me away from any temptation?

We need to pray often that God lead us away from temptation. We need to hear ourselves praying those words because prayer changes us more than it changes God. The magic of prayer is what it does to us, how it helps us re-form and re-shape our patterns of behavior and decision-making.

We are always tempted to think that we make ourselves holy. The truth is we don't. It is God who makes us holy. The only thing we can do is to open our hearts and souls to His Presence. Unless we are filled with God's Presence abiding in us, seven devils worse than the first will come and occupy our souls. The simple effort we exert to move away from temptation is not enough. The natural must be filled with the supernatural in order for anything spiritually significant to transpire.

Prayer has a very great effect on us. It changes our dispositions; it changes our way of seeing things; it changes the object of our attention; it can even change our direction. Is that not the essence of conversion, the adopting of a new version of living? This, I believe, is the reason that Jesus teaches us to ask that God not lead us into temptation. As we ask God not to lead us into temptation perhaps we will thereby lead ourselves away from temptation. When we pray that God will do something we actually begin to conform our will to His.

To voluntarily and tenderly give ourselves over to the ones we love is to be God-like. For He Himself tenderly, compassionately, and in great hope, has given Himself over to us in self-emptying love. That is the message of the crucifix, the icon of Love itself. The opposite of this love is hellish and demonic. The opposite is sin-full, and causes us to throw the other out of our communion of

265

love, to distance ourselves, to reject, humiliate, ignore, snub, shun, and thereby excommunicate those who are looking for our love.

"Lead us not into..." is another way of praying, "Lead us out from...." During the time of temptation, please lead us, Father. Give us the graces necessary to face the trials and tests that life hurls at us. Help us to get out of here, out of this place of temptation.

The World

The earth is both good and beautiful. Animals are innocent and good in themselves. There is a natural goodness that constitutes the goodness of nature. The world, simply as it is in its being, is good.

In biblical language, "the world" that is bad is that part of creation that has been withdrawn from God's dominion. It is the world removed from God's loving Presence. Satan claims it as his. In his arrogance he claims "I will give it to you" as he tests Christ out in the desert. That is the world in which God is avoided, ignored, or actually defied.

> Then the devil took him up to a very high mountain, and showed him all the kingdoms of the world in their magnificence, and he said to him, "All these I shall give to you, if you will prostrate yourself and worship me."*
>
> At this, Jesus said to him, "Get away, Satan! It is written: 'The Lord, your God, shall you worship and him alone shall you serve.'"
>
> **Matthew 4:8-10**

The world removed from God's Presence tests us, God doesn't. Perhaps the idea that God "tests" us comes from the fact that He has allowed us the freedom of our choices. Given the nature of our world and the fact that the choices of others have an impact upon us, all of life is filled with tests. If we blame God for all that is wrong in our world then we have only ourselves to blame.

All sin and temptation comes to us from the surrounding world in which we live, the world we have fashioned apart from God. Ultimately they come from the Evil One, the one who claims ownership and control over the world.

The Western world today is hugely narcissistic. The Imperial Self dominates. It is reflexive, reactionary, power-obsessed, overfed, fragmented into isolationist sub-cultures, because it is rootless, it is superficial. Its inhabitants are, for the most part, pleasure seeking, self-gratifying, concerned with immediate results, distrustful of intermediaries, and overly concerned with self-image and appearances.

As we have discussed earlier, many in our day regard sin as a medieval concept, quite outdated and irrelevant in the world of modern decision-making. And temptation to sin is even more on the periphery of our consciences. The world is

> Then to what shall I compare the people of this generation? What are they like? They are like children who sit in the marketplace and call to one another, "We played the flute for you, but you did not dance. We sang a dirge, but you did not weep."
> **Luke 7:31-32**

suspicious of moral norms. If you have them, then they are your private "opinions" and should apply to no one but you. If you really pray, and are truly devout, if you live a life that is integrated with God, then the cultured despisers of religion will call you a "fundamentalist" or a "fanatic."

In spite of this rather distressing assessment, if we are honest with ourselves many of us will admit that meaning is missing from our lives. We know we must discipline our appetites. We know that license has led to child abuse, that we are sexualizing our children at ever-earlier ages and thus depriving them of childhood. We have seen that selfishness has led to political, corporate and societal scandals causing great damage to our cultural ethos.

267

Where are the commonly held set of mores and values we once shared? There must be more to life than immediate and superficial pleasure. These appetites have not made us happy.

The Johannine view, with its emphasis on the other world, mystery, and the symbolic, is now facing the present-day ascendancy of the Lucan concern for the marginalized, the poor and oppressed, those who are in immediate need of God's saving providential love. Until recently John's Gospel has enjoyed the pride of preference in Catholic liturgical and spiritual life. Today more and more attention is being paid to Luke's Gospel. We are re-discovering that God has not sent His Son into our world to condemn it, but to redeem it. "For God did not send His Son into the world to condemn the world, but that the world might be saved through him" (John 3:17).

God offers, what is our response? I fear we too often pray that God do this or that for us, thereby making God responsible for what happens or what does not happen. Too often we do not act with the gifts He has given us. We fear responsibility. We even fear freedom and flee from the demands that freedom's responsibility puts upon us, preferring to make others, even God, accountable.

> Why comes temptation, but for man to meet and master and make crouch beneath his foot, and so be predestined in triumph?
> **Robert Browning**

God sees within us a power, a strength, and a glory that we usually we do not see within ourselves. Go to Matthew 15:21-28 and consider the exchange between Jesus and the Canaanite woman. Far from demeaning the woman, Jesus exalts her, and ends by praising her: "Woman you have great faith." In her persistent following of Jesus she realized, as did those around her, what God had placed within us when He created us, namely, the

268

power and the glory that come forth from within us when we allow Him to lead us.

The Flesh

In biblical language, "the flesh" is that aspect of human nature that is under Satan's dominion, dominated by our urges, drives and lusts. In the world of the flesh, feelings reign supreme, overruling convictions. Logic and rational thought are flattened, steam-rolled by our

> For from the heart come evil intentions: murder, adultery, fornication, theft, perjury, slander.
> **Matthew** 15:18-19

drive for immediate pleasure rather than lasting happiness. "The flesh" is found in the Temple of Lust, a temple in which the idols of adultery, fornication, and gluttony are worshipped. We are spending our inheritance, the treasured gifts our Father has given us, on things that prostitute our souls in a land far distant from our Father's house. We waste our selves, our talents, and our resources on food that is fed to pigs, on wine that brings depression instead of joy. We, like the prodigal son, have been reduced to poverty, poverty of spirit and soul. We are malnourished and thirsting for a few drops of genuine happiness.

> But when we ask that we may not come into temptation, we are reminded of our infirmity and weakness in that we thus ask, lest any should insolently vaunt himself, lest any should proudly and arrogantly assume anything to himself, lest any should take to himself the glory either of confession or of suffering as his own, when the Lord Himself, teaching humility, said, "Watch and pray, that ye enter not into temptation; the spirit indeed is willing, but the flesh is weak."
> **St. Cyprian**, d.258 Treatise IV. On the Lord's Prayer, 26.

The irony of our spiritual stories is that God is all around us. We thirst and are hungry because we, continually entertained by media spectaculars, look for God only in what appears to be spectacular.

269

The reality is that God comes to us in the ordinary, in ordinary bread and wine, in ordinary people, and in ordinary events. Read the Gospels closely and note how Jesus rejected what is spectacular, even telling the recipients of His miracles to keep quiet about them.

The flesh, in biblical language, is human nature wounded and weakened by sin. It is our unredeemed human nature that has descended to us from Adam and Eve and not as yet returned to God. Human nature is not corrupt in itself; it retains God's original blessing, just as the descendants of Abraham still remain under the blessing of God's original covenant. But though not corrupt, it is weak, diseased by sin, suffering with sin's leprosy, blinded in the darkness not yet under God's Light. It is prone to sin, supine under sin's weight.

God doesn't have to lead us into temptation; we do a very adequate job of it all by ourselves. He doesn't need to expend His energies in tempting us. Rather He leads us away from evil and the temptation to do evil. So are we willing to let God lead us? Perhaps therein lies our trouble. We don't allow God to lead us; we want to decide for our selves what is evil and what is not. We decide that in the time of temptation we can take care of ourselves on our own power. When we ignore God's presence, power, and love we do not allow Him to lead us in our moments of temptation.

In our arrogant sense of self-sufficiency we are in effect saying: "Do not lead us in the time of temptation." Pride, again, is our undoing, our downfall. Adam and Eve are not that far removed from us. Their sin is ours, and ours is theirs. How foolish it is to blame them when we ourselves stand in their stead. Their sin is our sin, we have acted no differently.

So when we pray to our Father asking Him to "lead us not into temptation" what we are asking is to become aware of His desire to lead us away from all that would cause us to abandon Him, all that would cause us to adulterate our love relationship, all that would cause us to "belong" to lovers other than Him. Actually, in praying those words, we are begging God to lead us back to Him.

And when you get right down to it, what's really happening is that we're hearing ourselves articulate our hearts' deepest desire. We're hearing ourselves put into words what is embedded within our hearts, namely

> The only difference between a saint and a sinner is that the saint keeps on trying.
> **Anonymous**

our desire to stay close to God and remain in His arms. "Lead us not into temptation" is the prayer of our own order to remain in His love, to stay with our hearts' real desires.

We suffer evils inflicted upon us that have been caused by the selfish decisions of others. Some of our worst sufferings are a result of rejection, particularly by those who claimed they loved us. This leads to significant, sometimes massive, self doubt. We hear the internal accusation that we are unlovable; no one will ever love us. We are total rejects.

Faith untested is no faith at all, just as love untested isn't really love. It is decisiveness that gives either its value. But decisiveness comes only with "testing," with costly decisions. The desire for love without hurt, faith without pain, and a life of complete ease is referred to in the Bible as "the desires of the flesh." Make no mistake about it, we are not talking simply about sensual or sexual sins but any number of sins, particularly those that seduce and capture our spirits, our souls. Sins of the spirit are far more deadly than sins of sensuality. We have our internal devils, the demonic within us; we suffer evils caused internally by our own decisions and emotions, our deep-down irrational, self-rejections.

271

The Devil

Is there a devil, a sort of cosmic Darth Vader? Many people today think not. They do not accept the idea that evil is personified in a unique person or being. Others characterize evil in cartoon form, or in Hollywood style. Then, too, there are people who suffer from beliefs about the devil that are at best neurotic and at worst psychotic.

The problem lies in striking a balance when it comes to recognizing the Evil One's presence. In the Bible we find the devil mentioned sixty times. Jesus speaks of the devil ten times. Satan is mentioned fifty-three times in the Bible and spoken of by Jesus eighteen times.

Lucifer's lust for independence and freedom from God is the foundation of his pride. His pride drives him to be free from dependence upon anyone, even God. This was the root of the temptation he put to Adam and Eve.

For many people it is too humbling to admit their faults and sins, turn to God, and seek forgiveness and restoration from Him. It's just too degrading, too much for the Imperial Self to bear.

> Lead us not into temptation": in other words, do not let us be led astray by the Tempter. Let us not even think that the Lord appears to be the one who tempts us – as if he were not aware of the faith of an individual or, even, were bent on disturbing it! That kind of weakness and malice belongs to the devil. Even in the Case of Abraham, God commanded the sacrifices of his son not to tempt his faith, but to prove it. In Abraham, God would set an example of that precept by which he was to teach, in time, that no one should love even his nearest and dearest more than God. Christ himself was tempted by the devil and unmasked for us that subtle master of temptation. He emphasizes this petition at a later time when he says, "Pray that you enter not into temptation." Still, they were tempted and deserted their Lord, falling asleep rather than persevering in prayer. Thus, the last phrase of this petition balances the first and points to its meaning: "Lead us not into temptation, but deliver us from evil."
>
> Tertullian, *On Prayer* 8 (Inter 200-206 AD)

Jesus Christ has justified us in asking for our Father's merciful and loving forgiveness. The Evil One whispers otherwise in our ears, telling us that we're still "rotten, no good, ugly and corrupt to the core." We need an Advocate, a Divine Lawyer, who will counsel us otherwise, who will plead our case for us in spite of our timidity, and fear-full paralysis. Without His counsel, without His wisdom, understanding, knowledge, and fortitude we will, in our own self-condemnations, fail to receive the justification Christ offers us. Once again we need to recognize the twofold paradox that evil disguises itself as good and that evil is the degradation and corruption of what is good.

The wolf comes in sheep's clothing in order to carry off his victim. He comes impeccably dressed, wearing a business suit, dressed to kill. What sin, after all, is not attractive? What evil is done when covered in beauty? Lucifer was "The Light Bearer," the one clothed in radiant light, God's light.

Here again we need counsel. We need to be able to distinguish; to receive the Holy Spirit's guidance in deciding between what is truly good and what merely appears to be good. This is a huge task in a culture that adores appearances.

When our house has been swept clean of its resident patterns of our bedeviling sins, it is empty. It must be filled with patterns of goodness, decency, and wholesomeness; it must be filled with virtues or else

> When an unclean spirit goes out of a man it wanders through waterless country looking for a place to rest, and cannot find one. Then it says, "I will return to the home I came from." But on arrival, finding it unoccupied, swept and tidied, it then goes off and collects seven other spirits more evil than itself, and they go in and set up house there, so that the man ends up by being worse than he was before. That is what will happen to this evil generation.
> Matthew 12:43-45

273

"seven devils worse than the first" will return to occupy our souls.

The Imperial Self prefers indifference toward considerations of morality, indifference when it comes to acknowledging or applying external standards of goodness and morality. The Imperial Self disdains moral constraints that are "imposed upon us by others." Indifference differs from outright rejection only in appearances. But we must remember that the Imperial Self deals in appearances.

Jesus Christ has given us His victory over the Evil One's influence and persuasive powers. By His passion, death, and resurrection Christ has empowered human nature with the ability to enter into the "freedom of the sons and daughters of God," a freedom He in His humanity won for us at such terrible cost.

Christ's self-sacrificial love is there for us, if we choose to accept it. It is in acceptance of this love that we have ultimate power over anything the Evil One can throw at us.

The Many Forms of Defiance

Our Ancient Enemy, sometimes called "The Accuser," induces us to sink into a downward spiral of self-accusations that lead to a complete loss of self-confidence and eventual despair. He accuses us of being hopeless sinners, those whom God has rejected. He accuses us of being rotten, no-good, and already forsaken. Why, then, bother with the effort to be good? It is too costly, he tells us; the effort to be good denies us the pleasure and happiness we deserve now. He is lying, of course.

The Accuser tells us: "You are a hopeless sinner, the worst of the lot, and God is totally disgusted and fed up with you. So go ahead and have a little bit of fun, even if it is 'sinful.' You deserve some pleasure so enjoy it while you can. Why struggle? All you have to do is yield and then you'll find rest."

One of the serpent's most seductive temptations is to induce us to simply give up, to surrender, to yield to our cravings, desires, and lusts for pleasure at no cost. When we do, we always find the pleasure to be momentary, the happiness fleeting. We quickly realize we've bought something that's very cheap. But do we want cheap love? Cheap grace? Do we want to give God a love without effort? We know the truth of the old saying, "You get what you pay for," and yet we still go for what is cheap instead of what is of priceless worth.

Love is not a feeling, it is rather a decision. Affection is a feeling, an emotion; love is a decision. Therefore, in order for God to be loved we must make decisions. We must give God decisiveness, not simply nice wishes or sentiments without substance. If God is to be loved then He had to create us with free choice, free will. Only in this sense can we speak of God "allowing" us to be tempted. But this allowance is never beyond our means. After all, God loves us, doesn't He? Does any lover demand the impossible of the one he loves?

Again, humility is required. We need to know our limits; we need to set boundaries. We are not omnipotent (another of the devil's seductive suggestions). We absolutely need God's help.

The Irrational: We Tempt Ourselves

Suppose that I am very much overweight. Does it make sense to sue fast food companies for making me fat? Suppose I don't feel like studying; should I sue the local school district for

> I can resist everything except temptation.
> **Oscar Wilde**

not giving me passing grades? Or I drive recklessly and have a terrible accident. Should I sue the automobile manufacturers for not making my car crash proof? This psychotic irrationality is gripping our culture. It puts thinking off-balance; it claims everyone else is responsible for the terrible things that have happened to me. If I feel guilty, the Church is to be held accountable. I am not happy, so God is to be blamed for my misery. I am a victim! I am not responsible!

The Imperial Self plays temptation games, goes shopping around in this world's erogenous zones, tests the principles of others who are principled, experiments with the forbidden, and finally comes out in direct defiance of God.

The radical sin is to refuse to love and be loved. Our prideful

> ...thus the work of the devil is one: to make trial whether you do will that which it rests with you to will. But when you have willed, it follows that he subjects you to himself; not by having wrought volition in you, but by having found a favourable opportunity in your volition. Therefore, since the only thing which is in our power is volition--and it is herein that our mind toward God is put to proof, whether we will the things which coincide with His will--deeply and anxiously must the will of God be pondered again and again, I say, (to see) what even in secret He may will.
>
> **Tertullian, An Exhortation to Chastity, Chap. II – The Blame of Our Misdeeds Not to be Cast Upon God. The One Power Which Rests with Man is the Power of Volition.**

refusal sends out the message: "I'm better, richer and fuller than you, and so I don't need your love." Such arrogance totally misses the only genuine lover's real call: "I love you and therefore I need you." The secular, worldly message is: "I need you and therefore I love you. You are useful to me, and therefore I love you."

To be sure, any lover wants to be needed. The spiritual question, however, is: "Why do I need you?" The genuinely good answer is: "I love you, and so I need you."

God doesn't play dirty tricks on us. He loves us and does not want us to face the Evil One unaided. That face-off occurred when Jesus faced Lucifer down in the desert. If we follow Jesus' lead we will be delivered from

> But it is not as if you live in the dark, my brothers, for that Day to overtake your like a thief. No, you are all sons of light and sons of the day: we do not belong to the night or to darkness, so we should not go on sleeping, as everyone else does, but stay wide awake and sober. Night is the time for sleepers to sleep and drunkards to be drunk, but we belong to the day and we should be sober; let us put on faith and love for a breastplate, and the hope of salvation for a helmet. God never meant us to experience the Retribution, but to win salvation through our Lord Jesus Christ, who died for us so that, alive or dead, we should still live united to him.
> 1 Thessalonians 5:4-10

that face-off with Evil's greatest and most powerful champion. To rely on our own strength is the ultimate foolishness. We are wrestling with principalities and powers on high and we will certainly fail if we try to do it on our own. If we confront Evil with Christ we will certainly prevail.

Our time and eternity's timelessness are constantly intersecting. In Christ we live in the interfacing between our limited human (chronos) time and the limitless (Kairos) time of God. When we were conceived we began to live in eternal time. When we are born we begin to interact with God and with each other in eternal time. When we are baptized we begin a new lifetime living in relationship with God. And when we die, time for us does not stop, it only changes.

Here in this life we simply must have the power of Christ Jesus in order to steer a course that saves us from the fate of spiritual death, the death of either Scylla or Charybdis. Without Christ there can be no deliverance.

It is in this context that we must set aside some time in our life to stop and consider who we are, what we are

277

about, and what our lives are all about. Does my life have meaning and purpose?

In our odysseys we are continually fascinated and attracted by the sirens of sin. We steer our courses hearing their calls and end up either being devoured in a series of sins, one leading to another, or being sucked down in the whirlpool of living in the continual state of sin. Both bring death with them, death in our hearts and souls, misery in our psyches and lives. It is so much simpler to steer another course, namely, that of following God's lead, for in doing so we find smooth sailing, serenity, contentment and, yes, happiness, something far more meaningful than merely placating desires for pleasure. Joy and contentment are the only things that will bring peace to our souls; satiating our senses is merely superficial and ultimately unsatisfying.

> This is what the Church is said to want, not party men, but sensible, temperate, sober, well-judging persons, to guide in through the channel of no-meaning, between the Scylla and Charybdis of Aye and No.
> **John Henry Cardinal Newman,** Apologia pro Vita Sua

We need to ask God to deliver us from defiant determination to take care of our needs in our own ways instead of receiving from Him what He wants to give us, that which will make us truly and lastingly happy. God waits to lead us when we are tempted to despair, or to give up, or to wallow in whatever pattern of sin we find ourselves. God will help us to remember that the only difference between a saint and a sinner is that the saint keeps on trying.

Recovery from any sort of addiction, as well as recovery from our own addictions to sin, our repeated behavior patterns that bring pain to others and self-hate to ourselves, rests on having eyes to see reality. Realism and truth are necessary in order for us to be set free: "...you will know the truth, and the truth will set you free" (John 8:32). The Evil One tempts; others tempt us; we allow others to tempt us; we tempt ourselves. Subsequently, in our misery, we choreograph our own little one-act drama of victimhood and play the blame game, claiming that others and God have done this to us. This charade is carried out so that we may live in denial, living in our own great lie.

* * * * * * *

PRAYER

O Father, we are tempted, sorely tempted to take your Truth, your Justice and your gifts into our own hands and use them just for ourselves. We are tempted to possess and control your Justice, your Mercy, your Truth as if they were ours, not yours. Help us to be your stewards and do what you want us to do, not simply what we want to do. Lead us to make your Truth, your Justice, your Mercy, and your powerful Goodness present in the world you have given us. Inspire us to be as you would have us be, not as we would. Help me, Father, to see that what I want is not necessarily what I need. Deliver me from the seductive lie that tells me what I want is in fact what I need.

* * * * * *

Questions

Who or what tempts me? When? Why?
Do I tempt myself? When? Why?
What can distract my attention when I am being tempted?
When I am tempted, do I ever pray?

DELIVER US FROM EVIL...

*The unconscious is not just evil by nature,
it is also the source of the highest good:
not only dark but also light, not only
bestial, semi-human, and demonic, but
superhuman, spiritual, and, in the classical
sense of the word, "divine".*
Carl Gustav Jung (1875-1961)

Does Evil Exist?

In politically correct circles evil is not discussed, nor taken seriously. Some think that if we took "sin" and "evil" seriously we would be on the road back to witch-hunting and burning people at the stake. Others carry the concept of separation of church and state beyond the Constitution's intent and claim that there is a separation between religion and society. Thomas Jefferson and the Founding Fathers of our nation had no such intention and any examination of their primary documents will clearly reveal this.

Some people attempt to dismiss the concept of evil as simply another form of psychological maladjustment, theorizing that evil can be explained scientifically via psychology. When I was a young priest I considered my thoughts to be infallible and spoke *ex cathedra* concerning the psychological and pathological causes of hurtful human behavior. Youthful idealism can do that. Now that I am an older and more experienced priest I realize that the causes are multiple and mixed; I can detect the Evil One's handiwork in our psyches and souls, in my own and in those of others.

281

Many remember the days when the Soviet Communists confined openly religious people to mental hospitals. But such attempts at suppressing Christian belief always fail. They skirt the central issue that requires us to look squarely at a reality that is present when some people do monstrous deeds, acts that result from the influence of a Monster. Can the actions of Hitler, Stalin, Pol Pot, and other tyrants be traced only to their misshapen psyches? Hardly! What, then, or more to the point, who motivated these tyrants?

When we pray, "And deliver us from evil," what is it that we call evil? From what do we need to be delivered? The nature of evil has been talked about since time began, but like the concept of "love," we don't seem to be able to comprehend it.

Some theorize that there are two cosmic realms, two "kingdoms" perpetually intertwined with each other and forever at war. At the end of time, on the "Last Day," they will be forever, totally, and irrevocably divorced from each other.

This theory, however, puts Lucifer on the same level as God, as a sort of anti-God. That is not the Christian vision. The Church's teaching presents Lucifer as one of God's creatures, a fallen mighty archangel, and forever existing in a state of loss. He is doomed to be eternally conscious of what he had, and now will never have. He lives in the hollow emptiness of his own rationalized self-justification, his own emptiness, having only his self to love and be loved. Hell in this view is non-being, loss, emptiness, hollowness, and deprivation. If we dare to ponder this, isn't that what evil is all about?

Evil, then, is the degradation, the deprivation and the loss, of what is good. We experience it when we become aware of our loss of innocence, when we deal with our troubled consciences, when we know we've fallen from the state of grace. Think of the pain of the loss of love, the loss of trust, the loss of hope, the loss of anything and everything that is good. In addition, we feel a particularly sharp pain when we

> We can believe what we choose. We are answerable for what we choose to believe.
> **John Henry Cardinal Newman**

regret what we have done, when we realize that our losses are the result of our own freely made choices. What bitterness there is in such a realization! An even greater guilt wells up within us when we consider that we have stripped others of their innocence and goodness, and that we have caused them to fall away from being in God's grace.

Jesus confronted the Evil One as no other human ever has. When asked why evil exists He responded, "An enemy hath done this" (Matthew 13:28). To blame God for the condition in which we find ourselves is unjust, unfair, mendacious, and blasphemous.

Christ Jesus bids us to make a conscious decision to place our selves into the hands of God and to actively reveal His kingdom here among us and within us. To respond to our Father as Christ would have us respond requires decisive action on our part. Far from stoicism or passivity it requires us to activate the powers the Holy Spirit has placed within us. For Jesus certainly did not sit back and do nothing in the face of evil. He made decisive choices. To live in His way, His truth, and His life, we must do the same. Evil, after all, must be deliberately overcome. Since evil is found in deliberate choices, it can only be vanquished by our own freely deliberated choices.

It is quite mistaken to think that God creates evil. An all-knowing, all-loving, infinitely caring God could not create evil. Evil springs forth from Lucifer's mighty "No!" to God, just as it does from Adam and Eve's analogous "No!" to God. The immediate result is negativity, nihilism, vacuum, loss, and emptiness, "nakedness" as the Book of Genesis puts it. Lucifer can only offer us what is illusory, the illusion of good, like a desert mirage. He is known as the "Father of Lies" because his enticements are nothing but phantasms containing emptiness, nothingness, and the pain of loss upon loss. Lucifer's non-servio, "I will not serve," is the rejection of God's presence, power, and love, the very essentials for which our souls hunger and thirst.

> The serpent was the most subtle of all the wild beasts God had made. It asked the woman, "Did God really say you were not to eat from any of the trees in the garden?" The woman answered the serpent, "We may eat the fruit of the trees in the garden. But of the fruit of the tree in the middle of the Garden God said, 'You must not eat it, nor touch it, under pain of death.'"
> Then the serpent said to the woman, "No! You will not die! God knows in fact that on the day you eat it your eyes will be opened and you will be like gods, knowing good and evil."
> **Genesis 3:1-6**

We know, too, that pride is the radical ground upon which we choose to say our own "no's" to God. We think we know better and we become addicted to our own power, the power to reject God's goodness, the power that gives us the illusion of being equal to God when it comes to the power of choice. Our Imperial Self rebels out of pride, the pride of believing that we can save ourselves. If you don't believe this then talk with an untreated alcoholic or drug addict. Or listen to and try to talk with an unrepentant sinner.

We all have patterns of behavior to which we cling or perhaps are even addicted. We struggle to rid ourselves of them and fail. We eventually are tempted to give up and simply live with them even though we dearly wish we were free of them. Is it drinking? Gambling? Sex? Smoking? Overeating? Addiction to anger, bitterness, and resentments? We feel powerless over them. And perhaps that is true; perhaps we cannot rid ourselves of them on our own power. We need a higher power. This is beyond a "wish" or a "want to," it is a need.

"Misery loves company" is an old aphorism we have all heard. It speaks a telling truth. The demons are bent on spreading a satanic realm of hurt, pain, loss, suffering, and misery. In some perverse way they derive "comfort" in causing others to join them in a world of hellish hurt.

We see hints of this when we observe how alcoholics make sure everyone around them is more miserable than they are. All who have had to endure living with an alcoholic know the put-downs, humiliations, and scorn they heap on those who are forced to live with them. The demonic world in which they live is passed down to succeeding generations in their families. Satan is the supreme drunkard, totally inebriated in his thirst for manipulation, power, and control over others. And as for drug addicts, it's the same, sometimes even worse.

Evil is found in the promotion of self, or the protection of self, at the expense of others. The Imperial Self is at work, depriving others of their rights, what is due them, what is rightfully theirs. Everything is to serve the Imperial Self. "It's all about me, isn't it?" The interests of others, along with their rights, are ignored, rejected outright, or directly assaulted. Injustice is evil; oppression is evil; rape and abuse are evil. Evil is the destruction and degradation of human life.

The Nature of Evil: The Denial of Goodness

God does not wish to inflict evil, pain, or suffering upon us. He is free to, of course, and perhaps there may be instances in which God must visit remedial punishments upon us, but such chastisements always come to us with healing intent. Mercy accompanies them. God gives us the opportunity to repent, and when we do so, when we turn to Him, He makes things right for us if we accept His remedies.

God loves us enough to chastise us and thereby present us with the opportunity to change our motivations. He knows ahead of time (being omniscient) which way we will decide, whether for good or for evil. Since He knows ahead of time, then, if we decide to choose evil, will He thereby withdraw His love from us? Of course not! It's not a question of what God will do; it's a question of what we will do. Will we bring ourselves to return, as did the prodigal son, to our Father's loving arms, to return to His house? Or will we remain defiant, separated and aloof from His love as did the elder son upon the prodigal's return?

When we look at the nature of our sins we cannot help but realize that sin brings its own punishment. Honestly, don't we have to admit that a whole lot of pain we suffer comes as a consequence of our own decisions? We also suffer a great deal of pain as the result of the choices of others, not God's choices. Most of the time God does not have to expend His energies in punishing us. Our sins bring with them their own punishments.

How do we respond when evil or suffering confronts us? Some opt for stoic resignation. "That's life," they say. "Just courageously accept it as it is. There is no God, no Higher Power, only human beings. Grit your teeth; survive with the fittest. Your courage and your strength is your divinity."

Others enter into a passive pietistic resignation, claiming that it is God's will that we suffer. "He's testing us," they counsel. "Just sit back and let God take care of things." Still others choose agnosticism or secularism. Evil, they assert, comes from a psychological maladjustment. There is no such thing as "sin" or "hell." They're even uncomfortable using the word "evil" because it smacks of "religious fundamentalism," or fanaticism. Our response to evil, they claim, needs to be based on sound psychiatric therapies that do not include God. Since sin is a "medieval concept," we change its name and think of it merely as a psychological maladjustment.

We are desensitized by a daily bombardment of enormous evils that stream through our television sets, newspapers, and magazines, interspersed with advertisements designed to make us feel good. This daily assault has a narcotic effect that takes us out of reality into a fantasyland that we call the "American Dream." As a result, our human spirits become dull. We cease the effort to seek God; we've lost our understanding of, or desire to live in God's grace, and we no longer feel the usefulness of any repentance. Living in a moral morass is the consequence.

The temptation toward either resignation or denial puts us, in our own odyssey, on a course of steering between either Scylla and Charybdis, a passage through life that offers nothing but loss and disaster. Many of our contemporaries are experiencing life in just that way -- rudderless, tossed about in moral storms, and feeling helpless.

Most sins are accompanied by automatic punishment and/or consequences. Although we often try to ignore or avoid the consequences of our sinful behavior, can we try to learn from them instead? Of course we can! For wisdom is hidden therein. Isn't it true that when we read of sins in the Bible we find God immediately

> Deliver us, Lord, from all that is wrong in our lives, what diminishes us, what brings misery and hurt into our own lives and the lives of those around us. For these things drain away our money, resources, energies, our self-respect, our self-assurance, our courage and finally our strengths. Help us, Lord to live constructive instead of destructive lives.
> **Anonymous**

thereafter offering reconciliation, forgiveness, and renewed blessings in His love? In God, justice, punishment, mercy, and love are all interconnected. Our spiritual task is to understand these concepts and their interconnectedness.

The most serious we can suffer in our sinfulness is the loss of our self-respect. When that goes our respect for others also goes and we begin to beat other people down as mercilessly as we berate our selves. Jesus, we must remember, did not tell us to love others. No. He told us to love others as we love our selves, knowing full well what we will treat others in the same way we treat our selves. We regard and respect others in the same way that we regard and respect our selves. Our self-respect is related to our respect for all human life, from its first moments in being until its last in natural death.

In J.R.R. Tolkien's epic The Lord of the Rings we are presented with the symbol of a powerful, magical ring that can unleash evil throughout the world. Paradoxically it also has the power to unleash wondrous goodness. The depiction is theological. It shows the awesome power of human freedom of choice, something so powerful that we humans can use it to cancel out God's loving offer to us, an offer in which He invites us to join with Him in completing His creation or rebel against Him and bring about horrible consequences that result in our rejection and deformation of His creation. At root is the problem of sin, the monumental problem built upon our egotistical pride. It stems from the notion that "we know better."

In the Lord's Prayer we pray that God will deliver us from evil. In the midst of terrible evil should we deliver ourselves from God? Isn't it something of a marvel that in the face of terrible evil we turn all the more ardently to the God who can deliver us? Perhaps this inclination is why so many pilgrims travel to Assisi, Italy, to the home of gentle Saint Francis whose life is a shining example of what can happen to any of us when we turn to our common Father and seek His deliverance of our sinful souls from the Evil One.

When evil befalls us we can take the occasion to develop our spiritual selves, just as Olympic and other athletes use pain to develop their strength, their endurance, and their skills. The paradox that strength and goodness can result from harmful or painful forces is true in many areas of our lives. From a spiritual point of view, we can use pain and suffering to draw closer to God. Just as Jesus on His cross converted all of His suffering for our redemption, so we too can redeem, or "buy back," our souls and turn victimhood into victory. This is the essence of His redemptive passion, death, and resurrection.

> Now he was teaching one day, and among the audience there were Pharisees and doctors of the Law who had come from every village in Galilee, from Judea and from Jerusalem. And the Power of the Lord was behind his works of healing. Then some men appeared, carrying on a bed a paralyzed man whom they were trying to bring in and lay down in front of him. But as the crowd made it impossible to find a way of getting him in, they went up on to the flat roof and lowered him and his stretcher down through the tiles into the middle of the gathering, in front of Jesus. Seeing their faith he said, "My friend, your sins are forgiven you." The scribes and the Pharisees began to think this over. "Who is this man talking blasphemy? Who can forgive sins but God alone?" But Jesus, aware of their thoughts, made them this reply, "What are these thoughts you have in your hearts? Which of these is easier: to say, 'Your sins are forgiven you' or to say, 'Get up and walk'? But to prove to you that the Son of Man has authority on earth to forgive sins, -- he said to the paralyzed man -- 'I order you: get up, and pick up your stretcher and go home.' And immediately before their very eyes he got up, picked up what he had been lying on and went home praising God.
> They were all astounded and praised God, and were filled with awe, saying, "We have seen strange things today."
> **Luke 5:17-26**

God doesn't have to waste a lot of time or energy throwing us into hell. Obligingly, we do that for Him. We inflict hell upon ourselves. We need to pray, hard and often, in order to overcome our tendency to place

289

ourselves "in the near occasion of sin," testing our selves. Usually, we fall. In our arrogance and pride we think we have enough spiritual strength and stamina to prevail, but of course we don't. There may even be a perverse drive to deliberately place ourselves into the clutches of temptation knowing that we will fall. Does not forbidden fruit taste all the sweeter precisely because it is forbidden?

The opposite of heaven is not to love, to ignore or actively reject the opportunity to love others, and to love God who dwells within them. ("I was lonely, I was thirsty, I was hungry...")

Forgiveness is God's gift to us in direct proportion to the forgiveness we give others around us. It is a part of our "testing." And so we ask God to deliver us in the time of our trial, not only in our travails but also in those moments when our hearts and souls are tried and tested, in those moments when we reveal to God our capacities for loving and compassionate forgiveness.

Hell is when I overthrow God and put myself in His place. "You shall be like God," declared the serpent.

Hell is when I pervert the Lord's Prayer and declare:

> *I am the Omnipotent One, the holy one who controls heaven and hell, the one who has declared that sin does not exist, and that God does not matter, living in my own self-made 'heaven.' My almighty will is to be done everywhere. I am Number One and all others are inferior to me.*
>
> *I decide what is right and what is wrong, what is moral and immoral. I decide what is truth and what is not. I recognize only those things that I admit to be true – and even then they are true so long as I do not recognize a greater truth.*

I provide my own daily bread. I forgive only those who have satisfied my ego and who submit to my conditions in order to be readmitted into my heart. I, and I alone, am the Arbiter of Reality, the Dispenser of Love, the Judge of Fairness.

Evil: The Corruption of the Good

When we ask our Father to deliver us from evil we need to have a good understanding of just what evil really is. Most of us do not have a good understanding and end up seeing in others an evil that really isn't there, or not seeing the evil that really is there.

Extremists and fundamentalists have hijacked our great religions in order to use them to justify fanatical and violent assaults against the basic humanity of others. The truth is that all of our great religions counsel peace,

> But I say this to you who are listening: Love your enemies, do good to those who hate you, bless those who curse you, pray for those who treat you badly. To the man who slaps you on one cheek, present the other cheek too; to the man who takes your cloak from you, do not refuse your tunic. Give to everyone who asks you, and do not ask for your property back from the man who robs you. Treat others as you would like them to treat you. If you love those who love you, what thanks can you expect? Even sinners love those who love them. And if you do good to those who are good to you, what thanks can you expect? For even sinners do that much. And if you lend to those from whom you hope to receive, what thanks can you expect? Even sinners lend to sinners to get back the same amount. Instead, love your enemies and do good, and lend without any hope of return. You will have a great reward, and you will be sons of the Most High, for he himself is kind to the ungrateful and the wicked.
>
> Be compassionate as your Father is compassionate. Do not judge, and you will not be judged yourselves; do not condemn, and you will not be condemned yourselves; grant pardon, and you will be pardoned. Give, and there will be gifts for you: a full measure, pressed down, shaken together, and running over, will be poured into your lap; because the amount you measure out is the amount you will be given back.
>
> Luke 6:27-38, (see also: **Matthew 5:38-48**)

understanding, and acceptance of others. Christianity, Judaism, and Islam all condemn terrorism and violence as sins. And yet fundamentalists and extremists continue to exploit them in order to dress up their hate in religious clothing.

What, after all, is evil? Most would acknowledge that evil exists, few agree on what it is in its very nature. Perhaps the greatest evil of our day is the concerted effort on the part of many to turn evil into little more than sentiment. Evil is the corruption, the perversion, of what is good. It defaces beauty and degrades what is decent. It tears away innocence. It oppresses one's inner soul and depresses one's feelings.

Is it evil to detest an idea, or a proposition that purports itself to be true? No, of course not. Is it evil to despise and reject certain forms of human behavior? Many tell us that it is, claiming that "we cannot judge; it's wrong to judge." Such notions are preposterous. The very ones telling us not to judge are making many judgments themselves. If we were to follow the dicta of those who tell us not to judge then we should immediately remove all judges from office and close down our courtrooms.

When it comes to judging whether or not a person is evil, however, we need to be more cautious. In all such determinations and judgments we must always do what Jesus would do, namely, love the sinner but hate the sin. Some behaviors are bad, and some are illegal. Damning a person to hell for bad or illegal behavior, however, is God's prerogative, not ours.

Illusions and Delusions

While it may seem cute and fun to depict the devil as a cartooned character, it is in reality a form of denial. The Evil One would like nothing better than to be not taken

292

seriously. Instead of disguising himself in sheep's' clothing he can be disguised as a buffoon, as a Hollywood ploy.

Far more insidiously, evil uses love as a disguise. Words of love are used in order to seduce. Love is corrupted into lust. Similarly, admiration is replaced by envy; self-worth is corrupted by prideful arrogance; the healthy need for rest is degraded by sloth; the desire for food and drink is co-opted by gluttony; the need for shelter and things useful for living well is taken over by greed and acquisitiveness; and when the Imperial Self feels threatened, anger rages forth from our hearts. The rightful desire in us to belong to others morphs into the will to dominate. Interdependence is replaced by absolute independence.

The consequences place us in a hellish life. Defiance of God and His love results in our withholding of love for others. That withholding leads us into withdrawal. We find ourselves in a desert of emptiness, our main reason for being, namely, to love and be loved, having been removed from our hearts. We become spiritually dry in that arid desert of our own making. We find ourselves thirsting and lusting after anyone or anything in order to slake our thirst and satisfy our hunger. At the bottom of this hell we find ourselves living in a horrible depression, the hell of loneliness and isolation.

Of course God wants to keep us away from evil. The question is, do we? It's a question of our own willingness to keep ourselves away from those persons, places, and things that we know will cause us to fall. We need deliverance from our pre-judgments, our prejudices, and our arrogant determinations that we know all about certain people before we even encounter them. Mark's Gospel speaks of a terrible loss in Nazareth because of prejudice, a tragically missed opportunity (See 6:1-6).

293

Jesus and Evil

Jesus, baptized by John and anointed by God's Holy Spirit, began his public ministry with these inaugural words:

> *The spirit of the Lord has been given to me; for he has anointed me.*
>
> *He has sent me to bring the good news to the poor, to proclaim liberty to captives and to the blind new sight, to set the downtrodden free, to proclaim the Lord's year of favor.*
>
> Luke 4:18-19

These words were taken from the prophet Isaiah. Jesus was quoting them because they were at the core of Isaiah's prophecies concerning the Messiah who was to come, God's *Christos*, God's Anointed One sent to redeem us. This inaugural address was delivered in the Synagogue of Capernaum and was Jesus' first public appearance after having spent forty days and forty nights in the desert wrestling with Satan, dealing with His identity. Evidently Jesus didn't have much of an identity problem.

Nor should we. After all, He suffered and died for you and me in order that we might see and understand ourselves in an entirely new way, in a radically different way. We are at the same time both loved and being-saved sinners. We are endowed by our Father in heaven with certain gifts and characteristics that no power in the heavens or on earth can take from us.

To whom, then, is your life dedicated? To what is your life dedicated? What part do you play in the great scheme of things? Would the people who know you succeed or fail in identifying who you are, what you stand for, and what your life is all about? If goodness were a crime there should be enough evidence to convict you.

Our Higher Power

The religious question is not whether we deal with evil, but rather how we overcome it. Religion (re-ligio) equips us with the power to "re-ligament" our fractured and dislocated humanity, to bring healing and wholeness into our lives. Vulnerable in our weaknesses, weaknesses exploited and used by our Ancient Enemy, we stand in need of our Higher Power. We are not omnipotent. Only the insane think they are.

There is nothing within us that is weaker and at the same time stronger than our will power. It is precisely here that the battle rages. Our Ancient Enemy's greatest victories are won in this venue, and it is precisely here that we must take hold of all that our Higher Power offers us in order to gain victory over our selves and the Evil One, he who constantly seeks to make us as miserable as he is.

Imagine you are a youngster at a beautiful lake, feeling that you really know how to swim. Your father has told you not to swim over to the west end of the lake because it is filled with reeds, grass, and a sandy bottom that can pull you down. Still, you want to swim over there and explore it — and you do, "just because."

Suddenly you find yourself in terrible trouble. The more you thrash around trying to get out, and the more you try to stand on the quicksand, the more you get pulled down. You are in a terrible panic; you're going to die.

Your father sees you and hears your cries. Your older brother, a strong and powerfully built young lad, is with him. They take a small boat and put it in the water, and your father sends his son, your older brother, over to you. Your brother finds you, and from the boat he gives you his hand. You grab on to it and together you are able to come up out of the sucking, clutching grasp of the weeds and sand... and you are saved.

How would you feel? Wouldn't you feel something more than relief? Wouldn't there be a great deal of joy in your heart and love for your

> But when he saw how (strong) the wind was he became frightened; and, beginning to sink, he cried out, "Lord, save me!"
> **Matthew 14:30**

brother and for your father? The joy and happiness of Christmas is that our Father in heaven has sent us His only Son to rescue us. We now have a way out from the mess we've gotten ourselves into because of our own arrogance, pride, and our false belief that we can do anything we want to. Humans who have ignored our Father have sinned, and in their sins have made many other people miserable.

Some people want to turn Christmas into the "Winter Holidays." Others tell us "Christmas is all about children." Well, yes... but more. "Christmas is all about family." Well, yes... and more. It is said, "Christmas is all about giving." Well, yes... and more. It is our joyful celebration of the fact that God our Father has sent us His Son to save us. In spite of the mess into which we've put ourselves, our heavenly Father still loves us. He has sent our older Brother to us. If we put our hand into His we can be saved. He will pull us up if we pull with Him. What a wonderful thing!

Relying on God

How far will we go in trusting God? The question needs to be put in the context of another question: How far has

God gone in trusting us? He has, after all, sent us His only Son. He allowed His Son to be placed in human hands. We crucified Him and yet God raised Him from the dead. That's how far God has gone! Will we, like Christ Jesus, give our Father the trust that Jesus did in saying, "If it be possible for this cup to pass, nevertheless not my will but Thine be done"?

What we see as a "test" from God can likewise be seen as an offer from God. He gives us the opportunity to trust Him in spite of our own perceptions. A crisis (as we see it) is composed of danger plus opportunity. In every crisis we need spiritual eyes in which to see opportunities to place ourselves in our Father's provident hands.

Peter, James, and John slept during the time of Christ's terrible travail in the Garden of Gethsemani. It was their own time of trial also. Yet they slept! Are we any different than they? Do we not put our consciences to sleep during times of temptation, preferring to delude our selves with "being

> O Lord, you did not create us to suffer. It is not your will that bad things should happen to good people.
> You do not want people to inflict evil upon us. Yet we do suffer – mostly from what others do to us.
> When suffering and evil come down upon us, help us to respond as you would have us.
> Help us to know that you are with us as we endure evil and suffering.
> You sent your only Son to become a part of us, to be with us when life inflicts its pain upon us.
> Dear Jesus, help me to be aware of you in good times as well as in bad.
> Help me to experience your Holy Spirit dwelling within me.
> Fill me with courage and strength.
> Do not allow the Evil One to use life's pain as an excuse not to trust you, to separate myself from you.
> Unite me with your Son on His cross and let me make my suffering a part of His – for the redemption of our world.
> With Him, let me overcome evil with good, and join me ever closer to Him in His resurrection.
> For He is risen, victorious over sin and death, victim no longer.
> Make me totally a part of Him in our Holy Communion
> **Anonymous**

ignorant" when deep down we know full well that we intend to succumb to evil?

The great evil of our day is sleepy indifference. "Whatever!" is a common response to any problem. "Everything is relative; nothing really matters"; a sort of fatalism pervades with its operative dictum, "Oh, well, that's life." The opposite is a fanaticism that leads us to think we can make ourselves worthy of God's loving forgiveness. It's the self-delusion of thinking we can make ourselves deserving by our own effort, irrespective of God, and then we shall present our selves to God.

Perhaps nothing tests our confidence in God more than when evil inflicts its terrible pain upon us, jarring us out of our indolence. And perhaps evil is never more acidic than when someone we trust betrays us and inflicts a form of hurt that sears our souls. Physical pain is bad enough. Most of us, however, find ways of coping with it. But when our hearts and souls are pierced with the lance of betrayal and malice, it is then that our faith is truly put to the test. You have experienced those moments and so have I. Even as I write these words I am experiencing that dark night.

> Jesus did not come to explain away suffering or remove it. He came to fill it with his presence.
> **Paul Claudel**

Does such an experience cause us to revert into an "eye for an eye" form of retaliation, or does it cause us to draw ever more deeply into a more profound reliance on God's saving power and love? Do we trust only in our selves, or do we enter into the core of Christ's response in the Garden of Gethsemani and as He hung on His cross?

Contrary to some popular preaching, we do not immediately move from baptism to the rapture. The bliss of beatitude is found in only one way, one truth, and one life. It is found in the way of Christ's cross. However much we shriek against it, we all suffer from the freely chosen decisions of other unredeemed humans. We all carry the awful burden of freedom of choice. We all find ourselves nailed by what others have done to us, suffering the consequences of their choices.

We should not let our suffering go to waste. Rather we should place ourselves on the other side of Christ's cross and join our sufferings into His. Redemptive suffering is the most powerful prayer we have and we can use it to bring Christ's message of salvation to others, even to those who hurt us, particularly to those who have hurt us. Was that not Christ's message as He hung dying on His cross?

Have you been betrayed? Christ was. Have you been rejected? Christ was. Have you suffered from the decisions of others? Christ did. Are you a victim? Christ is the Victim. Imagine what follows if you join all of your pain and suffering into His! His redemption is effected and made present in our world through you. Moreover, with Him and in Him you will be raised with Him in Easter's victory, victim no longer.

We all need God's saving power to get us out of the quicksand bogs in which we find ourselves. The more we thrash around trying to get out, the more we are sucked down into

> ...that creation itself would be set free from slavery to corruption and share in the glorious freedom of the children of God.
> **Romans 8:21**

them. Our bogs may be habits of thought, they may be attitudes, or may be behavior patterns. Whatever their nature, they hold us in their grip.

God wants to give us the gift of decisiveness. He is saddened to see us when we are victims. Living in a state of victimhood does not please Him. He wants us to live in the "glorious freedom of the children of God," having the virtues (powers) that enable us to choose what is decent, right and good. St. Irenaeus spoke of the glory of God as men and women fully alive, fully in life, living fully in the human nature God intended us to live in when He created us.

So that human sin might not thwart His original intention, God established a New Creation, establishing it in His Son who became as we are in all things except sin. He brought His divinity to our humanity in order that we might be able to start over again in Christ.

God gives us the gifts of art, music, and poetry, things of great beauty which are the gifts of our imagination. With imagination we can image and picture things, create them so they speak to us far more profoundly and extensively than mere words, information, and data.

These wonderful, wonderful images, pictures, sculptures, and other creations emanating from our souls inspire and deepen the souls of others, bringing them to see through our human mirror, however dimly, the Ancient Beauty from which all that exists emanated in the first place. What a fantastic gift we have from our Creator, what noble dignity, that He has given us the power to join with Him in creating. For what would be beautiful if it did not come from Beauty itself? What would be truthful that did not come from Truth itself? And what would be just if it did not come forth from Justice?

PRAYER

O Father, strengthen my resolve, my will to choose what is good. Help me out of my compulsions, my attractions to self-indulgence, my urges and desires. Be with me when I am tempted, when I want to yield to desires for immediate pleasures and instant gratifications. The serpent offers me what is only apparently good, what is merely instant and not lasting, what is superficial and not satisfying. The serpent offers me what in the long run brings misery, isolation and hell.

Deliver me, Father, from my defiant determination to take care of my needs in my own way, instead of receiving from you what you want to give me -- lasting happiness and deep fulfillment in you and in your love.

* * * * * * *

Questions:

What evils surround me and touch me?
How do I confront evil?
Do I just passively accept suffering, or do I use it for good?
What sort of deliverance from evil do we expect from God?

Printed in the United States
69083LVS00003B/50